PRESUMED GUILTY

A leading defence barrister, over the last two years alone Michael Mansfield QC has represented Judith Ward, five of the Birmingham Six, the Risley Fifty-five, the Winchester Three, a defendant in the Battersea bomb factory case, one of the Tottenham Three, one of the Cardiff Three and a Trafalgar Square poll tax 'rioter'. All were acquitted. His past cases include the Price Sisters, Operation Julie, Bradford Twelve, Newham Seven, ABC Official Secrets, Orgreave miners, the Brighton bombings, Bettany Spy, Angry Brigade, Operation Countryman, Roach Inquest, Mangrove trials, Arthur Scargill, the conspiracy to assassinate Gandhi and the Knightsbridge safety deposit trial.

PRESUMED GUILTY

The British Legal System Exposed

MICHAEL MANSFIELD
and TONY WARDLE

Mandarin

A Mandarin Paperback
PRESUMED GUILTY

First published in Great Britain 1993
by William Heinemann Ltd
This edition published 1994
by Mandarin Paperbacks
an imprint of Reed Consumer Books Ltd
Michelin House, 81 Fulham Road, London SW3 6RB
and Auckland, Melbourne, Singapore and Toronto

Copyright © Michael Mansfield 1993
The author has asserted his moral rights

A CIP catalogue record for this title
is available from the British Library
ISBN 0 7493 1253 X

Printed and bound in Great Britain
by Cox & Wyman Ltd, Reading, Berkshire

To everyone I've ever represented

CONTENTS

INTRODUCTION

Over the past few years, the tally of appalling miscarriages of justice which have come to light has mounted steadily. It is not a new phenomenon but has been an integral part of our criminal justice system for centuries.

The litany is not yet finished, there are more to come, there always will be more to come under our present system.

Miscarriages of justice can never be justified and few people ever really attempt to justify them. But whenever a failure of justice comes to light, excuses are quick to trip from the lips, tumbling over one another, jostling with platitudes for space: 'We have to remember the public mood at that time', 'the police were under tremendous pressure to come up with a result', 'there was a terrible mood of revenge in the air'.

They are designed to draw the sting of abject failure and to ameliorate the unthinkable suffering handed down in the name of justice. The Guildford Four, the Maguire Seven, the Birmingham Six and the Tottenham Three were subjected to the most appalling miscarriages and were then faced with complete intransigence when those miscarriages became public knowledge.

Perhaps even more terrifying is that it was not the criminal justice system which, in the end, recognised its dreadful mistakes and moved resolutely and contritely to correct them. It was not the police, it certainly was not the politicians, it was not the State and it was not the so-called responsible members of society who eventually demanded justice. It was the victims themselves, their families, friends and supporters who never gave up fighting despite the passage of so many years.

It is a chilling thought that one reason why these cases have caused such a furore is that the victims are still alive to fight their corner. Just a few years ago they would have been dead – hanged!

But it is not just over big cases that the criminal justice system falls apart, it does so even when stumbling along on a day-to-day basis. Miscarriages of justice can and do happen to anyone, at any time, for any offence! The deficiencies of whole squads of police which have been disbanded, suspended or relocated reflect the size of the risk.

Throughout the whole process of police investigation, interrogation, forensic examination, charge, trial and appeal there are faults so deep and so fundamental that revolution is the only solution.

Following the Court of Appeal decisions in the Guildford Four and the Birmingham Six, the government has set up a Royal Commission. It is not the first time – we had one in 1980 and it had very little impact on police malpractice. This Royal Commission has been given a brief to look at the criminal justice system from top to bottom and I firmly believe that it should seize this unique opportunity to recommend entirely rebuilding elements of a system in which the public has little or no confidence. This is not the time for compromise or cosmetic tinkerings. Central to genuine change has to be a commitment to principle and to human rights.

What should be at the heart of our judicial system is a basic principle which we seem to have lost sight of. It is very simply, very glibly stated, but it is often swept to one side. It is that we are presumed to be innocent until proved guilty.

If that principle were to be the main tenet, the main thrust, the main momentum of the judicial system, then a lot of other factors would fall into place. What is essential to the protection and preservation of this principle is the right to trial by jury. For it is only twelve jurors who have the power to displace it by their verdict. Serving on a jury remains one of the few ways in which we can still exercise true democracy and that is no doubt why it is perceived to be a threat and why it is constantly being attacked, marginalised and weakened, to the extent of abolition for some offences in the North of Ireland.

A jury, however, is only as good as the evidence presented to it and the rot begins long before a case reaches trial. It starts almost as soon as an incident has occurred. The approach, the procedure, the thinking, the preparation steadily relegate principle – particularly the presumption of innocence – to the back seat.

The murder story you are about to read took place on an average Saturday in April 1989 in an unremarkable town. There was little publicity surrounding it; no scope for tabloid newspapers to presume guilt and scream for retribution. No scope for government ministers to raid the thesaurus for condemnatory adjectives, for public outrage to inflame the situation and inflate the demand for retributory blood. Above all else there were no exceptional demands on the police to bring the guilty person to book. And yet once more the system was lining up another miscarriage of justice, propelling one more anonymous victim towards a life behind bars. But for the relentless efforts of his solicitor battling against the system this case would certainly have gone unnoticed and ended as just another criminal statistic.

As the story unfolds I attempt to show how the things that go wrong in this case are mirrored in many other instances and what sort of changes are required to ensure that you will not be reading a similar story in twenty years' time.

Since the first publication of this book it is clear that none of the lessons it highlights arising from the miscarriage cases has been heeded, and sadly its predictions about Government policy have been borne out. The position has deteriorated to such an extent that further wrongful convictions are guaranteed.

Nothing has been done to alleviate the risk of unreliable confessions; to establish a properly funded and resourced independent science service; to ensure independent supervision and accountability of police investigation; to alter the structure and composition of the judiciary; to remedy the Court of Appeal's shortcomings in fresh evidence cases.

Instead, what is suggested is the abolition of the right to silence which will once again concentrate police minds on interrogation; the abolition of the right to jury trial for large numbers of defendants; and the abolition of the right to bail for certain categories of alleged offender. At the same time the police will be encouraged to devote more time to 'targeting'; to prosecute rather than caution; to limit disclosure and the burden of paperwork. Conversely the defendant will be obliged to make advance disclosure; will be enticed by sentence discounts to enter plea bargains; will be faced with restrictions on legal aid and ultimately more prison 'because it works'. Essentially there is a transparent attempt to achieve a political quick fix with no regard for the quality of justice.

Above all, the combined effect of the Runciman/Howard proposals is a complete denial of the basic principal of the presumption of innocence and is predicated on a belief that assumes knowledge of who is guilty and that this way they will be convicted.

The pain and courage of those who fought for so many years from the isolation of prison cells to alert the world to a system badly in need of radicalisation must not be overtaken by the market forces of expediency. Fortunately a new generation is prepared to continue the struggle and in the Autumn of 1993 many assembled in Manchester to launch a campaign under the banner 'Innocent'. They deserve all our support.

ONE

The Incident

Sitting neatly to the north of the M40, between London and Oxford, High Wycombe has some impressive neighbours. To the east is considerably posher Beaconsfield and to the south the scarcely poorer Marlow. Not much more than a good, loud 'yahoo' away is Eton and next door to that the royal retreat of Windsor. Also straddling the Thames, to the south-east, is Henley.

Since the time, some hundreds of years ago, when bodgers eked out a miserable existence in Buckinghamshire's beech woods, making tatty tables and chairs, High Wycombe has grown and prospered. But posh? Never! And as for exciting . . .

None the less on 22 April 1989, at the International Café in Desborough Road, High Wycombe, a man was killed – murdered, said the police. Another man, a young man, was arrested and tried for that murder.

The case did not arouse huge interest nor did it capture the headlines outside the locality. The local newspapers puffed themselves up with self-importance for a day or two and covered the story largely as it was told to them by the police. A thirty-year-old man of West Indian descent had been knifed to death, possibly by an eighteen-year-old man of Asian descent in a petty squabble over the dead man's stepson.

Desborough Road is not prepossessing. It is the kind of road which was never designed, it just happened, and it exists in almost every town, somewhere near the city centre. It appears suddenly from around a right-hand bend, straightens for a hundred yards or so before darting away to the left and disappearing up a hill.

Red-brick buildings are skirted by narrow pavements. The small shops, an Asian grocer's here, a newsagent's there, have little scope to encroach on to the foot path with their stalls. On one side of what could be a warehouse is the Caribbean Kitchen take-away and on the other, the Top Cats night club. Both names are displayed more in hope of what the establishments could be rather than what they are. Much the same is true of the International Café. Lacking any commercial identity, it is a place which most people probably pass without even noticing. The entrance door is not directly on the frontage of the shop but to the right, in a recess which also gives access to the adjoining shop. It is the kind of doorway where people shelter on rainy days when waiting for their bus.

Inside the café, its narrow length allows room for little more than a couple of pool tables and a few fruit machines. At the end, furthest from the entrance, is a serving counter no more than four or five feet long adjoining a half-length swing door which leads through into a small kitchen. Wall decoration consists of a series of plastic laminate panels in differing shades of mock wood grain.

Behind the counter, tall, slim and usually smiling from behind his solid gold jewellery, is Shabir Kayani, more commonly known as 'Superfly'. A man in his mid-thirties, he is the café owner, its law maker and enforcer and general mister fixit.

On almost any day of the week the clientele is the same; young men, youths really, mostly of Asian descent, some black youngsters and a few white boys. The International Café!

It is a place where people gather, play pool, talk, plan, scheme and drink tea and coffee, which they usually make themselves, moving unchallenged between café and kitchen. It is a place to be with friends and to kill time, particularly when you are unemployed. It is cheap, predictable, friendly and safe.

On this particular Saturday, shortly after 9 p.m. on a dark night with rain threatening, uniformed police constable Ken Johnson was on patrol in a marked police car with his colleague, P.C. Michael

Buddle, when he received a radio message to attend a disturbance near the International Café.

Putting up their blue light and sounding the siren, they sped down Desborough Avenue, swung round to the right into Desborough Road where, a little way ahead, they could see a crowd of people gathered on both pavements. They were quiet, watching, huddled crowds, not the material of riots or insurrections.

Lying prone in the road between the International Café and Top Cats night club was a black man. They could not see his face as he had his back towards the police car. Kneeling over him in the road was another black man, also with his back towards them. Standing close by was Superfly. P.C. Johnson brought his car to a halt some ten meters away and he and P.C. Buddle leaped out and ran over to the men.

As the police approached, the kneeling man turned his face towards them. The right-hand side was drenched in blood and his right eye was closed. He said nothing.

The man lying down was on his right side in the foetal position, but he was writhing around as though in great pain and attempting to sit up. The kneeling man was trying to restrain him. Both his head and his clothes were covered in blood and on the road beneath him was a large pool of blood.

P.C. Johnson looked up at Superfly and asked what had happened. Superfly replied that the two men had walked into his café carrying knives and had then started waving them about. There was a fight and everyone had ended up out in the street. When asked who had taken part, Superfly indicated that five or six Asian lads were involved.

When asked what had happened, the kneeling black man said that his friend had been stabbed. When P.C. Johnson moved the stabbed man in order to try and staunch the flow of blood, he saw a small hole in his right side just below the rib cage from which blood issued freely.

At this point an ambulance arrived and the crew put the injured man on a stretcher and placed both him and his friend in the ambulance. They were taken to High Wycombe general hospital.

With the body removed, the policemen noticed the end of a broken, blood-soaked pool cue about twelve inches long lying on the ground beneath where the body had been. They did not touch it.

One of them walked over to a group of black youths who were standing nearby and asked if any of them had seen what had happened. They all turned their backs and slowly walked away without replying.

In the middle of all this, P.C. Colin Brooker arrived. He was beckoned to and called over by a woman standing near a car parked outside Top Cats night club. It was Karen Ray and she was in no doubt about what had happened.

'I saw it all, they beat them up and then ran back into there.' She pointed at the International Café. 'Lots of them were beating them up and that one there was hitting the one on the floor around the head with a bat.' She indicated Superfly.

P.C. Brooker did not interview Superfly because he was needed to travel to the hospital in the ambulance with the two black men. The one with the stab wound continually coughed up large amounts of blood and what P.C. Brooker took to be pieces of body tissue.

The ambulance man, Basil Dean, attended to the injured men and was aware that the stabbed man was in a serious condition and began work on him. He noticed that the stab wound was no longer bleeding freely but that the man was now bleeding heavily from the mouth and complained that it was filling up with blood.

Dean placed an aspirator down the man's throat and immediately blood began to pour from his nose. Slowly the injured man began to quieten down, slipping quietly into unconsciousness. Dean tried to administer oxygen but, owing to the copious bleeding, unsuccessfully. On arrival at the hospital the man was completely unconscious.

At the hospital both injured men were undressed and then treated. P.C. Brooker took the opportunity to seize the clothing belonging to the less seriously wounded man.

Unbeknown to P.C. Brooker, another man had just arrived at High Wycombe hospital and was also being treated. He was Talat Sarwar who had a stab wound in his neck only two centimetres from the jugular vein. There was also a cut to one of his fingers, the ring finger on his left hand. He had been driven to the hospital by two friends, Suklain Azad and Arif Ali Khan.

Yet another police constable was at the hospital, P.C. Gary Young and one of the nursing sisters whom he happened to know told him that there were three men in cubicle B who might know something about the fight. Young entered the cubicle and found Talat with Azad and Khan. He asked what had happened.

Azad replied that there had been a fight and Khan interrupted him, saying: 'Shut up, don't say anything!' Khan then explained that Talat had been attacked by two West Indians with knives.

P.C. Young took the two Asian youths along to the off-duty doctors' room where three out of a rapidly growing band of policemen guarded them. Talat was now alone in the cubicle.

Another policeman who had responded to the radio message which reported an incident in Desborough Road and who had arrived there at the same time as the ambulance, was D.C. Snelling. After watching the two injured men being put into the ambulance he drove up to the hospital.

As soon as he walked into the building he was shown Talat's two friends, Azad and Khan, and arrested them on suspicion of Affray. They were handed over to other policemen and taken off to High Wycombe police station.

The time was now 10.40 p.m. and D.C. Snelling found Talat Sarwar in his cubicle. The cuts to his neck and finger had been stitched, but complications had developed with the neck wound and he was waiting to be taken to the operating theatre for an examination under general anaesthetic. P.C. Snelling carried out a preliminary interview. He asked Talat how the wound had happened.

'It was the West Indians. They just went mad. They came in with knives.'

'Why?'

'Because of the fight at the fair.'

'Were you involved in that?', asked P.C. Snelling. Talat indicated that he had been, whereupon the policeman cautioned him. He then asked him what had happened at the fair.

Talat explained: 'We were at the waltzer and three coloureds were spitting at my mates on the waltzer. I went and told them to stop and we got arguing. Then a coloured came up and told them to leave it out because I was all right. A bit later one of the coloureds came at me with a large screwdriver and I hit him with a bit of metal I had from work.'

'What metal?'

'It was about eight inches long and a quarter of an inch thick.'

'Did you cut him?'

'No, I didn't have a knife.'

D.C. Snelling then asked Talat Sarwar what that had got to do with this night's happenings and Talat said he was not sure. He went on to explain what had happened.

'I was stood by the door and these two came in flashing knives. They came at me and I grabbed a chair to protect myself but one kept stabbing round it and he got me in the neck.'

'Then what happened?'

'I don't know, I was brought here by my mates.' Talat went on to deny that he had injured anyone that night: 'I was jumped by them, it was so sudden.'

At that point the interview was ended by the medical staff arriving to take Talat Sarwar to the operating theatre. Under anaesthetic they found that the neck wound was not as straightforward as they had believed and that a small artery in the middle of the partially severed sternocleidomastoid muscle was cut through. It was tied off and this stopped the bleeding. After the operation, D.C. Snelling took up guard outside the door to Talat Sarwar's room.

The less seriously injured of the two black men was being treated at the same time as Talat Sarwar. His name was Lewis Pinnock, from Aylesbury. Doctors found three major lacerations on his head, one over the right temple, one on the front of his head just above the hair line and one on the back. They were all surrounded by swollen tissue and the edges were ragged, all consistent with having been caused by a blunt instrument. Pinnock claimed they had been done with a hockey stick.

He had not been knocked out and did not report any nausea, headache, vomiting or blurred vision – but he was not very happy.

He was to be even less happy after his wounds were stitched and his head bandaged for as he left the treatment room with the intention of going home, clutching a piece of paper entitled 'Head Injuries, What to Do', D.C. Snelling, having forsaken his vigil outside Talat's room, arrested him. The charge was suspicion of Affray and Actual Bodily Harm. Together with P.C. Brooker, Snelling took Lewis Pinnock to High Wycombe police station.

The stabbed man had arrived at the hospital at 9.20 p.m. and from Lewis Pinnock, the admissions clerk was able to establish that his name was Lloyd Waite and he was, in fact, Pinnock's half brother.

Doctor Stuart Hall immediately took charge of Lloyd Waite and hurried him into the resuscitation room where he found him to be in shock and unresponsive. As well as the stab wound to his stomach there were lacerations to both wrists. With the aspirator removed from his airway he again began to bleed profusely from the mouth.

Dr Hall immediately sent out a cardiac arrest call and fast bleeped a surgical team. Waite was intubated and ventilated and given an intravenous fluid. There was no heartbeat and the team began external cardiac massage. There was no response so a chest drain was inserted in his right-hand side.

Resuscitation attempts were kept up for nearly thirty minutes but at 10.05 Waite had no pulse, his pupils were fixed and dilated and there was no activity of any kind from his heart. Dr Hall pronounced him dead. What had been the International Café incident was now being referred to as the International Café murder.

At this stage, barely an hour after the whole drama had begun, police, participants and possible witnesses were all over the place. Police cars were chasing between the café and the hospital, the hospital and the police station, the police station and the café.

Several policemen attended the scene within minutes of the first emergency call and each of them noticed additional people, events and objects. It was hoped that all these separate accounts, after notebooks had been filled in and reports written, would add up to a clearer picture of what had taken place.

D.C. Gareth Daniel, together with his immediate superior D.S.

Pattinson, had arrived at about the same time as D.C. Snelling. However, he spent considerably longer at the scene.

In addition to the two injured men and the group of West Indians already reported, D.C. Daniel noticed a large group of Asians standing at the corner of Cedar Terrace and Desborough Road. In the entrance to Top Cats night club was a group of white people in formal dress – probably bouncers. He also noticed a white Fiat Uno.

The car's windscreen and most of its other windows were smashed and the middle of it was staved in.

After the ambulance had departed, D.C. Daniel had a look around the area. In addition to the short, blood-soaked piece of pool cue there were several other pieces of broken cue strewn about.

On the ground, right next to a car which was parked outside Top Cats, he saw a wooden-handled, open knife about three or four inches long.

His sergeant, D.S. Pattinson, was talking to a group of Asians outside the café and D.C. Daniel went over to join them. The sergeant eventually asked Daniel to drive Superfly, a man called Ruksar Ahmed and Susan Ray to the police station and take witness statements from them.

Detective sergeant Pattinson had already radioed through to the police station and asked for the senior detective inspector to be notified and for the scene of crime officers (SOCOs) to come to Desborough Road.

His talk with Superfly had shed a little more light on what had happened. Superfly maintained that the two West Indians had come into his café carrying knives and were looking for someone. There had been a fight with an Asian lad who had been chased up to the counter of the café where he had been stabbed.

D.S. Pattinson's reaction was immediate: 'I want this café closed and the door locked.' Superfly ejected two West Indian lads who were still inside the café playing pool as though nothing had happened and did as he was told but he could not add a great deal more to what he had already said. Asked what customers had been inside the café, he was unable to help: 'I don't know who was in my café.'

Pattinson asked him what had happened after the fight: 'They all ran out and I followed and saw the man on the ground and the white car opposite with broken windows.'

'Where've all the Asians gone?' asked Pattinson.

'I don't know. They ran off!'

Sergeant Pattinson was not convinced and asked Superfly to go to the police station and make a statement. He then looked around the area again and saw a road scattered with pieces of broken pool cue, large quantities of blood and pieces of broken glass. The Fiat Uno was still there, windowless, and rain was looking more imminent by the minute. He instructed the road to be covered with sheets of polythene to await forensic examination and had the names and addresses taken of the remaining people who were still standing around and were possible witnesses.

While this was being done, detective chief inspector Short arrived to take charge of the incident.

Down at High Wycombe police station, Superfly was interviewed by detective constable Peter Tinley. They talked together and at some point during this conversation, Superfly brushed his right-hand trouser leg and D.C. Tinley noticed a quantity of broken glass fall out of the turn-up. He picked it up and placed it in a piece of folded paper.

He then turned to Superfly and said: 'I am arresting you on suspicion of murder,' and then cautioned him. Superfly replied: 'Yes, I understand.'

Shortly after Superfly had been driven away from Desborough Road, P.C. John Haines, a SOCO and a photographer, turned up and was joined by sergeant Clare. Under D.C.I. Short's instructions Haines took coloured pictures of the car, the wood, blood, broken glass and anything else which they thought might be relevant to a murder investigation. A video film was also made.

He and Clare then began to gather together all the bits of evidence and placed them in plastic bags. From the car they took notepaper and a Filofax and a sample of blood from the front bumper. The car was then covered with plastic sheeting and taped down in the hope of making it weather proof. At 2 a.m. on what was now Sunday morning, the car was towed away but the evidence-gathering continued.

A hat, sunglasses and a jacket were taken from the café and a series of fingerprints collected from the pool tables, ashtrays and the counter. By 2.40 more pictures had been taken of the café's interior and the SOCOs called it a day.

When everything had been brought together, there were 135 exhibits including knives, clothing, jewellery, glass, nail clippings, blood, stomach contents, urine, road sweepings and fingerprints and statements which would eventually be made by the accused.

TWO

Targeting

What happened on Desborough Road, High Wycombe, is typical of what happens in almost any allegedly criminal incident anywhere in the country. It does not really matter what it is, it does not have to be a murder or a bombing, it can be as simple as a car theft or even the scrumping of apples from an orchard.

Nearly all of them are dealt with in a similar way, which stems from a peculiar mentality which afflicts all our police forces.

It is an unexpressed but completely accepted genus of thought which is best illustrated through the remarks made by Leslie Sharp, a senior policeman in the Strathclyde force. In a recent after-dinner speech he joked about the difficulties of being a cricket umpire and the possibility of using robots. The problem with black ones, he suggested, was that they might be too busy mugging old ladies in the bus queue.

It is a way of thinking which permeates their structure, their education and their training and is fundamental to their method of operating. It is called 'targeting'.

Targeting essentially means that police concentrate their attentions on the individuals or families, groups of people or even whole communities who they think are most likely to be responsible. It is a kind of labour-saving short circuiting but the problem is that it does not work. It not only signally fails to capture offenders but leaves the community unprotected by locking up the wrong people. Inherent in its operation is a presumption of guilt and a determination to make the facts fit the theory.

This results in the discarding of evidence which does not fit the theory, putting pressure on witnesses and the accused to alter their statements to support that theory and a handicapping of support services such as forensics by providing them with wrong or incomplete information, pointing them in the wrong direction and by slanting the evidence which they do provide.

At the bottom end of the targeting scale is the village Bobby who is certain he knows who has pinched the apples from the orchard. Next time he is in the culprit's area he may well call on him and, round the corner out of sight of parents, give him a good shaking, a clip round the ear and a stern warning not to do it again. It is the sort of romantic scenario that so many people hanker after – the all-knowing, all-understanding, old-fashioned village policemen. And of course it is a myth.

At the other end of the targeting scale is CII criminal intelligence unit. It was brought into being by Scotland Yard with a specific brief to monitor the activities and movements of particular supposed criminal families. Any large crimes were laid at their door as it was believed that they were the only ones with sufficient money, influence and clout to set them up and there may well have been truth in this.

CII never became involved with the families or in police operations of search and investigation, they simply watched and waited and their files grew thicker and thicker. The information, supposition and opinion which they gathered was fed to the flying squad and would essentially dictate when to move in on the families and associates.

Alongside files on the families were files on solicitors with whom they might or might not have dealings. The word went out to police stations to make life as difficult as possible for these lawyers and they were, wherever possible, to be dissuaded from entering stations when anyone connected with the families was being held.

Parasitic on all large and powerful organised criminal families or syndicates are the peripheral small fry. Despite all the time, money and energy devoted to these monitoring exercises it was mostly only the tiddlers who were pulled in and very often these had to be fitted up to obtain a conviction.

Of course it is totally legitimate to keep tabs on outfits with known criminal involvement but this should be done through a genuine intelligence department which receives, absorbs and analyses information, not one which is acting on predispositions and which sets out to see how it can obtain a conviction. This book is littered with examples of this method of policing.

What is not legitimate, however, is when other covert organisations such as MI5 and the Special Branch are involved in targeting groups for political purposes, such as the telephone tapping of CND or the pursuit of Hilda Murrell, a perfectly innocent and legitimate anti-nuclear protester. Perhaps the most blatant example of this was during the miners' strike when the assumption was made that any striking miner was a law breaker and a whole series of actions were set in train by the Association of Chief Police Officers (ACPO).

Road blocks were set up as much as 150 miles from the Midlands coal fields, in fact at the Dartford Tunnel. Any miner from Kent who was heading north, or anyone seen as being sympathetic to the miners or anyone they thought might possibly be a miner, was turned back. Similar obstructions were used to seal off virtually the whole of Nottinghamshire despite the fact that to picket, to demonstrate or simply to travel the nation's roads is not illegal.

What was perhaps one of the most astounding aspects of this whole operation was the arrogance with which it was carried out. There was nothing surreptitious about it, nothing cloak and dagger, not even a passing sign of guilt or of concern at its inherent illegality.

There is, in fact, a culture of arrogance which is encouraged and defended by both government and the judiciary. In any public order situation such as Orgreave, Stonehenge or the Trafalgar Square poll tax demonstration, the Home Secretary, the Prime Minister and others immediately condemn the demonstrators and praise the police, regardless of the reality of the situation. Such blanket support, often in the face of gross incompetence and extreme brutality, gives a clear message to police – 'You are inviolate and have the full political backing of government regardless of what you have done.' Of course it leads to arrogance.

In one classic court case in which I appeared with the distinguished barrister John Platts-Mills, in whose chambers I had the pleasure to practise for a while, he had the temerity to challenge police evidence. He suspected the police of planting a fingerprint and asked if it was technically possible to do so. The reply was that with very specialist equipment and under laboratory conditions it might be possible but it was a complicated procedure.

John Platts-Mills produced a roll of Sellotape and two glasses and asked if this was the specialist equipment to which the officer was referring. He then asked the officer to place his fingerprint on one of the glasses. Platts-Mills then took a piece of the tape, placed it over the fingerprint, raised the tape and stuck it on the second glass. He then removed the tape and showed the court that he had successfully transferred the policeman's fingerprint from one glass to another. He had proved his point.

The judge made it clear that this was reprehensible conduct by the Bar and all counsel associated with it would have their fees reduced for the time taken in making these allegations against the police.

There was a wonderful scene from a documentary called 'Taking Liberties' (*Open Space*, BBC 2) when a BBC camera crew in a minibus approached a police road block in South Yorkshire. The policemen knew the camera was running because they complained about it but did little to change the way they behaved.

With the crew was a miner, acting as guide to the area. When asked if any of them had any connections with the strike they volunteered this information quite openly. That was sufficient to produce debate and discussion amongst the police and the crew were first told they could proceed and then told they could not as a helmeted copper went backwards and forwards between his superior and the van.

In the end the crew were instructed to turn their vehicle around at the nearby roundabout and head back the way they had just come. They would be followed by a police car and if they failed to do as instructed they would be arrested. When asked for what reason, the answer was: 'Obstructing the police in the execution of their duty.'

The irony of this whole strike saga is that the actions of the miners were legal and the actions of the police lacked any statutory authority. Of course, it did not take the government long to introduce legislation to permit the setting up of road blocks for political purposes with the Police and Criminal Evidence Act, 1984, which came into effect in 1986.

At about the same time, the most appalling scenes of violence appeared on the early evening television news as police blocked the road to a convoy of travellers heading for Stonehenge, forcing them into a bean field. In full riot gear they then set about them with truncheons and riot shields, assaulting men and women, including a pregnant woman, and terrifying children. They then systematically destroyed these people's homes.

By the later news bulletins the worst of the footage showing police brutality had been edited out and no one ever mentioned that the actions of the police in stopping the convoy were totally illegal. They were acting in anticipation of a Bill which was going through parliament and had not received assent. But no one was called to account.

The worrying footnote to this story is that when, in 1991, an independent television company came to make a programme about the battle of the bean field, the original, damning footage, given only one airing on television news, had disappeared completely and no one could account for it!

Running alongside this blatant abuse of the law was an even greater one – the use of phone taps and outdated information on anyone perceived to be a legitimate target during the miners' strike, namely a 'subversive' – a category in which I have little doubt my own file languishes.

The phone taps were illegal but again the government introduced legislation under the same Act which allows phone taps for 'the economic well-being of the State'. The ramifications of this little clause are extraordinary and could be used to justify eavesdropping of almost any kind if, in the government's judgement, it stood to lose a bob or two.

What is quite astounding is that the people who operate these systems never seem to learn anything from their previous mistakes, which they make over and over again. Forget the legalities or lack of them for a moment, but if we are to have covert, dubious organisations imposed on us in the name of national security, the least they could do to justify the huge amounts of money lavished on them is to be accurate in their targeting.

In the midst of all the Gulf War jingoism of 1991, ninety Iraqi nationals living in this country, some of them resident for many, many years, were whisked away and imprisoned. It was reminiscent of the US treatment of Japanese and our own treatment of Germans at the outbreak of World War Two.

Of course, when the Iraqi people had been bombed to pieces and the conflict had come to an end, it was admitted that much of the information was wrong, totally outdated and in some cases related to the wrong people. In short, these people had been deprived of their liberty unnecessarily. Then came the excuses – 'But of course you can't take risks in wartime', 'Their loyalties are bound to be with their own country', etc., etc.

This might seem a far cry from High Wycombe and the International Café but it isn't. It is about assumptions and guesswork rather than decisions and actions based on knowledge. The problem with assumption is, if you are wrong, innocent people have their human rights infringed and time, energy, resources and manpower are all wasted. And just as a bonus, the guilty get away scot-free.

Not only is it a lousy basis for justice, it does not catch the right people. The High Wycombe police not only made an assumption that the culprit was to be found in the Asian community, but within hours of the incident taking place they had made up their minds who was the guilty person. From that moment their whole investigation was geared towards proving his guilt and when eye-witness statements did not fit the scenario they were called back again and questioned for hours until their evidence did fit.

Just as the Asian community was targeted in High Wycombe and people were pulled in in their droves, so the Irish and black communities, throughout the country, have all been subjected to similar harassment.

In the wake of the Birmingham pub bombings, the six accused men were arrested and held in custody on the same night as the bombs went off. Their houses were searched but their families were not told that the men were being held. Nora Power, wife of Billy Power, remembers it all very clearly:

> It was very late at night, the early hours of the morning, and there was a terrible storm raging. It was making so much noise that at first I didn't hear the police banging at the door. Then four or five of them burst in and started to look around the house. They showed a lot of interest in something one of my little girls called her whistle, in fact it was the top of an old light switch. They looked in some pots and pans in the kitchen but it was all a bit half-hearted. My brother had been baby-sitting and he was still in the house but they didn't take him away. I wasn't at all upset by it and after they'd left I just went back to bed.

There is obviously nothing unusual about police searching the house of a suspected criminal, although it is bizarre that they did not say that they had arrested Nora's husband. But just imagine the situation. You are sitting at home after an evening out and five policemen virtually break into your home, search it, ask you and your children questions without telling you what it is about and then leave. Do you think you might be a little upset, perhaps a little concerned or maybe even rampagingly angry?

The reason Nora was not upset is that she had heard about the bombings and had assumed that police were raiding every Irish home in Birmingham. In fact they had originally called at the wrong house and had torn apart the home of a neighbour who was also probably not surprised. That is what targeting means to some groups in Britain, a resignation to the fact that at fairly regular intervals, without evidence or explanation, you are likely to be raided, arrested, questioned or followed.

The reaction of Paddy Hill's wife, Pat, to the night's raid

says even more about the way people have learned to live with targeting. Pat had six children under eight years old and the whole family was asleep – it was 3 a.m. Pat was awoken by one of her little ones crying that someone was trying to break down the door. With that the door burst open and the house was filled with police.

> Two of them kept asking me questions while the others searched the house. They asked me what Paddy was wearing and where he'd gone and things like that, two of them firing questions at me. Then one of them saw that I had a 'phone and accused me of getting it from the IRA. I told them I'd got it from the GPO but they didn't like that. Then they said I'd got my carpet off the IRA so I showed them the HP agreement. Then they just tore the house apart and their attitude to me and the kids was terrible.

The bizarre thing about this experience is that Pat Hill, knowing that Paddy 'loved a drink', thought he might have called in at one of the bombed pubs before catching the train to Heysham on his way to Belfast. She actually thought that her husband might be dead. However, being part of the Irish community, although herself a Brummie, she accepted, despite being angered by, the treatment she received. It did not cross her mind that if Paddy was dead she could expect a sympathetic, understanding, sensitive visit in which the news would be broken to her with feeling.

Those of us who are not marked out as being part of some targeted minority by our colour, our name, our accent or where we live cannot conceive of the intimidation which is inherent in such a policy. The automatic assumption by the police is one of guilt.

Prior to the implementation of the Public Order Act which legitimised targeting actions taken against miners, Sir Kenneth Newman, one-time commissioner of the Metropolitan Police, set up his own public order review.

In this review, he quite blatantly set out target areas in the metropolitan boroughs. These were the areas that the police believed housed potential crime and potential criminals.

It does not come as a great surprise to hear where they were – Broadwater Farm in Tottenham, Peckham in South London, Toxteth in Liverpool, St Paul's in Bristol, Handsworth in Birmingham – all target areas and usually housing estates. But that was not the end of the story.

To go along with these chosen, targeted, heavily policed communities went a new type of policing and a comparatively new type of policeman. They formed into special squads which might be referred to as special patrol groups, tactical support units, instant response units or Tottenham/Brixton/St Paul's support units. It does not really matter what names they are using at any given time because those names change to give the impression that the type of policing has changed and that the tactics are different. But at the end of the day it is all the same type of policing wherever it is or by whatever name it is known. It is policing by riot squad.

The police tactics which are employed came to light during the Broadwater Farm trial, although the revelation received little publicity. The police have contingency plans to deal with social disorder in these target areas by containment – social containment operated by riot policemen. The implementation of these plans had already started at Broadwater Farm and elsewhere prior to the 'riots'.

Conducted in exactly the same way as a military operation, including heavily armed and equipped back-up troops, the police swamp the estates in strength before any 'riot' or public unrest has even happened and begin a policy of 'containment' and intimidation. They justify their actions by issuing statements for which there is never any proof.

These claims are usually variations on the theme of the 'enemy within' and blame is laid at the door of outside infiltrators or Trotskyists or political insurrection or criminal conspiracy, anything which provides an excuse for going in. Of course no conspiracy is ever proved, no Trotskyist ever brought to trial and the outside infiltrators vanish into the air. They are allegations which again surfaced with the Oxford Blackbird Leys disturbances and other 'rioting' incidents.

What this means is that should those who feel the strain and frustration of unemployment, poor housing, irrelevant schooling, poverty, despair and social dumping on those soulless estates ever express these feelings, these areas will be swamped with riot police. All exit and entry will be controlled, snatch squads will operate with impunity and any civilised notion of what constitutes human rights will be suspended. Overnight, they will find they have more in common with the residents of South Africa's impoverished townships than with those of Esher, Cheadle or Morningside. The people on these estates and in these communities, whether guilty or innocent, will have all their basic freedoms curtailed, freedoms which are considered the yardstick by which civilised societies are judged.

These are freedom of assembly, freedom of speech, freedom of movement, freedom of thought, freedom from physical assault, freedom from arbitrary arrest and detention, freedom of association, freedom to withdraw one's labour, freedom to own and dispose of personal possessions and the freedom – the right – to be treated fairly and equally in the courts including the presumption of innocence in criminal trials and the right of access to legal advice and representation from the moment of detention. This latter right was blown clear out of the water in the investigation and trial for the murder of P.C. Keith Blakelock, where the majority of those detained were denied access to legal representation and in the case of the six who appeared in court accused of involvement in murder, five were denied access.

The problems that exist in these target areas are blatantly never going to be cured by concepts of saturation policing and the suspension of human rights. People on estates such as these see police as the instruments of their oppression and an increased profile does nothing to reduce crime. In the last decade alone, reported crime has increased by one hundred per cent. The police response is yet more policing, tougher policing, new laws to remove old freedoms, more technology and a more militaristic approach. None of which will have any impact at all but will simply stoke the fires of discontent and alienation.

After decades of policing on the basis of minimum force – only sufficient force to overcome resistance, or to ensure a person's safety – an enormous and fundamental change has been made in the way police are trained. This change has never been subjected to public debate or even parliamentary scrutiny; it has never been revealed to local police authorities and the Association of Chief Police Officers (ACPO) has tried, with great success, to keep it almost entirely secret.

The change in police training tactics emerged during the trial of fifteen miners at Sheffield on charges of riot. During the course of the trial, which arose as a result of the mass picket of British Steel's Orgreave coking plant on 18 June 1984, assistant chief constable Anthony Clements, the man in charge, insisted that policing methods on that day were the same as they had always been, nothing had changed, nothing was different. This, despite the huge number of injured miners and the unprecedented scenes of violence.

Fortuitously, a few pages of a new and secret police training manual came into our possession and despite every attempt by the police, the Crown and prosecuting counsel to have them excluded from the evidence, the judge supported defence insistence that they were at the heart of what happened at Orgreave.

The manual was never produced in its entirety but the few pages that were available provided sufficient information to show that British policing had stepped into a new, militaristic and very frightening world.

It advocated containment – rounding people up into confined spaces with all exits, entrances and boundaries controlled by police. It sanctioned the charging of police horses into densely packed crowds. It introduced the concept of short-shield units (what this really means is riot police) who could charge into crowds using their shields and truncheons to knock people down and then grab supposed ringleaders. It sanctioned the use of police dogs, not to chase escaping criminals or sniff out drugs but to intimidate and bite people. Perhaps most disturbing of all, it legitimised the beating and injuring of innocent demonstrators. This recommendation was wrapped up in slightly less inflammatory language but it advocated the 'incapacitating' of demonstrators.

These methods of policing are not restricted to use against an invading army, they are for use against ordinary citizens of this country expressing their democratic rights through demonstrations, pickets and peaceful assembly.

These tactics, developed in Hong Kong and on the streets of Belfast, have also been used in varying degrees against nurses demonstrating over working conditions and cuts in the NHS in Central London, against travellers in the battle of the bean field and against poll tax demonstrators in Trafalgar Square.

Perhaps the most telling way to illustrate the outcome of these changes is to compare Britain with Eastern Europe. One by one, the people of the satellite countries – East Germany, Czechoslovakia, Hungary, and so on – have toppled their governments. And they have done it in the most democratic manner possible, by taking to the streets in overwhelming numbers and peacefully demanding change. It could not happen here!

Public demonstrations of that scale would not be tolerated and injunctions are increasingly being granted where it is intended that more than half a dozen people should gather together. More than this number is seen as intimidation. There are also clauses in the new Public Order Act which could effectively be used to nullify the right of public demonstration.

The irony of Orgreave and the new methods of policing is that all the mainstream media were uninterested in investigating the real story of that day, the real journalistic 'scoop'. They fell back on the politically predictable cliches of the 'bully boys', 'thugs' and 'mob rule' and the BBC even edited news footage to give a completely different impression of what had really happened.

News footage showed a series of events which led viewers to an obvious conclusion. It began with miners throwing stones, was followed by the setting on fire of a Portakabin and finished with mounted police charging the demonstrators. The assumption is obvious. In reality what happened is that mounted police charged into thousands of miners without provocation and without warning. They repeated the charge and miners, who were trapped with nowhere to go, tried to repel them with stones. The charges continued and eventually miners tried to block the road with a dilapidated Portakabin.

It took until 1991 for the truth to emerge in a Channel Four programme, 'The Battle for Orgreave – The Sequel'. The BBC's comment was that the changes were a result of the pressure of trying to put together a news programme under very demanding conditions. The consequence of the media's concentration on picket line violence is that the secret training manual remains secret and police continue to be trained in incapacitating demonstrators.

There was, however, some sense of justice when the prosecution case against the miners fell apart in farce and disarray forty-eight days into the trial and before they had even finished presenting it, and all subsequent riot trials toppled in the same manner. But miners who had been beaten, falsely imprisoned and maliciously prosecuted had to wait a lot longer for any recompense for their grievances. It was not until 1991 that the South Yorkshire Police agreed, in an out of court settlement, compensation payments totalling £440,000 to the miners. The policy of targeting, backed up with a new and deadly form of militaristic policing, again slipped through the net of scrutiny and public debate.

The second track of a twin-track approach to targeted areas is to remove as many expressions of local democracy as possible. Only by gathering power around a central administration can authority be maintained, appears to be the theory. The abolition of the Greater London Council and other metropolitan authorities was one of the first shots in that campaign. Without a sense of involvement in their communities, where institutions are perceived to operate impartially for the benefit of all, and over which they have some control, people are gradually alienated.

This has been followed by a complete emasculation of local government, a reduction in the status and funding of caring services (reducing them to little more than social policemen, there to keep the lid on any explosion), the financial starvation of the voluntary sector so that law and advice centres and Citizens Advice Bureaux have withered.

Even police authorities, the only expression of democratic and public control over policing and police tactics, have been completely marginalised. Simply by appealing to the Home Secretary, chief police officers in any area of the country can override the democratic wishes of their locally elected representatives. If, after public debate and discussion, a local authority decides it does not wish its police to be armed with CS gas, water cannons, plastic bullets and riot equipment, the Home Secretary can and does intervene and the police get what they want. As a result, almost every police force in the country is now equipped with gas, plastic bullets and the whole panoply of so-called riot control.

It seems there is a determination to bypass all those avenues through which the police might be held accountable. A vision of what this could result in, if taken to its logical conclusion, was provided by ACPO's policy of 'mutual aid' – again during the miners' strike. Through the National Reporting Centre, all requests for assistance were matched by providing manpower from anywhere in the country and police tactics were centrally planned and controlled. It was, in everything but name, an embryonic national police force.

It provided a rudimentary model of what senior policemen and some Conservative politicians are constantly floating as the way forward, a police force where every last vestige of democratic accountability is removed. These same concepts form the basis of the present Home Secretary's thinking on Police restructuring leaked at the beginning of 1993. But of course, we are told, a national police force would be accountable to the Home Secretary.

Leon Brittan illustrated clearly what that accountability could entail – the jeopardising of normal, run-of-the-mill policing such as preventing or detecting crimes of rape, assault, robbery, burglary and murder for the sake of political ends. There is no other way of explaining why 14,000 police were removed from their normal duties to police the miners' strike, or why as many as 2000 officers escorted one solitary miner to work at Cortonwood colliery on 9 November 1984.

The last decade or so has seen the snuffing out of local institutions which are perceived to offer any kind of leadership or which provide a rallying point around which the discontented can organise. Equally, the police appear determined to stamp out individual, spontaneous exhibitions of leadership. Usually these happen in response to intolerable situations which the police have failed to control. Prime examples are the cases arising in Newham, East London.

Young Asian children on their way to school were subjected to racial abuse, intimidation, beatings and the usual range of disgusting tactics employed by racists. After parents had continually reported the incidents, nothing happened and the same old tired excuses that can still be heard were proffered: 'There is no evidence that the attacks are racially motivated'. 'It's the kind of thing that happens between school kids' and so on.

In the end the Asian community became tired of the excuses and set out to protect their little ones by using their older brothers to escort them to school and back again. They were successful. But the racists responded by producing older, harder thugs and the scene was set for a more serious confrontation, which of course happened. The outcome was that a group of young Asian men were charged with assault and faced long prison sentences. Fortunately the accused were found not guilty.

Similarly, with the case known as the Bradford Twelve, those who defended themselves against unprovoked racist intimidation finished up in court, accused of being the guilty ones and again the racists were never charged with any offence.

This incident sprang out of a march by the National Front through an area of Bradford heavily populated by Asians. It could not be seen as anything but frightening, provocative and highly intimidating and yet was allowed to take place escorted by police. Anyone uttering the word 'scab' in front of police on a picket line is liable to arrest. In Bradford the most base of racist insults were carried on banners and shouted out loud without one policeman raising a finger to stop it.

Again those Asians accused of assault were found not guilty but not before they had spent months weighed down with the fear of what the future might hold.

The prosecution of these people, whose crime was to defend their communities, had a familiar ring to it – and so it should. In the 1930s heyday of Sir Oswald Mosley, his blackshirts would pick parts of London's East End with high Jewish populations and then march through them in force. The slogans were much the same, only the nationality was different. In unison these thugs, who were largely recruited from the unemployment queues, would chant: 'The Yids, the Yids, we've gotta get rid of the Yids', all accompanied by a posse of good old British Bobbies.

Of course people reacted, of course people resisted, of course they tore up paving stones and pelted the fascists. And who in retrospect could consider them anything but brave and correct? But in these cases it was Jews, socialists and other ordinary people of the East End who finished up in court, not the blackshirts. One case was too much even for the magistrates of the 1930s and they acquitted the accused, a bystander at one of these marches. His offence? Blowing his nose in an offensive manner!

But that was sixty years ago. It could have been yesterday!

Less obvious, but still a reaction to anything which could possibly be seen as social subversion, was the police response to acid house parties. Suddenly it became a fad, a craze, a life-and-death example of vital police work – not attending the parties but trying to stop them. The usual venue for a party was a remote warehouse and finding how to get there involved a complicated game of dashing from point to point and phoning for the latest information. It also meant dodging police tails, road blocks and raids. One man was accused of being the organiser of one of these parties on the strength of having a box of orange juice cartons in the boot of his car.

Acid house became synonymous with decadence, drug taking and potentially dangerous situations. Drugs were used as the first excuse to swamp motorways with manpower. When their trawls produced little more than a meagre selection of drugs, no more than would be found in almost any gathering of young people, the motivation became safety.

Perhaps the clearest example of targeting with which I have had personal dealings was that of the Mangrove Club in Notting Hill, London, which combined elements of racism and targeting all in one. It involved a black man called Frank Critchlow.

Back in the 1950s he set up a café at a time when black people were not being particularly well received in London. It provided a safe haven for them in an area which had known race riots and where attacks on individuals could take place on almost any street.

Frank Critchlow is a man of considerable charisma, a political man who was not afraid to speak out or to represent the interests of black people who found themselves in trouble with police or in front of the courts. He became an advocate for the Notting Hill community and was liked and respected by both black and white. But it appears that the police saw him as a threat to their authority.

The harassment began with a whispering campaign that the Mangrove was a den of vice and presumably a linchpin in a world-wide white slave trade. But the local community did not lock up their daughters and before long the accusation changed to that of after-hours drinking. Presumably being aware that after-hours drinking was hardly the stuff of Sodom and Gomorrah, the attacks changed again to accusations of drug taking on the premises.

It was at this point that the police campaign took targeting to its ultimate obscenity and used large numbers of uniformed policemen to saturate the area. They simply poured men on to the street where the Mangrove Club was and had them permanently patrolling up and down both pavements. They moved in on any vehicles which looked as though they might even consider stopping and posted a group of policemen outside the entrance to the club, which was also a café and restaurant. Anyone entering or leaving the place was subjected to a body search or, if they refused, were taken along to the police station.

Imagine attempting to run a business under these circumstances! It was only a matter of days before no one went near the place and the principal purpose of the operation was beginning to succeed – Frank Critchlow's economic ruin. When challenged by him and others as to the reason for the blanket coverage, police response was as predictable as it was cynical: 'We're enforcing the parking regulations!'

What was not known at this time was that very senior policemen, including the chief constable of the Notting Hill area, Mr Pearman, were carrying out an unremitting covert operation against Frank Critchlow and the Mangrove Club.

The essence of this campaign was to persuade people in the locality not to patronise, support or encourage operations which the police, in their infinite wisdom, saw as being 'not the right type'. It has come to be known as enterprise policing and essentially involves helping to close down shops, businesses or meeting places which are seen as being subversive and driving out those who are of no economic importance – in other words the poor. In Notting Hill this paranoia extended to trying to put out of business a one-man operation making T-shirts with slogans on them.

In 1988 the pressure was increased and the Mangrove Club was raided. Frank Critchlow was thrown to the floor, face down, and held there while his pockets were filled with heroin. The stakes had now been raised and Frank faced his fourth major court case, his umpteenth if all the minor attempts at harassment were included. He had been found not guilty in all the previous ones but this time the charge was dealing in drugs and the sentence a possible twenty years or more. Perhaps it was coincidence, perhaps not, that the raid took place in the same week that Frank was to retire. It could have been seen as a last chance to get him – or not . . .

Again Frank was acquitted of the charges against him. Had the secret dossiers which the police have on call been accurate, they would have chosen a different charge. As their evidence stumbled and faltered in the court room and prosecution witness contradicted witness, people from the local community came forward in their droves – black, white and every shade in between. Throughout his time in Notting Hill, Frank Critchlow had always spoken out against drugs, was known by all to be anti-drugs and had never allowed drugs on his premises.

But the irony is that the police won in the end. During the months it took for the case to come to court Frank was held in custody and all his assets frozen. The Mangrove had to close down and the Notting Hill carnival, which had grown spontaneously out of the community, passed into the hands of a new breed of middle-class black person – a breed seen by the police as being acceptable. Suddenly conversations were about cash flow, return on investment and diversification, and a little more of the life blood had been drained from the veins of the local community.

Of course you might say that this has absolutely nothing to do with the High Wycombe killing and that all I am doing is to air some kind of radical agenda, to ride an anti-police, anti-establishment hobby horse and that there is no conspiracy only a cock-up. That is not the case at all, rather that I feel it is essential to understand how and why and under what influences police and judiciary operate and what agenda is set by government if there is to be any hope of meaningful change. What happened in High Wycombe was a direct result of nationwide policing attitudes and methods. My views are formed from twenty-five years as a criminal defence lawyer, after being in court day after day, pulling apart prosecution cases and being exposed to the less attractive aspects of life.

I think it is vital to know the type of sentiment which informs government debate. Sir Alfred Sherman, not just any Conservative party politician but one of its hierarchy, head of the Thatcher-inspired Centre for Policy Studies and one of the key voices in policy debates, let his views be known, in confidence, to Russian diplomats. His thoughts were delivered to Arkady Maslennikov, London correspondent of the Communist Party newspaper *Pravda* at, of all places, the Reform Club. Of course he was not to know that the Soviet Union would disintegrate and its records become public property.

I have not seen the records of these conversations but Sir Alfred's words have been reported and he has confirmed most of them. In essence he believes it is wrong to go on spending money 'on the parasitic state sector and branches of the economy which have outlived their time. The government should be more decisive in cutting funds to the civil service, the bloated and inefficient educational system and the collapsing National Health Service.'

He also believes that there should be cuts in pensions and unemployment benefits but is not concerned too much about the possibility of a social explosion:

> The unemployed and the lumpen proletariat never have been a revolutionary force. If the unemployed get lower benefits they will be quicker to start looking for work and they won't turn to political trouble making. As for the lumpen coloured people and the Irish, let's face it, the only way to hold them in check is to have enough well-armed and properly trained police.

Although this statement zings through the air like a hot line from the last century – 'keep the wogs in their place and send in a gun boat' – the only comment made about it by Sir Alfred is that he cannot remember advocating cuts in pensions and maintains that he did not say 'well-armed' when referring to the police. It is chilling to know that these views have been proffered to the government of the day and have not only been discussed seriously but have obviously formed the basis of policy.

I will not pretend to offer all the answers to society's problems here, but I will offer a way forward for our criminal justice system, of which I am a part. It is only one of the many institutions which need to be reformed and my changes to it are predicated on genuine democracy, a respect for the rights of the individual and a search for truth. If all the other major institutions in our country were to be reformed with these basic tenets as the guide then I think we might start to see change for the better.

THREE

The Next Day

At 10.25 the next morning, Sunday, Iain West, a consultant forensic pathologist from Guy's Hospital, London, attended High Wycombe Hospital and began a post mortem on the body of Lloyd Waite. Sergeant Clare was in attendance. Before beginning the post mortem, Dr West studied a police video tape 'depicting the scene where the deceased had been found and the interior of the café where I understand a disturbance took place'.

Dr West went through the normal procedures which begin by listing descriptions based on simple observation and measurement ... 'a heavily-built black man (although he did not specify his actual weight), five feet seven-and-a-half inches in height dressed in the remains of a blue sports top and white and blue undershorts. There were two yellow metal bracelets on the right wrist and yellow metal rings on both ring fingers and both middle fingers ...'

Dr West listed all the external features he could see including Waite's injuries, of which there were plenty, before tackling the stab wound. It was a one-inch wound which entered one-and-a-half inches below the left rib margin and out of which protruded a small section of intestine. The track of the wound was inwards and upwards, penetrating the abdominal wall and into the greater curve of the stomach where there was a seven-eighths-of-an-inch wound in the stomach wall to the left of the duodenal cap.

The stomach had been distended with a mixture of food and blood clot. Whatever had caused the injuries then continued through the rear wall of the stomach, pierced the head of the pancreas and opened up part of the duodenum. It continued upwards and to the left, transfixing the inferior vena cava and cutting into the aorta just above the right renal artery. About three-quarters of the circumference of the aorta had been severed and there were two-and-a-half litres of blood in the peritoneal cavity. The wound showed evidence of having been caused by a single-edged stabbing instrument.

The length of the wound track measured five-and-a-quarter inches and there was bruising around the rib area where the instrument had entered the body. This probably meant that the person who had inflicted the wound had forced the knife in and had had their fist tightly wrapped around the handle of the knife, or that the knife had some kind of guard on it between the handle and blade. Dr West thought that the knife was probably considerably shorter than the wound. If the weapon had been sharp tipped, he believed it would have taken only moderate force to cause the damage it did.

There were also cuts to Lloyd Waite's hands which Dr West believed were entirely consistent with him having tried to block blows from a knife.

Following the post mortem, Sergeant Clare returned to the International Café with P.C. Haines, took numerous finger prints and samples and found another knife. Later that same day they examined the Fiat Uno and took similar samples and prints from that. These would all be listed, numbered and entered as exhibits when the case, if there was a case, came to trial.

As the weekend drew to a close, a full-scale murder investigation was underway. All the information so far available was from police observations, statements from witnesses and some exhibits. Some observations seemed to be a little contradictory, others did not tie up and there appeared to be a lot of people facing very serious charges. But perhaps this is the normal situation when a large number of people each see a segment of a picture and no one person has the advantage of a total view.

In this instance perhaps the one person who might have had a broader view than anyone else was Lewis Pinnock, but strangely enough, he was not to make a statement until nearly two weeks later – on 3 May – and the police were never to offer an explanation for this delay.

So far no one had employed the services of a lawyer to represent them.

Meanwhile, police stood guard outside Talat's hospital room waiting for the doctors to certify him well enough to be discharged.

The police held a press conference on the Sunday morning at about 11 a.m. at which they expressed the belief that Waite had been stabbed with a sharpened billiard cue. In reality this was surmise. It does not appear that Dr West had even been asked to express any opinion about the possibility of a billiard cue being consistent with the injuries he found. Furthermore there is no record that those at the scene, neither inside the café nor outside in the street, were asked for fingerprints, blood or personal samples, nor that there were any immediate attempts to fingerprint the wooden-handled open knife.

At this early stage it was becoming apparent that police were focusing their attention on Talat Sarwar as the prime suspect in the death of Lloyd Waite.

FOUR

The Investigator

The first thing which must go, then, is the way in which the police force is trained and operated, and top of the list is its obsession with targeting. There is an alternative way of conducting investigations – not a theoretical, think-tank alternative, but a living, working, practical alternative which is at the heart of the French criminal justice system.

The French method is to place responsibility for investigating crime in the hands of an independent person who is not part of the police force. In France that person is called a *juge d'instruction*. He or she – and of the 500 *juges d'instruction* in France 50 per cent are women – is responsible for the investigation of a crime and in theory, although no doubt not always in practice, they are looking for the truth; they are looking for who did it rather than starting from the premise of 'we know who did it and we'll get the evidence to fit'.

I have no illusions that someone in this position could be susceptible to political pressure from above and to police manipulation from below, but when compared to the way in which the Guildford and Birmingham cases were conducted, their methods of operating are much more likely to discover the truth. Rather than some senior police officer homing in on the people who he probably genuinely believes is responsible and as a result focusing on the need to find the evidence to support that contention, there is a genuine investigation conducted under rules which are both fair and sensible and which everyone knows. However, I do not wish to import all these rules to England

and Wales but to develop rules of our own which are more pertinent to us.

So, stage one of the changes which I advocate is to ensure democratic control of the police and I suggest that it is not done through the police force at all but through somebody who is independently appointed. I believe that a system based on elements of the *juge d'instruction* would be infinitely better than the system which we currently operate.

I visited a *juge d'instruction* in a small town about a forty-minute drive from Paris. Senlis is one of those pretty French towns which appear to have stuck firmly at some point near the beginning of the last century. Stone-built houses spread outwards from the cathedral along narrow, cobbled and twisting streets. Windows are flanked with peeling wooden shutters and whatever the time of year you expect to see a flock of screeching martins come hurtling around a corner. Canopied restaurants with names like Le Scaramouche and Hotel du Post fill to overflowing at lunchtime and serious waiters serve serious food with quiet efficiency.

On the edge of Senlis, set in parkland, is the rough-cast concrete, two-storey, smoked-glazed court house which, strangely, does not look particularly out of place in the shadow of medieval walls.

Catherine Samet is one of two *juges d'instruction* who control all serious criminal investigations in a wide geographical area. It stretches from Senlis with its burglaries of smart houses belonging to foreign royals and diplomats to the new town of Creil. Huge tower-block estates pile up on either side of the Seine valley as the brown river heads towards Paris. Brightly coloured paints, murals, *boules* parks and maturing, municipally planted trees cannot disguise the essential nature of Creil. It is a stressed concrete and building-block attempt to meet a housing problem, executed on the basis of build 'em high and build 'em often.

Between Creil and Senlis and for many miles around is a sparsely populated, agricultural hinterland dotted with remote farmhouses and unsmiling farmers. The criminal product of this urban/rural mix covers the whole spectrum – from incest to abduction, drug dealing to robbery, burglary to murder. Catherine Samet is in charge of investigations into any or all of these.

Thirty-three years old, six foot tall, with bobbed hair, round, wire-framed spectacles, a loping gait and an accent like Inspector Clouseau's, she is not quite what you expect a criminal investigator to look like. For those of us reared on Morse and Taggart and Van der Valk and even Maigret it takes a while fully to comprehend that this young judge is a formidable and committed investigator.

She has not come up through the ranks of the police but was once a lawyer who applied and was accepted for training to become a judge. Being a lawyer was not a necessary qualification, it just so happened that she was one. To those of us who are used to judges being chosen only from within the legal profession by secretive and backstage methods – and only then at an age when most other professionals are thinking of retiring – it comes as a bit of a shock.

Seeing adverts for the judiciary phrased in a similar way to recruiting posters for postmen or miners also has a certain shock value initially – 'Why not become a judge?' Why not indeed!

It is a career with its own structure like any other profession and with its own school in Bordeaux – Ecole Nationale de la Magistrature, with a branch in Paris literally within the shadow of Notre Dame. It provides a two-year training with an ensuing probationary period.

Had the International Café murder taken place within Catherine Samet's jurisdiction, its early stages would have been handled very differently. As with High Wycombe, the first senior policeman on the scene would have made a simple decision – had a crime been committed or was this simply an accident? That is where the similarity with British policing ends.

As it was a crime, he would have immediately sent for the *procurateur*, the public prosecutor, and cordoned off the area, creating a *cordon sanitaire*. He would have dealt with any emergencies, taken the names and addresses of any witnesses and unless someone was standing in the middle of the road holding a knife shouting: 'I did it, I did it', it is unlikely that anyone would have been arrested.

On arrival, the public prosecutor, who is also quite likely to be a woman, would confirm that it was a crime and appoint the police force she thought best suited to begin essential preliminary work. Having done that she would then send for the examining magistrate, the *juge d'instruction*, hand all responsibility over to her and withdraw from the scene.

On her arrival, the investigation proper would begin. In France there are two police forces, the national police and the *gendarmerie*, which is part of the military structure. The judge would decide which of these two services would serve her purposes best. Police have good local knowledge and contacts while the *gendarmerie* have excellent manpower and resources such as helicopters and transport.

If the incident necessitated a huge search, a door-to-door operation or complicated logistics then she would almost certainly appoint the *gendarmerie*. Either way, the decision would be entirely hers and she could change the decision taken by the public prosecutor. With the café killing, it is likely she would have appointed the national police.

At the point at which we left the café case, under Judge Samet almost certainly no one would have yet been charged and probably no one even interviewed. The real detective work would just be beginning, with the police acting entirely under her instructions.

FIVE

Outside the Café

Since the night of Waite's death, police had taken statements from some fifteen people, nearly all teenagers, who had been at the fair referred to by Talat Sarwar and were treating the incidents at the café and the fair as inextricably linked.

The first statement was by Jason Waite, the 'son' of the deceased. In fact Lloyd Waite was living with Jason's mother and had simply given her son his name.

Jason Waite had gone to the fair with his ten-year-old brother Rowan and two friends, Jason Lane and Gasnel James. At the fair they met up with four other friends and spent most of their time standing around the waltzer. Also at the waltzer was a group of Asian lads, about seven in all.

Apparently, trouble had developed between the two groups without Jason Waite being aware of it. The first he knew was when some pushing and shoving developed between one of his friends, Mark Baptiste, and an Asian lad. Jason explained: 'The Asian boy then walked towards me as I was standing alongside Mark and he pushed me out of the way and walked past me down the steps. I took hold of his right shoulder and said, "Don't push me." He turned round and said nothing at all to me and then he struck me on my forehead with the underside of his right fist. I heard a metallic "cracking" sound and I felt pain on my forehead in two places.'

After this the Asian boy ran off together with his friends but other Asians began to appear from different parts of the fair, many of them carrying metal bars. In the event they followed the others and disappeared into the crowd.

Jason Waite finished up being taken to hospital where nine stitches were put in the two cuts on his forehead.

Jason Lane's version of what had happened was not quite the same. According to him, three Asian lads, including one called Suk, were riding one of the waltzer cars while Jason and his friends were dancing on the side of the waltzer. Suk stuck his hand out of the spinning car and slapped Jason Lane on the cheek as the car spun past him.

When the ride stopped and Suk and the other two Asian lads got off, Jason Waite and Mark walked over to them followed by their crowd of black lads. After an exchange of words, Jason Waite took one of the Asian lads by the shoulder at which the Asian boy slapped him on the forehead, twice. Then the Asian boys ran off followed by four others, two of whom were carrying metal bars. He heard one of them shout: 'Get the gun.'

Mark Baptiste's version of events supported that of Jason Waite including the observation that the Asian lad had hit Jason with his open hand.

Andy Aherne reckoned he had heard Jason Lane say, about three Asian youths riding the waltzer: 'One of them Pakis just punched me in the face.' At this one of the black lads began spitting at the boys on the ride. Then, according to Andy, after a bit of squaring up between a black boy and an Asian, each of them went their own way but Mark Baptiste followed the Asian and confronted him on the edge of the waltzer. A gang of black lads gathered around this confrontation between Mark and the solitary Asian. There was no one standing between the Asian and the steps of the waltzer so he could have left whenever he wanted.

When the ride stopped, the three Asians got out of their car and the lone Asian suddenly moved backwards. Andy then noticed that Jason Waite had two gashes on his forehead, looked at his bloodied hand and said: 'The man's drew my blood.' The Asian who had done the damage walked down the steps holding a knife in his right hand. He waved it and said: 'If anyone fucks me they're dead.' The knife was five or six inches long, double-edged and very shiny but he could not see if it had a handle.

Julian James, another of Jason Waite's crowd, said that he saw the solitary Asian on the side of the waltzer surrounded by black lads. Jason Waite, however, was standing between him and the steps down from the ride. The Asian boy shouted 'Move', pushed Jason out of the way and walked down the steps. Jason then took hold of the Asian by his shoulder and pulled him back. The Asian boy then put his left hand into his rear left hand trouser pocket and pulled out a knife. He used his right hand to open the blade. He then lashed out at Jason with a slashing movement.

Another of their crowd was Leon Henry and he also saw the lad he recognised as Talat slash Jason with a knife. It was about four inches long with a black handle. He also saw an Asian with a long screwdriver and heard another one shout: 'Get the gun.'

Gasnel James, also one of the group of black youths, saw Talat standing with his hands in his pockets before pulling out a black-handled Stanley knife about six inches long with a triangular shaped blade about one inch long. He flicked it at Jason's head before walking off.

Mark Jackson had also joined up with the crowd of black boys and Jason Lane spoke to them from the other side of the ride: 'This Paki punched me in the mouth.' He was holding his mouth as he said it. Some of the gang then spat at the Asians riding the waltzer. Talat then came up to Gasnel and told him not to spit on his mates. He did not see the assault.

Another member of the crowd was Dean Fountain. His story varied in some details from the others but according to him Talat slashed four times with a silver knife about four inches long with a black handle. As Talat walked away after the attack he pressed a button on the knife one handed and the blade folded away. He also heard the shout of: 'Get the gun, get the gun.'

Kevin Howell's statement offered nothing new except that it was two slashes which had caused the injuries to Jason. Daniel Priest, however, maintained that Talat had lashed out once and then, after Jason had let him go, slashed him four more times.

The doctor who treated Jason Waite confirmed two wounds on the forehead which needed stitches and recorded Jason Waite's belief that they had been done with a knuckle knife.

Despite the number of Asian youths at the Booker Common fair, statements were taken from very few. Sukhpal 'Suk' Singh Sandhu was one of them.

Although he was nearby he did not see what actually happened but ran to the car with Talat when he realised the urgency of the situation. In the back seat of the car, as it was being driven away by a friend called Rasool, Talat said that one of the black lads had pulled out a screwdriver on him so he had slashed him. He said that he had cut himself accidentally as he had got the knife out and there was a small cut on his right hand between his thumb and first finger. Suk did not see Talat's knife.

Another Asian to give a statement was Rasool Ghulam, the driver of the car. According to him there was an argument going on between Talat and a slim West Indian, who said something like: 'Why did you go down there?'

Talat answered: 'Because you were spitting on my friends.'

Rasool then said to Talat, in their language, that he didn't want any trouble. Talat passed this on to the black youth to whom he was talking, saying: 'Move, I don't want no trouble.'

With that Talat went to walk down the steps but another black lad stepped in front of him and blocked his route. Talat pushed past but the lad then grabbed Talat's collar from behind and pulled him.

With that, the black gang then began moving forwards towards Talat and Rasool heard one of the Asian boys shout out: 'He's got a screwdriver, he's got a screwdriver.' The next thing he knew was that the West Indian who had tried to stop Talat was holding his forehead and was shouting: 'Oh, he's got me, he's got me!'

Rasool, Talat, Saeed and Sukhpal all ran to the car and drove off. During the drive Talat asked for a tissue because he'd cut his hand and someone opened the windows without any apparent reason, allowing cold air to rush in.

They suddenly realised that a friend called Anser had been left behind and were debating whether to go back for him when he appeared running along the road. As he got into the car he said to Talat: 'What happened to your hand?' to which Talat replied: 'I've cut myself on the knife.'

Saeed Kayani, a cousin of Superfly, told a very similar story as to what had happened at the fair but with some essential differences. The black youth who had taken hold of Talat was, according to Saeed, carrying a twelve-inch screwdriver in his right hand. On seeing it he shouted out to run, which they all did, leaving Anser Khan behind.

When they were in the car they remembered Anser but Talat didn't say anything and he didn't appear to be carrying a knife.

That same evening of the Booker Common fair, the night before the café incident, P.C. Norman Rush went to Lloyd Waite's address following a complaint by a young Asian man. Waite explained what had happened to Jason and said that Jason had given him an address of someone involved in the incident. Waite had gone to that address but he could not quite remember now where it was and the young bloke who lived there had given him another address where he might find someone involved. He had this address written on a piece of paper together with the description of a car. It was Talat's name and address and Talat's car.

Waite did not tell the policeman the name of the person who had given him the piece of paper because he could not remember it. He could also no longer remember the address where this person lived. It was, in fact, the person who had made the complaint against Waite. P.C. Rush then left to discuss the matter with the CID.

Returning to the house at 1.15 a.m., P.C. Rush again spoke to Lloyd Waite. Waite said he had visited the address (the one which he could no longer remember) with friends but the young man who lived there (whose name he also could no longer remember) had been unwilling to help them identify the person who had attacked Jason. They had taken him from his house so that he could help them identify the assailant and he had then become more helpful. They had visited the International Café and the address on the piece of paper but did not find the person they wanted so they had taken the young man back home.

Perlina Francis, Lloyd Waite's common law wife of fifteen years, also made a statement about that evening. She said that when Jason had turned up on the doorstep covered in blood, she telephoned Lloyd's brother, Houghton. Lloyd, Houghton and Lewis (Pinnock) then came to her house and Jason gave the name of one of the people involved in the accident. Jason was taken off to hospital and the three men went in search of this person. They did not seem to be gone very long and when they returned Lloyd said the man they wanted was not in.

Perlina Francis then moved on to talk about events leading up to the incident at the café. She, Lewis Pinnock and Lloyd Waite all had dinner together and then the two men went out, saying they were going to Aylesbury to see Waite's mother to give her some money. As Waite was dressed up she asked him if he intended going anywhere else but he said he did not. That was the last time she saw him alive.

The witness statements which were taken by police following the stabbings at the International Café revealed a variety of different observations, some of which were completely contradictory. But there is an old saying that if you ask six witnesses to the same incident for a description of what they saw, you will get six different versions.

Brian Cordice, a twenty-nine-year old plasterer, had been inside the café to begin with and only left it after most of the others had run outside following the fight. He saw someone smashing the windows of the white car with a baseball bat or something similar and thought it was Superfly but he admitted that his mind was completely confused and dazed.

Lewis 'Looy' Pinnock was inside the car and trying to start it. The engine wasn't running but it was jerking towards Lloyd Waite who was lying in the road in front of it. He tried to get out of the car but Cordice told him stay where he was.

He noticed his friend, Andrew Gumbs, using his car phone to

call an ambulance. He then went over to Waite, felt his neck pulse and noticed a wound where his jumper had risen up. 'It was on his side and looked like a knife wound but there was no blood, there was just dry, pink flesh against his West Indian skin.'

Andrew Gumbs had locked himself out of his flat and went looking for his brother Eurich at the International Café. Eurich wasn't there but Andrew sensed trouble and immediately left. He drove around aimlessly for a while before finding himself back outside the café and saw the smashed white car rolling towards Waite. He got out, helped stop the car, phoned for an ambulance on his car phone and drove off.

Sixteen-year-old Alex Till had gone to the Top Cats night club to help out moving some furniture around. In payment he was allowed to play pool free of charge. The pool room was on the first floor and overlooked Desborough Road and he saw two black men coming from the direction of the café followed by a crowd of Asian lads carrying what looked like pool cues.

The larger of the two black men fell to the ground and was obscured from view by the white car. He thought he may have been hit before falling but once he was on the ground it seemed as though five or six people gathered around him and started to hit him with pool cues. 'I saw sticks being raised and blows raining down on the man on the ground.'

The smaller black man was standing by the open car door when, after a hesitation, someone struck him on the back of the head with one of the sticks. Others then joined in, aiming blows at his head and body. He felt sure that one of the crowd was using a hockey stick.

The smaller black man, Pinnock, sat in the driver's seat with his legs sticking out and one of the crowd began to beat his legs with a stick. Perhaps two of the crowd began smashing the car windows and after that everyone began to disperse quickly.

After the ambulance had arrived Alex left Top Cats and as he passed the scene he noticed what he thought to be a knuckle knife lying in the road near the white car. He later changed this description and said he believed it to be an ordinary knife three to four inches long.

John Newell had taken his thirteen-year-old daughter, Donna, to the Desborough Road Bingo Hall and they were about to enter when he noticed a white car stop in the road and then reverse into a building entrance. Two stocky West Indians got out and walked across the road towards the café but, before entering, stopped to talk to a small group of Asian lads standing outside.

Soon afterwards, both men exited from the café and the smaller one had his arm around the other one whose shirt was pulled up and whose side looked red. They both stepped off the pavement and the larger man fell over. A group of about six Asians then came running out of the café carrying pickaxe handles and one was carrying a machete-type knife – he was an older man, lighter skinned and wearing an apron.

Those with the pickaxe handles then began to beat the two black men and smash the car windows after which they got into a blue car about the size of a Ford Escort and drove off.

Karen Ray was in the passenger seat of a car driving along Desborough Road when, just past Top Cats, the car in front swerved around something in the road. It was Lloyd Waite. An Asian youth struck Waite twice with something that looked like a snooker cue and a taller, older man was ushering a group of Asians into the International Café.

Another Asian youth with a large plank in his hands was standing near a white car. A black man with blood on his face was getting up off the ground and was trying to get into the car. The Asian youth with the plank, which measured about four feet by three inches, smashed the windscreen of the vehicle with it. She put his age at between twenty-one and twenty-three.

After parking the car and calling the police she returned to the scene and spoke to a policeman, pointing out to him the tall man who had been ushering the youths into the café. She wasn't sure if the policeman had heard her.

Almost a month later Karen Ray made another statement in which she clarified what she had seen:

I saw three Asians, one was holding something that looked like a snooker cue hitting the person lying on the ground. Another Asian was ushering lots of other Asians into the café. He was not holding any weapon. The third Asian was smashing the windscreen of the car with a plank of wood.

After I had called the police and returned to the scene, the Asian (Superfly) which I pointed out to the police officer was the one who was ushering the Asians into the café. I did not see the other two Asians, the one smashing the car or the one hitting the West Indian, at the scene at all. I did not say anything to the police officer other than: 'I saw that Asian man ushering other Asians into the café.'

In P.C. Colin Brooker's report of the night's events he had written down the following conversation with Karen Ray:

'I saw it all. They beat them up and ran back into there.'
'Would you recognise any of the offenders if you saw them again?'
'I think so if I saw them.'
'What exactly did you see?'
'Lots of them were beating them up and that one (indicating Superfly) was hitting the one on the floor around the head with a bat.'

Two other witnesses made statements but neither was able to provide much detail. An American military policeman, driving along Desborough Road at the time, was able only to describe one of the Asians who was handing out a beating as being between five feet ten inches and six feet tall and another as being five feet eight inches tall.

A man on his way to the bingo hall in his car saw the white car smashed by Asians, one of whom was wielding an iron bar. They ran off, passing either side of his car.

SIX

A Search for Truth

Someone new to the workings of a police investigation, suddenly presented with a huge file of papers which include witness statements and the essence of the prosecution's case, might themselves need to be a detective to make sense of it all. But of course what is contained in that file is only one half of the story, the other half being the defence case. But even the combination of the two halves do not add up to a whole. There are other, unwritten, unrecorded, uncommunicated happenings which mould and form an investigation from its very beginnings.

The case of the International Café was no different.

In the early hours of Sunday morning, just a few hours after the incident, John Davis, a principal in the local firm of solicitors of Davis Walker & Co., was contacted by people in the local Asian community. They were extremely concerned as large numbers of Asians had been arrested and were being held at High Wycombe police station on suspicion of murder. Families had been denied access to them and their impression was that there had been a sweep through the community with as many people being arrested as could be found.

Confusion obviously abounded and it was not clear if it had been a gang fight. The first thing the solicitors did was to contact the police and ask for clarification, particularly about who was being held in custody. Police response was at first reluctant then vague and then obstructive, maintaining that none of those being held had requested the services of a solicitor.

It seemed incredible that anyone arrested on such a serious charge would not want a solicitor and so permission was asked to talk to those being held to see if that really was what they wanted. It was refused.

Under the workings of the Police and Criminal Evidence Act (PACE) the police were within their rights to refuse access where they claim a detainee does not wish to see a solicitor. If a detainee does wish to see a solicitor he or she may request a named solicitor or the duty solicitor but the police may still delay access on a number of grounds (e.g. interference with enquiries).

When someone is admitted into custody the only record of whether that person asked for a solicitor or refused the option is a signed box on the Custody Record. Even the duty solicitor does not have the power to confirm that decision. You can imagine the scenario:

'We only want to ask a couple of questions. You haven't done anything have you? So why do you want a solicitor, you'll be here all night waiting for them. The sooner you sign this the sooner you can go home!'

John Davis was extremely concerned about the seriousness of this case and cancelled his intended visit to Lords that same day to watch the first match of the season. At the request of their parents, he felt it vital to gain access to those who were detained as soon as possible and start the process of discovering exactly what had happened. He was being asked to act by parents of those detained who had been refused access to their sons, some as young as sixteen and seventeen years old.

A series of further telephone calls to High Wycombe police produced no result and so a letter was written to the Superintendent of the station and immediately sent to him. Suddenly, all obstacles evaporated.

It transpired that those arrested were being held at both Amersham and High Wycombe stations and so representatives of Davis Walker were sent to both. The moment it was known that Talat Sarwar was in the local hospital, medical staff were contacted and they gave an assurance that they would not allow police to interview him until he was fit enough. A brief meeting was arranged with Talat in the presence of police and he was advised to say nothing until he was well and his solicitor was there.

Being present at various police interviews Davis Walker were now beginning to glean scraps of information which they could collate to provide the outlines of a picture. But it still was not known who or how many would be charged with murder or other offences such as affray.

One thing became abundantly clear; there was a need for quick and decisive action if Davis Walker were to stand any chance of mounting a worthwhile defence should anyone be charged as a result of the International Café incident.

What they wanted was an independent post mortem of Waite's remains; a restriction on the release of the body without their consent; the right to investigate the scene of the incident; access to all forensic samples taken from Waite or from anyone else for that matter; to identify the type and extent of Talat's injuries and to have them officially recorded and, if necessary, photographed so that a clear record would be available in any trial; and the right to interview as many witnesses as possible who were at the scene while events were still fresh in their minds.

These requests were made to the police and elicited no response whatsoever. Even worse, they were considered to be an intrusion into a very serious crime and the implication was that their actions stopped only one pace short of aiding and abetting the guilty. The police made it clear that they had a set procedure for investigating crimes such as this and no defence solicitor was going to disturb it. They also appeared to be completely bemused by the efforts Davis Walker were making on behalf of the Asian community. They should not have been because Davis Walker had acted for both Asian and West Indian communities at different times.

At this early stage it was obvious in which direction the investigation of Lloyd Waite's death was heading. It was to be a battle between police and defence, with no concession by police that defence lawyers have a right to and a need for information if the interests of justice are to be properly served.

But of course it does not have to be like that and under

the system of a *juge d'instruction* it is not like that.

Had this case been handled by Catherine Samet she would have been in complete charge of the investigation into the death of Lloyd Waite. The local police, regardless of their seniority, would have been under her instruction.

On arrival at the scene she would have issued a series of instructions as to what she wanted done. In essence they may not have differed that much from what any investigating officer would do. She will make decisions about the need for forensic examination and fingerprinting, ensuring that arrangements are made for an autopsy which she will attend; she may give instructions to the pathology department and eventually go to the laboratories and discuss the case with the professor responsible.

But the main point is that Catherine Samet is not a police woman, not a member of the CID, but a judge. Her instructions have to be followed out and any information resulting from them is fed back to her. She has total control of the investigation and her aim is not simply to secure conviction after conviction but to seek out the truth. Her role is explained best in her own words:

> The principles on which I operate are essentially to be free from all external pressures, to have no ideas and no hunches, to be totally practical and know nothing about anyone. My whole intention is not to be prejudiced, not to come to a case with preconceptions and above all to protect the rights of people. In the process of questioning someone I might be rude, I might be aggressive but I am only playing a game, a game which assists me in discovering the truth.
>
> I always strictly apply the rules because once you allow yourself to indulge in a personal interpretation of an event, the ground beneath you becomes very weak. I had a recent case of a car accident in which four people died. In front of me was a young boy who had made one mistake – his concentration had flagged and he had shot across a crossroads and hit another car. I had to ask myself if it was right to continue with this case and almost certainly send this boy to jail for what was a momentary slip. In the end I applied the rules, which is what I always do.

Once an investigation is underway, police can only properly act under the instructions of the *juge*. They can question suspects with her authority or follow a particular line of enquiry but only for a set period of time which she decides. Once that time scale has come to an end so must that line of enquiry. If they do unearth something they will telephone immediately, regardless of the time of day or night.

The term of duty for Catherine Samet is ten days on and ten days off and she may have up to 150 serious crimes under investigation at any one time. So it is not surprising that mobile phones and disrupted sleep are part of her life.

Central to the work of any *juge* is a dossier for each case. Everything which happens, every piece of information which is gleaned, every statement, report, finding and every instruction, whether to the police or anyone else, is included in this dossier. It is one of the most vital elements of the work of a *juge d'instruction* and the relevance of it will become obvious later in the book.

Just as in our system, police will frequently claim that they know who is responsible for a certain crime, perhaps because of their previous history and in these cases the *juge* will insist on seeing some additional proof. Again, if police feel they have a case against someone they will ask to see the *juge* and ask for permission to pull them in. If she feels that on the basis of the information they have there are two or three suspects and one has obviously been targeted, she may insist that the investigation is widened before making an arrest.

There are those who believe this system to be too expensive but in reality I believe it to be considerably cheaper than ours. There is absolutely no need for magistrates' courts and as over 80 per cent of our cases are handled by magistrates' courts there would be an enormous saving here alone. In addition, there is no need for summary hearings and because the *juge d'instruction* is a judge, she has the knowledge and confidence to weed out weak cases before taking them to court. In England and Wales, magistrates rarely have the confidence to do that with serious cases (as we shall see) and refer them on to very expensive higher courts.

If it does appear that one of the suspects is a likely candidate she will authorise the police to arrest him and hold him in custody. This is one element of the French system with which I disagree but at this point the accused will have no access to a lawyer. They can be kept *incommunicado* for twenty-four hours and this period can be extended to a further twenty-four hours but not without obtaining permission from the *juge*. In the case of a drugs charge this period of detention can be as long as four days and in my opinion is totally unsupportable. This period of detention is called *garde à vue* and I am certainly not advocating that.

When I expressed my concern to Catherine Samet she responded with Gallic nonchalance:

> The difference between your system and ours is that I am a judge and I know the person is in custody. Although they cannot phone for a lawyer at least someone reasonably independent knows where they are and why they are there. The reasons for keeping them away from a lawyer are quite simple, it's a means of putting pressure on them.
>
> I would never authorise it if there was no strong evidence or we had nothing to challenge the person with. Certainly I would never allow someone to be held simply because they were in the vicinity of a crime or at the scene. What would be the point of bringing someone in unless we had a very strong case to put to them? Certainly to extend the period of detention to a second twenty-four hours I would need some very conclusive evidence.
>
> This whole process can be very painful for the accused but often I just have to do it and I liken it to an exploratory operation in hospital – not pleasant but necessary.

If, during the period of detention, the accused confesses, the police are forbidden to question him any further and must telephone the *juge* immediately with the information. They are obliged to apply article 105 of the French penal code and take the accused person in front of the *juge*.

For most people, their impression of the interior of an interview room is probably drawn from a thousand television police dramas and as far as the British model is concerned it is fairly accurate. Sparsely furnished, windowless, flaked gloss paint barely concealing years of neglect and a locked door – they do exist. This is perhaps by design – fear has to be instilled in those who are unused to the confrontation which is so much a part of interrogation.

Confrontation may also be a part of the French model but the physical surroundings, certainly at the court of Senlis, are very different. Firstly, it is an office, not an interrogation room. One wall is comprised almost entirely of glass and overlooks the grass, trees and shrubs of the landscaped gardens which surround the court.

The *juge* sits with her back to the window and the accused faces her across a desk. Around the walls are shelves full of files and the room contains all the normal paraphernalia of a working office. At right angles to the window and facing both *juge* and accused is Madame Herbert, Catherine Samet's clerk, a woman probably in her late thirties and normally viewed through a cloud of cigarette smoke. She sits, fingers poised at her typewriter keyboard. Wherever Judge Samet goes so does Madame Herbert, ceaselessly taking notes. The *juge* may not talk to the accused without her clerk being present.

Standing by the door is a policeman, not one who is involved in the investigation but a court policeman whose role is to ensure the security of the *juge*. He takes no part in the proceedings and stands silent throughout.

The first interview is very formal and is a statement of rights and of the situation as it currently stands. The accused is informed that he has a right to a lawyer either of his own choosing or, failing that, one will be appointed for him under legal aid. He is then given the option of continuing the interview without a lawyer being present or of waiting until one arrives.

Under French law, a person is considered a witness until such time as they confess to or are charged with an offence, when they become the accused. In both cases the option of speaking with or without a lawyer must then be posed. If a person has confessed they will be asked to repeat the confession in front of both the *juge* and their lawyer. If pressure, either physical or psychological, has been put on them to admit a crime, they have the chance at this early stage to refute it. But in France, nowhere near as much importance is placed on confessions as in Britain where a large proportion of all cases are supposedly resolved with an admission of guilt.

> I think in your system you pay much more attention to wit-
> ness statements and confessions. We don't really need confessions
> because the case will be built on material evidence. Simply to
> confess isn't enough as you might be shielding someone or it
> might be because you have psychological problems or because of
> pressure.
> I never believe a confession and I never believe what a witness
> tells me until I have other concrete evidence which supports what
> they say. Humans are very complex and I cannot rely on their
> words, I need material evidence. Everyone when he comes into
> my office for the first time will generally not tell the truth. I know
> that so it is a factor which I have already included in my logical
> thinking. So, a confession doesn't mean you are guilty and it is
> my job to find the truth. I cannot stress it enough – I am neutral.
> I apply exactly the same thinking to witness statements. I
> know that people might be a bit slow, become confused and
> say the wrong thing but in the end a logical statement will make
> sense when it is backed up with material evidence.

Throughout an interview the accused is not obliged to say any-thing but the pressure to do so is great. The role of the *juge* as an independent investigator, trained to sift evidence in a search for the truth, places the onus on the accused to participate in that search if they are innocent. Although the same principle applies in France that is supposed to apply in Britain, namely that a person is innocent until proved guilty, a decision to remain silent would not be seen as normal.

Ironically, because police investigators in Britain frequently set out to mould an accused's words to fit the preconceived idea of what happened, lawyers quite rightly instruct their clients to remain silent.

To speak is often to play into the hands of the investigators, allowing them to confuse and befuddle you and turn innocent inaccurate details or lapses of memory into proof of guilt. In France, however, lawyers frequently advise their clients not to remain silent and to cooperate with the *juge*.

Catherine Samet emphasises that normally, when someone initially chooses to remain silent, her logical arguments as to why they should speak are accepted.

Throughout the course of an interrogation, which could last for several hours each time and take place over a prolonged period, the accused will always have the right to have his lawyer present. At any time he may stop and speak to the lawyer out of ear shot of the *juge* and if the accused is held in custody the lawyer has the right to unrestricted visiting.

Perhaps one of the most important aspects of this system is that every single piece of information relating to the case – witness statements, forensic reports, the *juge*'s instructions to the police and their responses – are all included in the dossier and the defence lawyer has access to it. Both parties are playing with exactly the same cards and should the case eventually go to court, the prosecution's case will be based on the information in the dossier and nothing else. Defence lawyers will have the same dossier and there will be no surprises, no secret witnesses, no last-minute evidence presented on the first day in court and, equally as important, nothing is secretly excluded from evidence which doesn't fit the prosecution's case. The withholding of information, together with uncorroborated confessions, has been a regular theme in Britain's appalling record of miscarriages of justice as we shall see.

Interviews are not recorded or video taped and notes are not taken contemporaneously, but every so often the *juge* will stop and dictate a summary of what has happened to her clerk who will take it down. The accused will be asked to verify its veracity. In my version of the system of *juge d'instruction* I would want all interviews to be video taped and I would preserve the right to silence.

To imagine that an interview with a *juge d'instruction* is a session where tea and sympathy abound would be completely wrong. Although only visiting, I did sample just a small taste of Catherine Samet's ability to command a situation. 'Of course, when necessary I can be aggressive, I can play the good guy or the bad guy and whatever else is needed to get at the truth. It is a little like being a member of an orchestra, you have to play your part. Sometimes you have to be nice and sometimes you have to be cruel.'

In pursuit of the truth, the *juge* is at liberty to use whatever experts she chooses – a radiologist, an expert in matters sexual, a biologist. They do not have to be members of the state forensic service but can be the most qualified experts in the country. Frequently they are university professors. 'I always send my forensics to Paris and I don't use anyone locally because of their lack of consistency. I want the latest in science and I want results quickly – and by that I mean "now".'

If she decides it is necessary she may use two experts in the same field in order to verify a finding. In theory, there is no limit on the money she can spend on any one case. Naturally, there is constant criticism of this freedom, particularly when the expenditure is on cases involving working-class people and in particular North African immigrants. Obviously in France also there is a presumption of guilt for certain groups of people from some quarters.

The relationship between the *juge* and defence lawyers is an interesting one. In the case of independent experts they have every right to ask the *juge* to seek a second opinion. They cannot insist on the expert she uses, they can only suggest. There would be no recompense within legal aid to pay for them to seek their own independent advice but if the request is placed through the *juge* then the cost would come off her budget. Ironically she has never had such a request in her five years of practice.

It is important to remember the difference in approach between our police-operated system of investigation and that of a *juge d'instruction*. In the latter case the search is for truth and not guilt. Because of this it would seem logical that defence lawyers would contribute to the well of knowledge by providing information on the innocence of their client. Again in five years no such thing has ever happened. I suspect that this says more about the quality of French lawyers than it does about the effectiveness of the system.

Ironically, in some cases there is a very close relationship between lawyer and *juge*. In company fraud it is obviously essential to have a detailed explanation of the financial dealings of an organisation and the lawyer might well have a great deal more information at his or her disposal than the *juge*. She may request in writing information from them and they would normally respond.

Catherine Samet's explanation of this relationship is, at first, a bit unnerving to a lawyer schooled in and exposed to the British way of doing things. She maintains that her first and most important dedication is to human rights and lawyers are aware of this. They rely on the *juge d'instruction* because they have confidence in the position and the ideals which the holder of that position represents.

One of the most damning indictments of the British judicial system is the large number of people held on remand. In this respect the French system appears to be little better. At the time I spoke to her, Catherine Samet's case load amounted to approximately 124 serious investigations involving some two hundred to three hundred people who might be considered suspect. Of this number thirty-four were being held on remand – not a particularly enviable record.

In deciding who is granted bail there is as much subjectivity as there is in Britain. The first thing the *juge* does is to consider what 'type' of person the accused is. The prosecutor will be the one to oppose bail and the process takes place in the form of a formalised meeting. There will be the accused, the *juge*, the prosecutor and the accused's lawyer if he wants him present.

The meeting has to take place within five days of the accused requesting bail and all the reasons for and against are given and noted. At the end the *juge* will make a decision and I suspect it will be on similar subjective grounds to the bail decisions taken in Britain. It is not a satisfactory way to deal with people who, at this stage, must still be presumed innocent – but more of that later.

An accused person can spend a year or more in prison awaiting trial but has the right to apply for bail on a regular basis – a right which is not much use if the request is continually refused. The reasons proffered for such an infringement of human rights are the slowness of the bureaucratic judicial system and an insufficient number of courts to handle the case load. Both excuses are totally unacceptable so this is another element of the French system which I reject.

It would be naive to pretend that the examining magistrate system of investigation, the *juge d'instruction*, is without faults and free from outside pressures. In fact there have been recent examples in which overt political interference has been exerted for *juges* to drop cases which could possibly embarrass government.

However, Catherine Samet is fairly sanguine about it:

> Indirectly I come under the prosecutor and when the prosecutor hands a case over to me, he or she can instruct me not to follow a particular line of investigation. The prosecutor is accountable to the Ministry of Justice and has political considerations. But once I am in charge of investigation I can do more or less what I wish and there is often more than one way of getting the same result.
>
> There can also be indirect pressure and it is important and quite possible to ignore this if it is not legitimate. But sometimes it is a question of doing what you can rather than what you want.

With a phrase which left more unsaid than said, she added: 'Mostly you can withstand political pressure but in the end you can only expect of people what they are.'

There could be similar reservations about the relationship between the *juge* and police. When working with the same people month after month there must be some risk of listening too attentively to their beliefs and perhaps giving in to their requests for the sake of an easy life. Again, her response indicates a subtlety of approach:

> Police obviously do have the ability to manipulate you whether you are experienced or not. So you have to tread a careful line which involves diplomacy. As a judge I am the head of an enterprise and I must know the people who are working for me; I must know their strengths and their weaknesses and I must be a bit of a philosopher.

I do socialise with police sometimes and in order to find the truth it is important to work together. To live in a state of permanent confrontation with the police would help no one.

There can be cynicism from some long-term, experienced police that a young person such as me can be in charge of an investigation. The whole point is that they are police and I am a judge and there is a world of difference in the way we approach things. But on the whole I don't find them resentful of my role.

Many of the criticisms which are levelled at me are simply not valid, particularly the one which says that you can't possibly investigate properly unless you've been through the police mill. Can you be a good doctor only if you've had a bad heart, and then can you only be a heart doctor?

I have no desire to be a police woman because my principal aim is to guarantee a person's rights. If anything I am an academic. What motivates me most of all is my love for people and criminals are men and women, members of our society. In my office I see them cry, I see them laugh, I see them suffer in prison. People are very complicated and I never forget this. Someone can do something horrible but for a very pure reason and I will try to get at this reason, I try to understand them. Despite my title, my role is not to judge them but to understand them.

I believe in justice and I believe in a democracy which works. I try to uphold the three pillars of the French constitution – Liberty, Equality, Fraternity – and to that you could add human rights.

To someone weaned on the confrontational approach of the British police, these ethics might sound too pure, too idealistic, too soft. They are the views of one particular *juge d'instruction* who takes her job of trying to find criminals very seriously.

The point is that in the role of the *juge d'instruction* we have a totally different approach to investigating crime, one which begins with an assumption of innocence; which does not depend upon confession to secure conviction; which upholds the basic principles of human rights; which is independent of police; and which could not possibly get things as badly wrong so frequently as our own system.

To anyone with even the slightest interest in policing, it must have become apparent that reports of malpractice are now almost a daily event. In addition to the now infamous miscarriages, and to which new ones are continually being added, dozens of cases involving individuals and groups of policemen flit through our newspaper columns.

The latest one at the time of writing involves accusations against several policemen at Stoke Newington police station. A local community group has claimed to have monitored offences which include drug dealing, drug planting, physical violence, fabricating evidence and inducement to give evidence by offering drugs. At this time, none of the thirty alleged offenders have been prosecuted but eight men have been moved to another police station, although we're assured that it has nothing to do with the allegations. Scotland Yard has launched what it claims is one of the biggest enquiries in its history into malpractice in the Metropolitan Police.

Only last year, in the same neighbourhood, seven policemen were dismissed from the force for beating up a window cleaner in a local pub.

That there is a crisis within the police force is now obvious and a little tinkering at the edges, a determination to 'root out the odd bad apple' is not good enough. The whole basis of the way in which investigations are conducted needs to be changed.

So, an end to targeting and the introduction of an independent investigating magistrate similar to the French *juge d'instruction*, who is democratically accountable through a Ministry of Justice. Police must no longer be responsible for supervising the investigation of criminal offences in Britain.

SEVEN

Inside the Café

Although not a regular visitor to the International Café, Brian Cordice was there on the evening of 22 April. He had picked up a take-away from the Caribbean Kitchen and was eating it in the café. There was a crowd of Asians around the place but the only one he recognised was Superfly.

He became aware that two people had entered the café, one of whom was a man he knew, 'Looy' from Aylesbury (Lewis Pinnock). He called out 'Hello Looy' but got no reply. 'I knew he had seen me because he looked round and I gained the impression that he didn't want to be involved in what was happening.'

Looy stayed near the door and the other man, Waite, went up to one of the Asians and, 'with a not very friendly attitude', put his finger under his chin and asked him some questions. Waite then came up to Cordice's table and asked him if he knew someone called Talat. He did not. Waite then went up to Superfly who was behind the counter and asked him something. Superfly answered: 'No, he's not here.'

Waite then walked back down the café towards Looy and they talked together before moving over to a group of five young Asians. One – five feet two inches small with a black bomber jacket – fitted the description of Talat. Waite turned his attention to another Asian and the one who fitted Talat's description suddenly pushed Waite and ran from the group towards the counter. Cordice did not see if he had anything in his hand.

The two West Indians followed him, tables and chairs went flying and a quick fight took place behind the counter. Cordice saw a knife flash but he could not see who was holding it or whether there was more than one knife because he was too busy trying to keep out of the way of the blood which was being splashed around.

The fight stopped almost as quickly as it had started and the two West Indians headed for the door. As they left, most of the Asians followed and many appeared to have suddenly acquired sticks or cues. Superfly was one of those who rushed out but Cordice was not sure if he was armed or not.

Arif Khan not only claimed to have seen most of what happened inside the café but accompanied Talat to High Wycombe General Hospital after he was injured. Arif went into the café looking for his cousin and he estimated that there were about twenty people there, most of them Asian but also some West Indian lads.

As he walked in he saw Waite and Pinnock chasing Talat towards the service counter. He went on:

> There was a lot of shouting and noise going on and people were crying out 'Stop it'. As Talat was running past the centre pool table I could see that the two black men were both lifting their arms high and were striking down at Talat. One of them had a knife in his hand, a knife about five inches long.
>
> Talat was sort of facing them, with his hand, I think it was his left hand, held in front of him sort of protecting himself as he was running backwards.
>
> Both men were like crazy men, lifting their hands over and over again striking down at Talat. Then Talat reached the end of the café and was inside the gap into the kitchen. Both the coloured men were behind the bar and in the kitchen as well and they were still hitting out at him. I saw the manager of the café go over towards them and others were shouting out for them to leave Talat alone and to stop it.
>
> I then saw Talat sort of slump over to one side and fall across a chair. The two men were still hitting out at him and I could see one of them had a knife in his hand.
>
> Then the two men seemed to think that Talat had had enough

because they turned round and started running back towards the door and past where I was standing. As they passed by me, over by the space invader machine, I could see that both men had knives in their hands. Up until then I had only seen one but as they started to run out I could see clearly that they were both holding knives.

All of the café chased after them and I could see that some had grabbed hold of pool cues. I looked around for my bag, found it, then went outside and Talat, by that time, had got up and gone outside himself. On my way out I saw a knife lying on the floor inside the café. I don't know if it was one of the knives the coloured men had, all I remember is that the blade was all bent.

As I got outside I could see that one of the coloured men was on the ground and you could hear the sound of the sticks as they were hitting him. I think the other man was on the ground as well. I could see that the café manager was in the group but I don't know if he was fighting or trying to break it up. Talat was in a group near the road but he wasn't fighting; he just seemed to be standing there.

I went up to Talat and said, 'Look, just go to hospital.' I could see that he had a large wound to the side of his neck and one to his hand. He was very unsteady on his feet and it looked as though he was going to pass out. I thought he was going to die, there was blood dripping from the wound to his neck. I opened my sports bag and took a T-shirt out and told Talat to hold it to his neck. Then Suklain (Sugi) said he would take us to the hospital.

On the way to the hospital Talat told him a bit about what had happened at the fair and said that Suk was with him. Suklain then said that he had driven past Suk's house the previous evening and had seen him being beaten up by a crowd of black men. His mother was looking on, screaming and crying.

Arif asked Suklain if he'd done anything to help and he replied that he had not. 'I don't blame you,' said Arif.

Ateeqe Zarif went to the International Café with Saeed, and after a quick trip to Southall and a few cans of lager, they were both a bit 'tipsy'. He recognised a few faces in the café – Talat, Superfly, Roger, a white man called Peter and a few others he knew by sight but not by name.

Ateeqe was standing near the window when he became aware of two West Indians standing by the café door. The bigger of the two men seemed very aggressive and grabbed hold of Saeed, shouting something at him.

'He then came to me and grabbed my clothing on my chest and was clearly very agitated. He looked very wild and I suddenly realised he was saying: "Where is he, where is he?" I didn't know what he was talking about but when I saw the weird look in his eyes I took it seriously. I also noticed that in his right hand was a closed knife. He was keeping it hidden to some degree but I could see some of it in his hand.'

With that Superfly intervened and told the West Indian (Waite) that Ateeqe wasn't the man he was looking for so Waite let go of him. Ateeqe then looked around for Saeed and saw him leaving the café. Ateeqe, probably wisely, immediately followed him.

Nasir Ahmed added a little more clarity to the events of the evening before the stabbing. On that evening he had also been in the International Café but had left at about 9 p.m. to get a kebab from the van at the top of Amersham Hill after which 'Sugi' ran him home. As the car was being turned in the road near the end of Pettifer Way he saw what he took to be a family squabble. 'Suk' Sukhpal's father and mother, Mr and Mrs Singh, were in front of the house.

Mr Singh was shouting and there were three or four young teenage kids running around in the garden and there were three or four West Indians standing on the steps leading up to the front of the house. Standing inside the front porch Nasir could see the shape of someone else through the glass. They were bending over and he could not recognise them. The next thing he knew, a white car which had been parked outside the house sped past them and it seemed to be packed with people but he could not recognise any of them. He wrote its registration number down.

As it sped away, Mr Singh ran after it, shouting. Mrs Singh

turned and walked into the house.

Nasir then moved on to the night of the stabbings. He was playing pool at the end pool table nearest the window of the café with Iftikar ('Ifti') Ali. Talat was sitting behind the door of the café.

He became aware that two black men had entered and were talking to Saeed, asking him if he knew who Talat was. The two men then moved towards the window and asked the same question of the lad standing right next to Nasir. They appeared to be angry and went over to where Superfly was standing at the counter. Superfly tried to calm them saying he did not want any trouble.

The two black men then moved back through the café, grabbing hold of people and asking if they knew who Talat was. Talat then came up towards the bigger black man and there was a scuffle and they seemed to be pushing each other. He could see both of Talat's hands and they were empty.

The black man pulled a knife from somewhere inside his jacket and the blade was already out. Talat ran up the café towards the counter and the black man followed him. He kept stabbing at Talat who had his arm up to protect himself and Superfly was shouting out to leave Talat alone, he had not done anything.

At one point Talat had hold of the man's arm and Superfly was trying to separate them. They then fell behind the counter out of Nasir's view. Just seconds later, the black man came from behind the counter, down the café towards the door and there was blood on his hand. The second black man asked him if he'd been hit and he replied that he had with which he lifted up his sweat shirt and Nasir saw a wound two to three centimetres long on the right side of his body just below his ribs. Blood was beginning to ooze out.

Superfly helped Talat up from behind the counter and there were blood splashes across Talat's face. Nasir then stopped watching the two black men for a while but when he next noticed them, the man involved in the stabbing had collapsed on the pavement. Most of the people inside the café ran out, including Talat and Superfly, who was carrying a hockey stick. Superfly then proceeded to hit the car and smash its windscreen.

Ruksar Ahmed was standing outside the café with Arif when a white car pulled up opposite, reversed into the entrance of the carpark and stopped, facing the café. Two black men got out and Ruksar gave quite detailed descriptions of them. The stockier of the two asked him if he knew Talat and Ruksar lied, saying that he did not know him.

They then walked into the café, the thinner of the two (Pinnock) waiting by the door. Ruksar also went inside and saw Waite turn on Talat, shouting: 'You're Talat!' Talat denied it. The black man then pushed Talat and went for him with a knife he was holding in his hand. He said the man might have waved the knife but he wasn't sure. Anyway, he chased Talat up towards the counter and Pinnock joined in, all three of them fighting, with Talat taking punches all over his body.

As they all disappeared from view behind the counter he heard Talat shouting out: 'Help me, help me!' The fighting then broke off and Pinnock and Waite ran towards the exit. None of the twenty-five or so people inside the café went outside carrying snooker cues. Twenty or thirty seconds later, when Ruksar left the café, he saw Waite lying in the road with Pinnock bending over him. Being afraid, he went home.

Ruksar made that statement to police in the early hours of the day after the incident. However, later that same day he made a second statement which did not look at all good for Talat. He began by saying:

> Last night I said things in a statement that weren't true. The bit about the man waving a knife at Talat wasn't true and when I said I didn't see anyone go out of the café with snooker cues, that wasn't true. I said these things in order to protect Talat. I realise now how serious this is and now I want to tell you what really happened. The black actually got hold of Talat and said: 'You know Talat, you know Talat, you are him.' Talat said 'No!' then one of the black men grabbed somebody else. Talat then came over to where I was standing with Farouk by the first pool table as you enter the door. Talat asked Farouk to give him the knife and somebody shouted 'Don't'. Someone else shouted, 'Give it to him' and Farouk unzipped his jacket pocket and started to take something out.

I was moving away at this time but the next thing I saw was the black man starting to turn round and Talat ran up and went for him. Before all this happened I had been standing where I could see the black man. I don't think anyone else saw it but he had a knife in his hand, tight up against the side of his leg.

The details of the fight were much the same as his previous statement but when the two black men left, Talat came out from behind the counter holding a hockey stick and there was blood on one of his hands. He was looking really angry and ran out of the café after the two men.

When Ruksar went outside he saw Waite standing in the road looking very shaky and then falling over. Talat was swinging the hockey stick at Pinnock. After this the description became very confused except that he maintained he saw Superfly with some sort of stick hitting the car and breaking the windows.

The testimony of Suklain 'Sugi' Azad also did not appear to do very much for Talat's case and was very similar, remarkably similar, to Ruksar's. Sugi maintained that after the two black men had entered the café and grabbed Talat they let him go. Talat then went up to Farouk and said, 'Quickly, give me the knife.' Someone shouted out, 'No, don't give it to him', but Farouk unzipped his pocket on the right-hand side of his jacket and took out a knife which he gave to Talat. Sugi continued:

> I heard all the conversation quite clearly from where I was standing. I saw Talat then open up the knife and I saw the blade was about four or five inches long. I think it had a black handle. I then saw Talat run up behind one of the West Indians and he stabbed him about half way down his back on the right-hand side. The one who had been stabbed then took a knife, I think from out of his jeans or trousers, and he stood there and opened the knife up by using both hands. Then he ran after Talat with the knife in his hand. Before Talat stabbed the West Indian with the knife he got from Farouk I hadn't seen the West Indians with any weapons whatsoever. It was

only afterwards that the one who got stabbed took out a knife of his own.

The story of the fight was then similar to other stories except that he saw Waite stab Talat in the neck and then terminate the fighting. Talat then picked up a hockey stick and ran out after Waite and Pinnock and began swinging the stick at Pinnock, hitting some of the time and missing at others. Sugi pulled him away. Superfly was hitting the other black man with a pool cue and there was a noise of breaking glass from the direction of the car.

'I don't know what happened to the hockey stick after I pulled Talat away,' Sugi explained, 'he didn't have it when we walked to the car and he didn't have the knife with him either. I think he must have lost that in the café because he didn't have it when the West Indians were attacking him there.'

Susan Ray, Superfly's girlfriend, also made a statement concerning a knife:

> I had received permission from the police to clean up the café and I was cleaning the corner below the till and noticed blood splashes. I cleaned it with a cloth and disinfectant then I pulled the juke box out to get some loose change which was in bags on the floor in the corner. I noticed a bag of change between the extension lead wires for the juke box. I reached over to pick up the bag and noticed a knife in the corner of the cupboard. It was not hidden by anything and it was on the floor.
>
> I was surprised that the police had left it. The blade had been bent ninety degrees to the handle. There was no sign of blood on the handle. I straightened the knife blade, cleaned the knife and put it back into use for cutting bread rolls. I thought about ringing the police but decided not to. I assumed that the police didn't need the knife.

Three knives had now made an appearance. The original knife found out in the road, a second knife found down a drain grating and now this one. All were in the hands of the police and would eventually be passed over to forensic scientists.

But there were still more witness statements to come, one of them from Iftikar Ali. It did not shed much new light. He had seen a jumble of bodies moving down towards the serving counter but hadn't noticed any weapons. After about a minute of fighting, Pinnock had said to Waite, 'Come on, let's go!' and they walked out of the café. Waite had blood on his right hand.

Outside the café there were some unidentified Asians smashing up the car with pool cues. That was essentially it.

Iftikar, 'Ifti', made this statement three days after the incident but four days later he made a second statement which was very different. In fact it was almost identical to the statements made by Ruksar and Sugi. After the initial questioning by Pinnock and Waite, Talat had lunged forward at Waite with something in his hand and had struck Waite in the stomach area to the side.

His testimony was vague from then on as his vision was obscured but as Pinnock and Waite left the café he noticed that Waite had blood on his hand. Ifti even included in his statement something which he had said to another Asian lad after the fight: 'Jerry asked me what had happened and I said that these two guys had come into the café and I think Talat stabbed one of them because he pushed his hand into the black guy's side and the black guy had a cut on his hand as he pushed Talat's hand away.' Perhaps even more concerning, he went on,

> I didn't give all these details in my first statement because I am really, really worried that my life will be threatened because of reprisals in the Asian community. I have not been threatened at the moment by anyone but I do not want to go to court because my family and myself will be very worried about what other families in the Asian community will do to us.

After numerous witnesses which at best supported Talat's innocence and at worst were neutral, suddenly witnesses' statements were appearing which seemed to condemn Talat in the clearest possible way. Iftikar Ali's statement, while not as detailed, appeared to support these more damning statements.

He had also seen Talat go over to Farouk and talk to him before the fighting started. After it was all over he claimed that Waite, as he left the café, appeared to be leaning over on one side as if he was hurt and Pinnock was saying 'come on' and was trying to get him out.

These statements were the basis of the police case against Talat Sarwar. Copies of them were furnished to the defence and it was up to Talat's solicitors to counter the more damning ones if Talat was to stand a chance of being found not guilty.

Talat was obviously alleged to have been one of a group of Asian teenagers at Booker Common fair on the Friday night. A group of West Indian lads were spitting at some Asians on the waltzer and Talat challenged them about it. One of the black lads, Jason Waite, although two years younger than Talat, was much bigger and had produced a screwdriver. With a sharpened tip, screwdrivers are sometimes carried as weapons of self-defence. If stopped by the police they can argue that the screwdriver is a tool which they use for their work.

In this instance Jason Waite is assumed to have threatened Talat who produced a Stanley knife or some other knife and as Jason Waite lunged forward he was cut across the forehead.

Both groups of youths returned home and Jason's common law father wanted to know who had attacked him. Jason gave the name of Sukhpal, having confused the two identities. Lloyd Waite, together with his half-brothers Lewis Pinnock and Houghton Pinnock, then set out to find Sukhpal and see about retribution.

Lloyd Waite had a number of convictions for violence and in 1983 had been sentenced to four years in prison for it. Both his half-brothers had received two years each for the same offence.

That night, Lloyd Waite armed himself with a knife and his brothers with bricks and they went to Sukhpal's house where they assaulted his parents. Sukhpal was dragged from the home, forced into the car and effectively kidnapped.

When it became apparent that Sukhpal was not the person they were looking for, they wanted to know who it was who had cut Jason and they threatened to kill Sukhpal if he did not tell them. In sheer terror he mentioned Talat's name and the three men drove around High Wycombe in search of him. They went to various locations including the International Café but Talat was not there and eventually Sukhpal was dropped off near his home, scared stiff but not physically harmed.

The next evening, Saturday, Lloyd Waite and Lewis Pinnock returned to the International Café. In his statement to the police, which was not officially made until 3 May, Pinnock didn't deny the kidnapping but maintained that on the night of his half-brother's death they were in fact driving to Aylesbury, with Pinnock at the wheel, when Lloyd Waite told him to turn in towards High Wycombe town centre. It was not until he was asked to pull over that he realised what was happening.

Waite then walked into the café, stopping to talk to a group of four Asians who were standing outside the café. Pinnock followed when he realised that Waite was continuing with his intentions of the previous evening. He left the lights of the car on and the keys in the ignition, although he maintained that he did not leave the engine running.

Pinnock walked past the group of men and entered the café, staying by the door with his foot keeping the door open. Waite was at the counter talking to the person who appeared to be the owner. He noticed a small group of West Indian males, one of whom was Brian Cordice who spoke to him but he did not answer as he was watching Waite.

At this point there was no sign of trouble and Lloyd had not mentioned anything to him about going inside to look for trouble or even about going to the place.

Pinnock went on,

> I would say that if he'd planned to go to the café looking for trouble I would have been alongside him and we would have been carrying weapons to defend ourselves and would probably have had a few friends to back us up.

It was obvious from the beginning that we were hopelessly outnumbered and I hadn't thought of any fight. I wasn't armed with any weapon of any description. Lloyd then walked to me at the door and I turned to leave. As we were about to go an Asian called out something, I can't be exact but I think it was, 'Get the fuck out of it.'

Lloyd went over to him and it was pretty obvious why because that was the person who'd spoken. Lloyd pushed him back against the wall and was clearly upset and told the Asian: 'Don't fuck about with me!' He also pointed to him in quite a threatening manner. Lloyd was obviously well annoyed at this man.

I moved into the room and got hold of Lloyd by his right arm and was trying to pull him back towards the door with me. At this time he had nothing in his right hand. He began to turn and at the same time I saw another Asian youth coming in from our left side. He was short, about five feet two inches tall, black curling hair with a black leather jacket done up with 'poppers'.

I saw he had a knife with a black handle and a blade about four inches long. I saw him stab Lloyd in the right side and almost immediately Lloyd reached into his right trouser pocket and pulled out his brown lock knife. He flicked the knife in the air and the blade shot out. He went after the Asian who had stabbed him. I recall thinking at that point that Lloyd wasn't badly hurt as he ran after the Asian, who had run towards the counter.

The Asian dropped his knife as he ran and I picked it up as I followed Lloyd. I didn't use that knife on anyone. I tried to throw it to one side so it couldn't be used by anyone else.

The Asian who had stabbed Lloyd ran behind the counter and I could see Lloyd stabbing at him. I can't say if the Asian had another knife when he was behind the counter. I pulled Lloyd away from him because it was a one-sided fight at that time. I can remember seeing blood but I can't say whose blood or where it was coming from. The Asian stood up straightaway.

I pushed Lloyd behind me towards the door and I walked backwards covering his retreat. As we walked out I lost sight of Lloyd and I assumed he had got out. As I moved, three Asians came at me, one of them was the owner of the café. They rushed me and I began to punch. I hit one, I'm not sure which and they all backed off.

As I stepped back I saw Lloyd's brown-handled knife on the floor. The blade was still out and I picked it up for him. I didn't try to close it as there is a knack to it but I didn't try to use it. I remember thinking two things; that Lloyd's fingerprints were on it and it was one less weapon for them to use on me.

I took about two steps back after getting his knife when I was struck on the back of the head with something solid. It wasn't a fist or anything like that, it was definitely a weapon of some sort. I was stunned. I recall dropping the knife in the club. I then got out of the door and as I got out on to the footpath I saw Lloyd laid on the pavement, his legs in the road. I could see his side was exposed and there was a wound with the pink inner flesh exposed but it wasn't bleeding.

I tried to talk to him but he wasn't well; he was clearly in a bad way.

Pinnock then tried to drag Waite across the road to the car by lifting him under the arms. When he got there he found difficulty in getting in and he noticed that the windows were smashed. He then saw several Asians coming towards them, one of whom was Superfly, and they were armed with a variety of weapons including a baseball bat, a hockey stick which Superfly was carrying and pool cues. Both he and Waite were hit all over and then the attack ended as suddenly as it had begun and everyone was gone.

He estimated that the whole affair lasted between five and seven minutes and that they were in the café for between two and three minutes before Lloyd was stabbed.

EIGHT

Ending the Confessional

So what did happen inside the café on the night that Lloyd Waite died? The defence assertion was straightforward. Waite and Pinnock, having failed to find Talat the previous evening, had headed straight for the International Café and were not, at the particular time, on their way to Aylesbury. Rather than an innocent party as he maintained, Pinnock was an integral part of the plan to punish Talat Sarwar for his alleged attack on Jason Waite.

Pinnock parked the car pointing into the road so they could escape quickly. The headlights were left on, the keys were in the ignition and it was alleged that the engine was running. Waite went into the café carrying a hidden lock knife and Pinnock took up a position in the doorway to prevent anyone else coming into the café and, perhaps more importantly, to stop anyone from leaving.

Not knowing exactly what Talat looked like, Waite went round various Asians in the café either accusing them of being Talat or demanding to know who he was. Everyone denied that Talat was there, including Superfly, as it was more than obvious that Waite was after trouble. Again it appeared as though he had missed finding the man he wanted.

Waite was on the point of leaving when he went up to one particular youth and demanded to know where Talat was in a particularly threatening way. The lad was so frightened that his eyes automatically looked to where Talat was standing and Waite followed his look directly to Talat.

Talat noticed that Waite had drawn a knife and was holding it down by the side of his leg and he moved smartly backwards to try and get away. Waite went in for the attack and there was a scuffle, then he was joined by Pinnock and they were both stabbing at Talat as he retreated up the café. He was eventually stabbed two centimetres from his jugular vein, but at this point he was not aware of how serious it was. The attack went on to the back of the café and finally Talat fell on the ground with Waite on top of him. There was a huge difference between them, Waite being thirty years old, extremely stocky and five feet eight inches; Talat was five feet two, eighteen years old and slightly built.

Pinnock realised that his brother might have gone over the top and pulled him off Talat and he and Waite then headed for the door, Waite emerging into the road first while Pinnock guarded his retreat. Pinnock was then hit from behind by either a pool cue or a hockey stick as the Asians inside the café realised that Talat had been stabbed and they were set on stopping the people responsible.

When it was realised that Talat was bleeding from the neck, which had partly been hidden by his polo-neck jumper, and was beginning to feel faint, his friends took him off to hospital.

Unnoticed by Talat, some of the Asians in the café armed themselves with pool cues and, it was later claimed, hockey sticks and chased Pinnock. As they came out of the café they saw Waite lying half on the road and half on the pavement, motionless. Pinnock noticed the cut in Waite's beer belly but did not realise how serious it was, so attempted to get him to his feet and into the car. He did not succeed and was dragged from the car, its windows were smashed and he was beaten.

All the events which took place outside the café were after Talat had been taken to hospital where he was soon to have two policemen placed as guards on the door to his room.

So how did this square with Pinnock's account? Why should he lie about his brother having been attacked first?

Both men had a record for violent crime and if Pinnock had admitted that they went to the café to cause violence he would have placed himself 'in the frame'. Similarly, if he had admitted that his brother was the first to pull a knife, unprovoked, and witnesses could swear that they were both carrying knives, he would have no defence whatsoever. He would be a party to a violent assault which very nearly resulted in the death of a young man. The only possible defence he had was that of self-defence.

But what of the eye-witness accounts inside the café which had stated quite clearly that Talat had gone to a friend and demanded a knife and was then seen to stab Waite in the side?

Davis Walker & Co. had managed to gather together names of people who had been in the café and had begun to interview them either at the law offices, in their homes or in the café. It came to light that some of those who were witnesses had originally been arrested on suspicion of murder and were threatened with prosecution as accessories. They claimed they had made statements which did not implicate Talat because they had not seen anything which incriminated him. They were then persuaded by the police to make other, different, more damning statements. This was their claim.

Some of them swore other statements in front of solicitors to this effect. One of them was Iftikar 'Ifti' Ali. In his police statement he had claimed that he had seen Talat lunge at Waite with something in his hand, that he pushed it right into the right side of his stomach and that Waite had pushed Talat's hand away with his right hand. He claimed that what he had seen in reality was Waite pushing Talat and being helped by Pinnock. After the attack was over both West Indians left the café walking quickly.

He claimed that after his initial statement to the police he was asked to make another one a few days later.

I was warned that if I was lying I could get seven years in prison for withholding evidence. I was held there from 6.30 p.m. until 1.30 a.m. when they released me and dropped me off at my home. I was so tired I don't remember exactly what I said. I can remember that I was agreeing with everything they said just to get out of it. My father had been locked up in the police station and beaten up about a year ago and I was afraid the same thing was going to happen to me.

Suklain 'Sugi' Azad, who claimed in his statement to police that he had seen Talat go over to Farouk and ask for a knife and then run up to Waite and stab him half way down his back, also made another statement. He had a very different story to tell this time. He maintained that Waite had pulled a knife on Talat. He was one of those who accompanied Talat to the hospital:

> At about 9.15 p.m. the police came to the hospital and we were told to stay where we were. Later, at about 10.15 p.m. we were taken to the police station and locked up. At midnight they took a picture of me but nothing else happened. I remained in the cell.
>
> I had not eaten all day as I had been at work nor had I eaten in the café. Nevertheless, the police didn't give me anything to eat or drink until the following morning at about 11 a.m. I was absolutely starving.
>
> I had never been to a police station before and I was extremely frightened about being locked in a cell all night long. I was virtually in tears.

Two policemen interviewed him and told him that he could have a solicitor present but he declined, believing that he had only a brief story to tell. He was also anxious to get away because he was afraid of losing his job as a security guard. He was not allowed to telephone his employers so asked if someone could tell them what was happening. This was promised but never happened and so he nearly did lose his job.

> I told my story but the police accused me of lying. They began

to put words in my mouth. They had their own idea as to what happened in the café. It had little relation to what I had actually seen. They were not interested in my story and all they wanted me to do was write down what they wanted me to say.

Eventually, I began to say yes to anything that was put to me. I was in a considerably distressed state. The interview went on for about five hours. There were many things which were said in my statement which were quite untrue. These were: that I saw people fighting outside the café immediately after the stabbing; that I identified the people who had been fighting; that I saw Talat run out of the café carrying a hockey stick; that Talat stabbed the West Indian first.

All these allegations were put to me by the police and I agreed they were true although I knew they weren't. I believed that if I didn't cooperate with the police I would be locked up and charged with an offence connected with the murder. This is what the police told me. I said yes to virtually everything they put to me because I couldn't stand the idea of being locked up in a cell again.

Seventeen-year-old Farouk Mohammed, the one reputed to have handed a knife to Talat, also made a statement. He strongly denied the allegation and had told the police so.

None of them wanted to make formal complaints because they felt they would not be believed and would almost certainly be harassed. Davis Walker listened to what they had to say but found themselves in a difficult position because if they acted for these people they would lay themselves open to accusations of trying to influence witnesses. Because of this they advised them to go to an independent solicitor and it is thought that some of them did.

Through their contacts within the Asian community, Davis Walker were able to find and talk to almost as many witnesses as the police. However, they did not know what information and evidence the police had. John Davis approached High Wycombe police and asked for a list of people who had been interviewed and copies of the statements they had made.

The police refused this request but then, according to John Davis, rumours began to circulate throughout the local white community, the Asian community and the legal profession that Davis Walker were interfering with the police investigation and were getting to witnesses first.

The implication of this is that the defence solicitors were in some way persuading witnesses to change their testimonies in order to help the guilty person or persons – the automatic assumption being that the guilty were of Asian descent. In view of the complaints made by several Asian youths that the police pressurised them into changing their statements to implicate Talat Sarwar, this appeared to stand reality on its head.

So far in this investigation no one had been charged and no one had confessed. In fact no one was to confess. However, if they were to be believed, several young men had been put under pressure to say things which were simply untrue and had left police custody frightened, dazed, dismayed and angry.

It is in precisely these circumstances that so many people make confessions, jeopardising their liberty simply to bring to an end the oppressive, intimidating and threatening atmosphere in which they are held. The desperate desire to be left alone, to have the incessant challenges brought to an end is sufficient to induce an admission of guilt from many people. Where this is done in the absence of a lawyer, the chances of securing a confession are infinitely greater and that is why innumerable obstacles are often placed in the way of lawyers attending interviews.

In recent years, case after case comes to light where convictions have been based on nothing more than confessions and in some cases the pressure has been not only psychological but physical as well. Not to put too fine an interpretation on it – confessions have been extracted from people and with virtually no other corroborating evidence they have been sentenced to long periods in prison.

Such is our system of justice that once an accused person has made a confession of guilt it is almost impossible to counteract it. In the case of Winston Silcott, one of the three men who came to be known as the Tottenham Three, it was not even a confession which secured his conviction, simply some remarks which could be interpreted as a little suspicious. Even though Silcott refused to sign it, the court saw fit to convict him on the basis of it.

Of course, on appeal, it eventually transpired, with the aid of an ESDA (electrostatic deposition analysis) test, that even these 'suspicious' remarks were unreliable and appeared to have been added to the interrogators' notes after the interview ended.

The immediate outcry is that the evidence was put before a jury – a system in which I have always expressed faith and the use of which I want to see expanded – and the jury failed to come to the right decision, so jury trial must also be at fault. That is something which I will answer in a later chapter.

What the Silcott case also shows is that when it comes to supposed confessions the police can be quite subtle. It is no longer a case of simply writing down: 'And the accused replied, "'Cor blimey, guv, it was a fair cop, you 'ad me bang to rights!"'

The main point is that the lack of credibility in so many supposed confessions has been known for years, scores of people have been convicted without any other corroborating evidence and have suffered appalling injustice as a result. Yet it is still a system which is allowed in courts, it is still being used and people are still being sentenced as a result of it. It is an affront to human rights and it is hardly surprising that uncorroborated confessions appear as an almost constant element in miscarriages of justice. Usually they are the principal cause of the miscarriage and their use must be ended immediately.

One of the most disturbing elements of alleged confessions is that when an accused is supposed to have made one and then denies it, the public reaction is often that of 'no smoke without fire'. And yet when it is eventually discovered that the person could not possibly have committed the crime, the significance of the confession and how it was arrived at seems to disappear out of the window. Rarely is anyone brought to account or even asked to explain their actions.

There is a long history of people being found guilty and sentenced purely on the basis of an uncorroborated confession. One of the first cases that ever went to the Court of Appeal was in 1909 and it involved a gentleman called Mr Verney.

Mr Verney was released from prison one cold and rainy morning and wandered the streets. He had no relatives to visit and no home to return to so he headed for the nearest Salvation Army hostel but unfortunately it was full. It was still raining so he decided on the local magistrates' court. One of the cases which came up was that of sacrilege and the accused pleaded not guilty.

Mr Verney looked out of the window and saw it was still raining, looked in his pocket and discovered very little and suddenly the prospect of prison with food and warmth of a sort became very appealing. He went round to the back of the court and surrendered himself, claiming that he was the one who was guilty of sacrilege.

Poor old Mr Verney was arrested and put on trial and was duly convicted. How or why it eventually went to appeal I don't know but that's what it took for the truth to come out. And the truth was that Mr Verney had been in prison when this very unusual case of sacrilege had taken place.

In Mr Verney's case the police accepted his confession because it was easier to do that than go out and engage in the real work of finding evidence. Their job was made easy for them. But sometimes they bring out this short-circuiting by leaping to the conclusion that someone is guilty and then, one way or another, forcing an admission from them. Take the case of Gerry Conlon, one of the Guildford Four.

On the day he was arrested in Belfast he was beaten and bloodied to such a degree that his parents had to bring him a change of clothes. He was transferred to Britain, where a reception committee of some twenty-five policemen awaited him, gathering around hurling insults.

> They made me take off my clothes in front of them all and they made sarcastic comments. Some were spitting on me. I was taken down to a cell where there was only a wooden bench and I was left

there until 12 a.m. the next day. It was cold and frightening. People kept coming down and looking at me like I was some animal in a zoo.

I was interrogated for two days and I couldn't believe that police officers, who are supposed to be serious, intelligent people could go down to that level. One said he would show me an old RAF trick and he put his hands behind my ears and pulled me off the chair by them. It was very painful. Another officer squeezed my genitals until I screamed.

But the real threats which made me sign two confessions came from a senior Surrey CID officer. He told me an accident would be arranged for my mother and sister. He said that if a soldier shot my mother it would be put down to an accident and British soldiers were never convicted in the courts.

I was never so relieved to go to prison and get out of that police station so they would leave me alone. I couldn't give them any information about Guildford because I'd never been there. I couldn't believe how anyone sensible could believe what we had written – people who lived in squats and hostels, people drunk on the Kilburn High Road. But even after the trial no one said, 'That's a strange Active Service Unit the IRA has there, spending their dole money on drugs.'

Frighteningly, the effect of duress does not stop with the person who is subjected to it and in the case of Gerry Conlon and the others of the Guildford Four, things they said were used to enmesh Gerry's father, Giuseppe Conlon, his aunt Annie Maguire and five other relatives and friends who collectively became known as the Maguire Seven. They also served long prison sentences and in Guiseppe's case, died there. They were also eventually cleared.

Billy Power, of the Birmingham Six, was stopped at Heysham, together with four of the others, he quite voluntarily went with police to Heysham police station and equally voluntarily allowed swabs to be taken of his fingers and hands. They were supposedly tests to ascertain whether he had been in contact with explosives.

When the results came back later that evening, the attitude of the police changed instantly.

Both in his evidence and subsequently Billy Power has maintained that he was taken back to an interview room and as he entered he was hit on the back of the head from behind and the abuse began. He was told that he might as well admit to blowing up the two Birmingham pubs because his hands were covered in 'jelly' – gelignite. He was in no doubt that the police genuinely believed that he was guilty of the bombings on the basis of this one piece of so-called evidence.

It was a piece of evidence which was later to be torn apart when it was shown that contact with playing cards, polished wood surfaces and plastic laminate could all give a positive reading as could soap if it was used to clean out the test tubes and residues were left behind. In this case the crucibles had been cleaned with soap. Perhaps just as importantly, the same test was being used elsewhere with similar results. I will also come back to that.

Once the police had the results of this 'scientific' test the pressure from the police which Billy Power described to the court led to a signed confession. Days later, when he was transferred to prison, still not tried and still not guilty of any crime, he was brutalised again by prison officers. No one has ever been convicted of responsibility for his injuries and Lord Denning blocked the men's civil action for assault with his now notorious words: 'If the six men win it will mean that the police were guilty of perjury, that they were guilty of violence and threats, that the confessions were involuntary and were improperly admitted in evidence and that the convictions were erroneous ... This is such an appalling vista that every sensible person in the land would say it cannot be right that these actions should go any further.'

Hughie Callaghan was also one of the Six but was not on the ferry with them, he had simply seen the others off in Birmingham. He was arrested that same night with a gun to his head.

Hughie Callaghan is, in every sense of the word, a gentle man. He is quietly spoken, polite and very much a family person. Physically he is not strong and has always been of a nervous disposition and at the time of his arrest was suffering from stomach ulcers.

The police did everything they could to make him nervous – shouting, threatening, making noises, punching but stopping just short of his face – but the cruellest thing of all was to tell him that his own daughter had died in the bombings. They accused him of killing his own daughter.

> Because of my ulcer, I kept asking for milk and biscuits to keep the pain under control but they refused so I was in severe pain the whole time. They started by twisting everything I said. I would tell them the truth and they would twist it. Eventually I became very confused and it was impossible to think straight. It was like a comedy script except that it wasn't very funny.

Eventually Hughie signed a confession:

> Even though I hadn't said most of what was in it I signed the 'confession' anyway. I was upset and crying and my hands were shaking so much that they had to hold the one with the pen in it so I could sign.
>
> From the time I was picked up at home until all the interrogations finished I was like a zombie. I just didn't know what was happening. I felt they could have done anything they wanted with me. After I'd made the 'confession' I was transferred to another police station and in the car going over a spaghetti junction I said they couldn't use the statement I'd just made because I'd been forced into it. One of them took a gun out and held it to my head and said that if I didn't shut up they'd shoot me. We were passing a lake or pond and another of them said: 'Let's throw him in there, nobody will ever know!' And the truth is, I believed they meant it and I did think that nobody would know or care.

The latest in what appears to be an endless line of miscarriages based around confession evidence is that of Stefan Kiszko, jailed for the murder of eleven-year-old Lesley Molseed. It now transpires that he could not possibly have committed the crime and the medical evidence is incontrovertible. And yet Mr Kiszko served sixteen years in prison, much of it in virtual solitary confinement as a segregated 'nonce' – a child sexual offender.

At the time of his trial, Stefan Kiszko was twenty-three and was described as being socially and sexually immature, was having hormone boosting injections and was said to have the mental age of a twelve-year-old.

He too was convicted as the result of a confession during his sixth interrogation by police. The day after his acquittal in 1992 he was asked why he had signed it. He replied that he wanted the questioning to stop, he just wanted to get out of the place. There were many more disquieting factors in this case, all of which are relevant to my proposals for a new type of justice.

Those who believe there is nothing essentially wrong with our criminal justice system, on hearing these allegations against it, will immediately reach for a copy of the Police & Criminal Evidence Act 1984 and wave it in the air. They will almost certainly claim that all these cases are old ones, long before PACE was introduced and the faults which I have highlighted have now been remedied. They would be wrong.

But this was not the only new law to be placed at the disposal of police. Following the Birmingham bombings on 21 November 1974, there was a huge media and public outcry for something to be done. That 'something' included banning the IRA, bringing back hanging for convicted 'terrorists' and launching a new police campaign against the IRA. There were also violent attacks on many perfectly innocent Irish people.

After the bombings a Bill was introduced into parliament by the Labour government which gave the police sweeping new powers to detain people whom they suspected of involvement in terrorism and it was passed without a division, becoming law the next day. It was called the Prevention of Terrorism Act (PTA). Why these sweeping new powers were needed, when the old laws had been sufficient to detain the six men supposedly responsible for the Birmingham bombings, was never made clear.

It was termed a temporary Act but a Conservative government made it permanent in 1991. Amongst other things, its provisions allow for a suspect to be held for forty-eight hours without charge and without access to a lawyer and if the Home Secretary chooses, the period of detention can be extended for up to one week. There is no right to have a friend or relative notified. Anyone entering or leaving the country can be detained for twelve hours even if police do not suspect them of anything. To extend the detention further they must have 'reasonable suspicion'. There are a host of other totally undemocratic and unjust provisions which are predicated on a presumption of guilt.

The Guildford Four and the Maguire Seven were held under this Act and Gerry Conlon was, in fact, one of the first people ever to be detained under it. The provisions of the Act have been made even more stringent since its early days so not only could the same thing happen to these people again it would be more likely to happen. The Birmingham Six would now also be caught in the net of the PTA had those explosions happened recently. For major incidents such as these the provisions of PACE are ineffective.

The main and worrying point is that the confessions of guilt were made quickly, within twenty-four hours, so it is here, right at the beginning of a detention, that protection is needed.

Many voices have been raised in concern at these powers, not least the European Court which believes that they breach article five of the European Convention on Human Rights. This stipulates that defendants must be brought promptly before a court. The British government's response to this criticism was to attempt to justify detaining people for up to seven days. This was not accepted and so our government, with little embarrassment, effectively said: 'Yes, we've noticed what you say and, yes, we did sign the European Convention but no, we're not going to do anything about it!' It is called derogation.

The irony of this bare-faced insistence on retaining the PTA provisions is that the detention period of its first victim, Gerry Conlon, was used to produce evidence which condemned him.

Similarly under PACE, there are unacceptable powers to detain and to prevent access to a lawyer. For a 'serious' offence, a suspect can be detained for twenty-four hours before being charged and this can be extended to thirty-six hours on the say-so of the police. Further periods of detention can be imposed, up to a maximum of four days, on the issuing of a magistrates' warrant. If the police think that their presence would interfere with the investigation, lawyers can be kept at bay for the whole of the thirty-six hours. Similarly, they can postpone informing friends or relatives of a person's detention for a similar period. There is nothing which requires the police to tell suspects of their right to a lawyer, thin as that right is.

In fact, very few people are detained for longer than twenty-four hours without charge because there is no need. The vast majority of accused people who make a confession statement do it within this period. PACE offers no protection during this first and most vulnerable twenty-four hours. So assurances that PACE protects the rights of the innocent are simply untrue, as the case of Anthony Everett, amongst many others, shows.

Mr Everett is a manic depressive and when arrested, so severe was his mental state that he was in a friend's attic, clutching the chimney breast and weeping. Within twenty-four hours he had confessed to six burglaries and a cheque fraud but he had also asked to see a doctor. The police did not provide one for another two weeks.

Having confessed to seven offences Mr Everett was charged but was neither granted bail nor sent to a remand prison. In fact he was kept at the police station for a further seventeen days during which time he confessed to a further three hundred and eighty-four break-ins and cheque frauds. These were supposedly TICs, offences he wanted to be 'taken into consideration'.

At his trial he was remanded for psychiatric reports and his health began to deteriorate rapidly until he was eventually taking a prescribed cocktail of heavy-duty tranquillisers. Not until after a seven-year sentence was handed down and he was moved to a more liberal prison regime, where he was weaned off the tranquillisers, did his mind clear. When it did he realised that he had been in prison serving a previous sentence when most of the TICs had been committed.

This case did wonders for the Essex police clear-up rate but little for Mr Everett and has yet to be resolved.

Another case which happened during the currency of PACE was the trial of five men for the alleged murder of P.C. Keith Blakelock at Broadwater Farm. Three of them were found guilty and became known as the Tottenham Three. They have subsequently been cleared by the Court of Appeal. Concerning as these three cases are, there were other people accused of murder in that investigation which are also worrying in their implications.

One of them was a thirteen-year-old youth. He was held incommunicado in a police station for forty-eight hours dressed only in underpants and wrapped in a vomit-stained blanket. He confessed to a part in the killing, was charged and tried. Fortunately for him his confession made little sense. It was filled with inconsistencies and was described by the judge as 'high fantasy'. What was even more sinister than his own confession was the way in which it implicated another accused, Winston Silcott.

'I didn't even know Winston Silcott but when I broke down they kept feeding me his name, telling me to agree he'd done this or that. I agreed to keep them off my back. They could have told me to name Prince Charles and I would have said it was him, I was in such a state.'

Another young man involved in that case also made a statement, a fifty-page statement which was extraordinary in its command of names, timing and details. He confessed not only to being at Broadwater Farm, to making petrol bombs and to throwing them but claimed he was an eye-witness to the death of P.C. Blakelock. It is worth looking in detail at some of the things he said.

> We went up Gloucester Road from Phillip Lane, down an alleyway between Mount Pleasant Road and William Road and came out in the slip road by Rochford. There was some big bloke who came

out of the community centre and was telling everyone what to do. He was about five feet eleven inches or six feet, big build, in his twenties, rough sort of beard, long bomber jacket with detachable sleeves and brown desert shoes. He was telling everyone to fight the police. He said, 'If you're coming to the riots be at the centre at six o'clock (or it might have been eight o'clock), they'll be giving out masks up there.'

After many more pages in which he describes the build-up to the 'riots', he begins to outline what took place on the night.

There were more crowds throwing stones and cans and whatever at the police. I threw cans and stones and whatever was on the floor – and I threw a petrol bomb. They were hidden behind a fence and there was a bloke there who was pulling them over. They were stored in a green Unigate crate. I didn't know the bloke but he had a green serge Tortini track suit, white with red colour and stripes on the sleeves and a red or blue sign. The bottoms had red stripes down the sides and had two black zips at the bottom of the legs. He was wearing a hat, black silky with a red ribbon round it. He had a rough beard.

They were the new kind of milk bottles, petrol in them with a rag coming out of the top soaked in petrol. I threw one over the back of the people in front of me at the police. It landed near their feet. I didn't get them properly because I can't throw very well.

Allegations had been made by the police that shots had been fired at them and the youth supported that view in his fifty-page 'confession'.

When I heard the shot I ran up to Griffin Road and threw a few things from behind the wooden barricade I made from the fence. I was there less than five minutes and I left the barricade behind and went through Rochford on the ground, through into

Stapleford and up the stairs on to the deck where there's a play area. When I got there I threw the petrol bomb over the side at a policeman who was walking with another one along William Road. It smashed on the road. It was the one I had from before when the geezer got them from behind the fence. A black guy was there throwing them but he wouldn't give any away. One guy got one from him (he mentions his name) and threw it the same way I threw mine. I gave him my matches to light them.

He then moves on to his eye-witness account of the death of P.C. Blakelock and in doing so names several people who were at the scene.

One had a ratchet knife, press a button and the blade comes out and it's locked until you press the button again. One had a kitchen knife in his waist. I couldn't see the colour of the handle. I went down the other stairs and ran underneath towards the Avenue and met (gives the name) by a small wall underneath Tangmere.

I just see a load of people hands up and down in the air. The geezer must have been on the floor, they were hacking down and chopping at him but I couldn't see the person on the floor. Most of them had knives. Some of them had sticks (names people). There was a big crowd, about twenty, but there were others just standing around talking. I was about twenty or twenty-five feet away. I could see what was happening because I was standing on a wall. That gave me about three feet more height than other people.

In this incredible fifty-page statement he names twenty-seven other people, some in the most minute detail, who also participated in the events at Broadwater Farm. He admits that he threw stones, he admits that he threw petrol bombs, he admits that he saw a petrol bomb factory and he admits that he saw the death of P.C. Keith Blakelock. The result was that he was charged with affray.

Once he got out of the police station he was able to pursue was nowhere near Tottenham on that awful night and was, in fact, drinking with his girlfriend and a male friend at a pub in Windsor. Only hard work by his solicitor uncovered the truth of that evening.

There are very few black people on the streets of Windsor. Fortunately for this young man, the pub where they were drinking also has very few black customers and the two black young men stood out. The landlord remembered them very clearly and confirmed that they had not left the pub until late in the evening.

Once they had arrived back in London, now penniless, a bus conductress also remembered them and was able to exactly plot the time they had caught the bus to get from the station to Tottenham, much too late to have participated in the events of that evening. The reason her memory was so good was that she had kept her ticket accounting accurate. She had run off tickets for the two black men who then told her they had no money. To account for the discrepancy, she marked the back of the till roll with the letters NNP – nigger, not paid. Some hoarding instinct had for years prompted her to keep the old till rolls and so there was the record of the journey and the time, clear and unambiguous.

It took time to collect the necessary evidence to prove his innocence and when his solicitors had finally constructed a watertight alibi, police dropped the action. There were no apologies, no enquiries, no investigations and apparently no concern that policemen had constructed a totally fictitious case against an innocent man. This all took place under the so-called protection of PACE.

Having proved to those who place their faith in PACE that all is not well, I know the next defence of the indefensible will be that the introduction of tape-recorded interviews has put everything right again. I am afraid not.

No sooner had tape-recording started to appear than a new phenomenon cropped up. It was the sudden and irrepressible desire of accused people to confess as soon as they possibly could – in the police car on the way to the station or at the police station before the tape recorders could even be used. No matter if the confession was not repeated in the formal, tape-recorded interviews, there it was in black and white in the arresting officer's note book!

There was the very recent case of two police officers who were on surveillance duty. Three men, totally unconnected with their specific duties, were arrested for assaulting one of these police officers, who had died in rather strange circumstances. The men were also charged with the theft from his car of an item of the policemen's martial arts equipment. The men made a tape-recorded confession of the theft and were held in custody for some twelve months while the case was prepared.

After this time, the wife of one of the policemen produced the supposedly stolen piece of martial arts equipment and said that it had never even been lost let alone stolen. It transpired that the assault charge was also totally concocted. The policeman who had died had consumed a huge amount of alcohol while on duty, so much so that he could not even walk straight. He had lurched, drunkenly, into a forklift truck, striking himself in the throat and had collapsed in a stupor – a stupor which cost him his life.

The confessions had been obtained by taking the suspects to a police station near to where they were arrested, frightening them into agreeing to make confessions and then driving them to the correct police station where their custody was recorded as having started on their arrival. In fact they had been in custody for several hours by this time. They were then made to sit down, were interviewed with the tape-recorders running and then confessed to a theft which had never taken place.

Besides confessions being induced or produced by these obvious methods it is only now becoming recognised that their inherent unreliability may also stem from an even deeper, more subtle defect – the psychological vulnerability of the interviewee to all kinds of intangible interrogation techniques.

Much of the pioneering work in this field has been carried out by three experts: Gudjonson, MacKeith and Tunstall. The following features are significant: impaired intelligence, borderline subnormality, abnormal suggestibility, abnormal desire to please, impaired social functions. Such features are never obvious and require careful observation and detection. They regularly go unnoticed by police custody officers and interrogators, defence solicitors and barristers, 'appropriate adults' required by PACE to be present during interviews of juveniles or those suffering from mental handicap.

Judith Ward demonstrated a remarkable propensity for confessing to all sorts of offences she had not committed. Yet no one observed the disability from which she suffered at the time. More recently, both subject to the PACE regime, were the cases of Engin Raghip (one of the Tottenham Three and now Broadwater Farm case) and Stephen Miller (one of the Cardiff Three). Both were young men from London with similar borderline IQs – effectively mental ages of ten to eleven, with the reading ability of nine-year-olds – and both were highly suggestible.

There was no solicitor present throughout Raghip's extensive interviews, it being claimed he did not want one. Miller had a solicitor of five years' experience for seventeen out of the nineteen taped interviews lasting about thirteen hours spread over five days.

Miller is the most alarming example. Until then (December 1992) everyone had imagined that the presence of a lawyer and a tape-recorder would provide the necessary protection against unreliable confessions and therefore could form part of the preconditions for admissibility of any confession.

Plainly no one at the interrogation stage detected Miller's vulnerabilities and at the trial stages (there were two trials) two High Court judges felt the presence of a solicitor constituted a seal of approval.

In fact the solicitor had said very little let alone made any attempt to intervene or stop what amounted to oppressive questioning.

Almost from the start, officers told Miller he was guilty, they knew the facts, that he had no alibi, that he was stuck in the police station running the risk of life imprisonment and that they could provide him with a nice way round (explanation).

What they did not make clear was the flimsy and limited basis for their claims. The only positive 'allegation' they had implicating Miller was one statement from a prostitute colleague of his victim. She had lied long and hard to the police prior to the statement and continued to do so thereafter. By the time of trial and during the trial her credibility was non-existent. The statement she had made naming Miller at the scene was contradicted in its lead-up detail by other statements. No other so-called witness named Miller at the scene. Although blood and fingerprints were found in the murder room, they were not Miller's. Above all the police had far more positive evidence linking a white male suspect who had been detained months before and who, according to the detectives interviewing him, had been on the point of confessing!

Despite over three hundred denials by Miller, the officers finally coaxed, cajoled and bullied him into submission.

It is not surprising that the police have regarded confession as the short cut to a conviction. It can serve to reinforce their own assumptions of guilt and it circumvents the need for other forms of detective work. They have been encouraged in this by trial court judges' attitude to that evidence. Firstly, judges have failed to sanction transgressions of the Judges Rules relating to interrogation and, until recently, transgressions of the Codes of Practice under PACE, by ruling resultant confessions inadmissible. Secondly judges have commonly advised juries that they could have no better form of evidence – why else would a person make a statement against self-interest unless it was true? Furthermore they have amplified their advice by recalling the accumulated wisdom of the bench which suggests that guilty men often wish to unburden their souls or consciences once apprehended by the long arm of the law.

Of course, one of the classic cases of confession is that of Timothy Evans in the murder of his wife at 10 Rillington Place, later discovered to be the work of Christie. He made five statements supposedly admitting his guilt and providing evidence of the crime and was eventually hanged for it. If capital punishment had still been in effect Billy Power, Hughie Callaghan, Paddy Joe Hill, Gerard Hunter, Richard MacIllkenny, Johnnie Walker, Gerry Conlon, Paul Hill, Carole Richardson, Patrick Armstrong, Winston Silcott, Engin Raghip, Mark Braithwaite, Stefan Kiszko and a host of other people would now be further monuments to an incompetent and flawed criminal justice system.

Its failures have been known for years. PACE was supposedly

introduced as a response to the report of the Royal Commission on Criminal Procedure which was set up in the wake of another infamous miscarriage, the Confait case.

Maxwell Confait was murdered and his house set alight, and, in the case which followed, one young man and two youths were found guilty. Colin Lattimore, aged eighteen but with acute learning difficulties, and Ronald Leighton, aged fifteen, were charged with arson and murder. Ahmet Salih, aged fourteen, was charged with arson. Lattimore was convicted of manslaughter on the grounds of diminished responsibility and was ordered to be detained indefinitely at Rampton Hospital. Leighton was found guilty of murder and was ordered to be detained at Her Majesty's Pleasure. All three were convicted of arson and Salih was ordered to be detained for four years.

Again, in this case, police blatantly disregarded the few existing rules for the conduct of interviews and interrogation, particularly with minors. Surprisingly, there were no clear rules to which police were required to adhere, simply a set of guidelines and basic principles known as the Judges Rules. Not only did police ignore them but they were encouraged to do so by a judiciary which frequently closed its eyes to transgressions of its own rules. And this is what happened in the Confait case.

The outcome was a public outcry which eventually led to the case being reconsidered, when it became obvious that the three accused could not possibly have committed the crime and they were released but not before they had served three years' detention. The ensuing Royal Commission was supposed to make recommendations which would ensure that a similar situation never arose again. With the introduction of PACE, the then Home Secretary, Leon Brittan, announced proudly that we now had 'The framework for modern policing by consent'.

In effect, little has changed and following the release of the Guildford Four and the Birmingham Six, another Royal Commission has been established. This time it must make the recommendations which are so obviously needed.

To my mind these are clear and unequivocal. Any confession is invalid unless made in the presence of a solicitor. It then has to be verified in front of an examining magistrate – a *juge d'instruction* – within twenty-four hours. It has to be tape-recorded and video-recorded. Only one police station in the country has the facilities to video-record statements but only with this medium is it possible to see the physical condition of a detainee and assess his or her demeanour. If required, they should be able to show their whole body so that any damage which has been done will be on record. Police should not be allowed to put statements into evidence unless these preconditions are met.

And there is another step which already exists in Scotland and must be introduced into England and Wales and that is corroboration. Even if you have a video-recording, even if it has been verified in front of a judge, even if it has been done in front of a solicitor, there should still be no prosecution. The judicial corridors will be rattling with that suggestion because the whole judicial system will probably grind to a halt as it relies so heavily on confessions.

They will say that if corroboration has to be sought out every time they will simply not get the convictions. Why is that? Because again they have made a presumption of guilt. Unless these safeguards are introduced we will continue to be faced with cases of innocent people serving long prison sentences, of politicians wringing their hands in supposed concern and of police claiming that there is not really a problem and it's all just the fault of the odd rotten apple.

It must now be obvious to all that there is a deep and fundamental malaise in our criminal justice system which produces a situation in which police officers regularly feel the need to lie in order to get results – a pressure exacerbated by the media's and Home Secretary Kenneth Clarke's current obsession with arrest rates and clear-up rates being reliable measures of productivity! They do lie and they do it regularly and until we build in safeguards which place a belief in innocence above the veracity of policemen then miscarriages of justice will continue on the grand scale.

NINE

The Accused

Back at the International Café, police continued with their investigation. By now it was Sunday 23 April, less than twenty-four hours after the incident and at Amersham police station, two policemen, D.C. Tinley and D.C. Daniel, conducted an interview with Superfly but this time his solicitor was present. He was still under caution.

Superfly was asked if he knew why he had been arrested and he replied: 'Last night I made a witness statement, I told you everything about it. I told you last night that I had nothing to do with this. I have been advised by my solicitor not to say anything.'

The policeman asked: 'I understand that you did give a witness statement last night. Is that the truth that you put in that statement?' Superfly made no reply and the interview ended after a few minutes at 1.21 p.m.

At 4.30 p.m. the two policemen had another go at interviewing Superfly who still had his solicitor, John Davis, with him. This time he was more talkative, in fact he made a full statement. This was on the advice of his solicitor and contradicts the assertion often made by police that solicitors obstruct police enquiries. In fact because of the cooperation Superfly was exonerated from the murder investigation.

He said that he was sitting at the serving counter watching TV when he noticed two Jamaican men. One was holding the door wide open and the other one was asking people inside the café if they knew a certain person. Both looked extremely aggressive. Superfly went over to the man asking the questions and asked what the problem was. The man replied that he was looking for a chap called Talat.

Superfly knew that Talat was there as he'd walked into the café five minutes before the Jamaicans. He admitted that he knew Talat but said that he wasn't there just then. The man obviously didn't believe him and walked over to Talat, saying, 'You're either Talat or you know who he is!' With that the other black man who had been guarding the door came over and joined them, saying to Talat, 'You tell me where Talat is!'

Superfly then interjected telling the two men to leave the lad alone because he didn't know anything about Talat. As he turned his back to return to the counter both black men, one of whom was extremely stocky and the other thin, began fighting with Talat.

The thin one pulled a knife on Talat who immediately ran away into the middle of the café by a wall. With that the stocky man also pulled a knife. Superfly said he shouted: 'Don't do it to him like this.'

Talat moved quickly up the café towards the counter followed by the stocky black man, who in fact was Lloyd Waite, and the fight reached the kitchen. Superfly wanted to try and stop Waite but was frightened, really frightened, because of the knife he was wielding. Talat was shouting out: 'Oh no, leave me alone, no, leave me alone.' Superfly was also shouting: 'Don't do to him like this, don't kill him, don't do to him like this!'

Waite then stopped stabbing at Talat, turned round and walked from the café. Superfly asked Talat if he was all right and he replied that he'd been stabbed and that he was leaving. With that he walked out.

The other people in the café then started to leave and, when it was empty, Superfly also walked to the front door and from there he could see Waite lying in the street so he walked over to him. It was obvious that he was bleeding so he went up to the skinny black man, Pinnock, who was sitting in the driver's seat of a white car which had all the windows smashed, and asked him if he was all right. He got out of the car and they both walked over to Waite, lying in the road.

Superfly told Pinnock to undo Waite's belt while he unzipped his top. He could see he'd been stabbed. He then shouted for someone to call an ambulance and the police. The police arrived first, after a couple of minutes, and the ambulance two minutes after that.

The two policemen questioning Superfly wanted him to expand on his statement and began asking him specific questions. What kind of knife was it, did Talat have a knife, did he see Talat being stabbed, did he see Waite being stabbed and so on. They kept coming back to the question of whether he had seen Talat stab Waite. One of the policemen then gave an indication of the direction in which their enquiries were heading. He said: 'Someone stabbed Waite in your shop and as a result he died and it's suggested by the SOCOs that it occurred in the kitchen.'

They then asked if Waite was walking normally when he left the café but Superfly hadn't noticed. They followed that by asking if he kept any knives in the shop and he admitted that he did and one was normally kept on the counter leading to the kitchen – it was used for cutting bread rolls. It was about three inches long, serrated, with a black handle.

The police then changed their questioning to what happened outside the café and asked him if he had smashed up the car. Superfly said that he hadn't and that it had been in that condition when he first left the café. So what about the glass in his turn up? 'I told you last night. There is only one way the glass got in my trousers, when the Jamaican guy opened the door perhaps the glass fell from the window. I was standing by the door.'

He denied that he had beaten the man, Waite, who was lying on the ground and he insisted that he hadn't seen who had smashed up the car. The police then asked him who was in the café before the fight started.

'I was asked that last night and I told them what happened in my premises. I was shocked and I couldn't think properly. I have been taken from my shop to the police station. Since then I've been locked up away from my family and I'm still here in the police station. My clothes have been taken away from me and I've been in an overall for twelve hours and I can't think straight as to who was present.'

'Are you so shocked you can't say who was in your café last night?'

'Some of them I gave to you!'

'Tell me them again.'

'I can't remember.'

The police weren't too impressed, it seemed: 'You're shocked so you can't remember the name of the people who were there but you can remember what else went on. Is it because you don't want to give me the names? Maybe because you're frightened of the people and the consequences, is that right?'

'I need the time to get myself together and then I can give you people's names and help the police in any way that I can.'

'Two West Indians come into your café and two people are stabbed a few feet from you and you don't see that. Both West Indians are beaten about the head and body by pool cues in your café and you don't see that. Both of them are beaten senseless outside by people from your place with pool cues from the café and you don't see that. A car is smashed up in the road outside your place and unfortunately you don't see that either. Is that right?'

'When you are in your shop and the curtains are drawn, nobody can see what's going on outside.'

The interview was brought to an end at 5.50 p.m., an hour and a half after it started.

The next morning at 10.03 a.m., Superfly was interviewed again with his solicitor present but this time he decided to say nothing further: 'I've made two statements already, I've been interviewed twice and I don't want to say any more. I had nothing to do with it whatsoever.'

The police continued to put suppositions to him: 'I'd like to point out to you that since your arrest many people who were at the scene have been interviewed and a number of those have made statements naming you as smashing the windows of the car and striking the West Indians with a hockey stick or billiard cue. Can you give any reason for that?' There was no response from Superfly. 'Are they lying, Mr Kayani?' Silence. 'Is Talat your cousin?' Silence. 'Do you intend answering any of the questions I'm going to put to you?' 'No,' replied Superfly. 'Is that because you're lying?' Silence.

The interview ended after only ten minutes but at a little after twelve noon, Superfly was interviewed again and this time he undertook to answer questions. In essence he repeated his original statement that Waite and Pinnock had come into the café looking for Talat and had pulled knives. He hadn't seen anyone actually stabbed and he hadn't seen Talat with a knife or any other weapon.

His account of what happened outside the café was also much the same as before. A man was already smashing up the car by the time he exited from the café and Waite was already lying in the road. He was insistent that he never had a hockey stick in his hand and that he never touched the car with a stick or anything else. In fact the only time he had anything in his hand was when he returned to the café after the arrival of the ambulance and he saw one of his pool cues in the road. He naturally picked it up.

'So you're telling me,' said the policeman, 'that prior to that you didn't have a stick or any other weapon in your hand?'

'No!'

'So everyone else is lying apart from you?' The questioning kept returning to whether Superfly had smashed up the car or not but he was adamant in his denial.

At 1.07 p.m. the interview was interrupted so that he could consult with his solicitor, John Davis. In fact, no other statements appear in the police records so, officially, Superfly was not interviewed again.

On the Tuesday, 25 April, P.C. Michael Orme was employed as a static guard at the hospital bed of Talat Sarwar. At 8.25 a.m. Mr Grogono, the consultant physician, told Talat that he was now well enough to leave the hospital and discharged him. As Talat was dressing himself P.C. Orme arrested him on suspicion of murder and cautioned him. They had to wait until Talat's dressing was changed and then P.C. Orme, together with D.S. Kitson, took him to High Wycombe police station.

Once there, the police surgeon took intimate samples – blood and saliva – and at 10.16 a.m., in an interview room off the cell block, D.C. Wenman said to Talat: 'I must also tell you, Talat, that I am arresting you on suspicion of an offence of Grievous Bodily Harm which occurred at the Booker fair on Friday, 21 April.' Talat made no reply.

At 2.40 p.m. D.S. Kitson and D.C. Wenman began their first interview with Talat. John Davis, his solicitor, was also present.

Surprisingly, the line of questioning began not with the café 'murder' but with something which had happened at Booker Common fair the day before Lloyd Waite had died.

This, then, was some of the background which the police had been following in the few days since the café incident. This is what they seemed most interested in pursuing in their first interview with Talat.

It all began politely enough: 'You've seen the doctor and she says you are fit to be detained. How are you feeling at the moment?'

'Not too well, I've got a bit of a headache!'

'Do you feel well enough to carry on?'

'Yeah.'

'If at any stage you feel ill then tell me and we'll stop. All right?'

'Yes.'

'I'm getting some headache pills for you and hopefully that will sort that out. OK? What I want to do is go through what happened in relation to two separate incidents, the first being at the Booker fair on Friday and the second at the International Café on Saturday. Firstly, do you understand why you've been arrested?'

'I've been advised by my solicitor that I don't have to answer any of the questions and I don't wish to do so.'

The questioning continued unabashed despite Talat's reply of 'no comment' to everything he was asked. Did he go to the fair? Did he go on certain rides? Was he on the waltzer when some West Indians started arguing with him? Had they tried to stop him from getting away? The policemen asking the questions were D.C. Nigel Wenman and D.S. Kitson and they sounded fairly sympathetic.

'As a result of them stopping you, you pushed past one of them because he wouldn't get out of your way. That seems reasonable to me and as a result one of them grabbed you by the shoulder which wasn't a very nice thing to do. Is that correct?'

'No comment!'

'As a result of that particular action you were seen to hit the man, or should I say the youth, with what appeared to be a knife. Could that be right?'

'No comment!'

'Why is it you don't want to defend your actions? Because clearly, to a certain degree, the West Indians were out of order. Do you agree with that?'

'No comment!'

'We've spoken to your friends who were with you that night and they confirm you were having some problems with the West Indians. Would their account be right?

'Can you just tell me this, I will give you a chance to deny or admit the offence which is hitting the West Indian with a knife causing two cuts to his forehead. Do you deny or admit that you were involved?

'When the incident was over you got into the car driven by Rasool and you had a conversation. As I understand it you had an injury to one of your hands and you said you had injured it on your knife. Do you recall that conversation?'

'No comment!'

'Are you saying no comment because that's the injury you got after the incident?'

Police then gave the first indication of the direction in which they intended to direct this interview. It was just a throw-away line to begin with.

'What do you think you should do yourself, not your solicitor?'

'No comment!'

'You see he wasn't involved in the incident and therefore can't tell me your side of the story so don't you think it would be a good idea to give your side? We have to give you the opportunity to do that.

'It's quite clear, looking at you, that you want to put your side of the story like anyone else would.

'I have no intention of trying to catch you out, I just want to hear your side of the story.'

Eventually the interview began to concentrate on the events at the International Café.

'As a result of the incident on Friday night, within half-an-hour of Sukhpal getting home to Pettifer Way, he was kidnapped by three West Indians, one being the father of the lad you assaulted with the knife at the fair and he was taken on a trip to identify you as the person who assaulted his son. I don't think you knew about that, did you? Did you know about that?'

'No comment!'

'Can you tell me how you got the injury to your neck . . . Is there a particular reason why you can't bring yourself to talk about it? . . . It must have been quite a frightening experience, a fight like that . . . As a result of that fight a man was killed. Do you have any thoughts on that? . . . Do you think the death of a man is worthy of "no comment"? That doesn't look good on you, does it? . . . Do you consider this to be a serious matter or not? . . . If you had not consulted with your solicitor do you think you would have given your account? . . . Why are you saying "no comment"?'

'No comment!'

The interview ended fifty-five minutes after it started, at 3.35 p.m. At 3.53 p.m. they began again, and again it was the fair incident which predominated.

The interview started with questions about whom Talat knew but still his response to every question, on the advice of his solicitor, was 'no comment'. It then turned once more to his silence.

'You're the only person who hasn't given an account of what happened at the fair. From an outsider's point of view, what do you think that looks like? . . . Does it look like a person who's innocent of an offence?'

One of the questioners put a proposition to Talat which appeared to turn reality on its head: 'You see, when you are the central figure in such an incident, it is for you to convince me that your intention and action at the time was lawful, that you had a right to do what you did. Now that might be so but I can't make up an account for you, it must come from you. There must have been a reason for you to take the action you did when confronted with the argument. Can you give me that reason?'

'No comment!'

The questions continued incessantly. Did he mean to injure Jason? Did he always carry a knife? What had he done with the knife? Had Sukhpal seen him slash Jason?

And then the pressure came again.

'You've had time to think about this incident since last Friday. I would have thought you'd have considered your position and would have some sort of account to give us. I'm sure you have but for some reason, and I think it's because you know you were wrong, you're not talking about it. Is that right? . . . Do you agree that failing to give an account looks as though you're guilty of some offence?'

'No comment!'

'Anyone outside would say to themselves, "Why doesn't he give his account of what happened if he hasn't done anything?" What do you reckon? . . . I can only take it from your attitude that you did and can't face up to it . . . If you'd acted reasonably, you'd tell us but you haven't. What is the true story?'

The session, in which not one question had been asked about the café, finished with an appeal: 'I can understand if the West Indians were to make up a story to say that you were out of order and that was how it started but they haven't. It's clear from what they've said that they were out of order to start with. If that's the case then say so because that does affect your case, doesn't it?'

It seemed that the hour-and-a-half interview had been dedicated to one topic only; extracting a confession from Talat that he did have a knife.

Two hours later, at 7.23 p.m. the questioning began again still with Talat responding with the words 'no comment' to every question. Finally questioning was getting closer to the café – in fact the hospital where Talat went after the fight. D.C. Snelling's notebook was produced and Talat was asked to read the section in which Snelling had written a conversation which he said he'd had with Talat. It was the conversation in which Talat is supposed to have told him about the fair and the reason for Waite and Pinnock coming to the café.

He read it out loud and was then asked if it was true. 'No comment!'

Immediately questioning was back to the incident at the fair and an attempt to get Talat to agree that his account of a West Indian having a large screwdriver was false. Numerous questions and propositions were then put, all attempting to show that his account to the police was a pack of lies. Finally questioning did get around to incidents surrounding the death of Waite. It began with questions about whom he knew and where he was standing.

'You see, it's of vital importance from your point of view to say where you were ... Did either of the West Indians assault you? ... In fact we know they did assault you because we have gone out of our way to find out what happened in that café because at the moment your back is against the wall. We know they came in looking for you. We don't know what they had in mind for you but they certainly weren't happy at all, were they? ... Now just think about what happened because it's extremely important that you give an account. We're not talking about a minor wounding, we're talking about a man losing his life.

'If at any stage you want to speak privately with your solicitor just say so but we have reached the point where you have got to make a decision and that is, what was your part in this man's death. Now what I'm going to do is let you have a chat with your solicitor while we get some refreshment for you. But just think on what I've said because it's a big decision.'

They took a twenty-minute break and at the resumption Talat was clear about what he wanted. 'I have had a word with my solicitor and I don't want to answer any further questions at this stage.'

'So you'll answer questions at some stage?' Talat replied 'no', but his solicitor intervened: 'I think in fairness you meant tonight.' Talat agreed, 'and it will be subject to advice from your solicitor.'

'So are we talking about tomorrow, or what?' asked the police. They were extremely keen to know if and when Talat would speak. No one could give them an assurance as to if or when as it depended upon Talat's full recovery from his stay in hospital. The police would not accept that: 'It seems to me that that will allow a story to be concocted to fit the circumstances so we'll interview you now. You'll have an opportunity to give your account now. Any later account wouldn't carry the same weight. This is a matter for you and not your solicitor. He's not answering the questions, you are, and it's you who's got to account for your actions on Saturday night. Do you understand?'

'No comment!'

Questioning began again about movements and happenings inside the café. ' . . . they were standing with their backs to you and you got a knife off a friend and you ran over to the West Indian and plunged that knife into his back. Is that true or untrue? . . . And you went to the back of the shop, didn't you? . . . And it's there that one of them slashed your neck. That's right isn't it? . . . You should tell us now who stabbed you, shouldn't you?

'Who's going to believe a story which emanates from you three days from now, a week from now, a month from now? I wouldn't believe it! You aren't so ill that you can't remember what happened on Saturday night and no amount of delay in telling us what happened is going to change the facts. I can only presume that the account you would give us now would incriminate you and you need a better story. Hiding under the cloak of being under the advice of your solicitor won't help you and that's a fact! Do you understand what I'm saying?'

'No comment!'

'If you give an account now it's fresh in your mind, just like the witnesses who've been seen already. If a witness gives a statement to us, say, a month or two months later, the accuracy of that statement will be in question. The criticism will be levelled at any statement you'd make after such a delay. Make a decision for yourself, be your own boss, won't you. Your solicitor is to advise you, you don't have to listen to him. What happened immediately before you got into the fight with the two West Indians in the café?'

'No comment!'

Questioning continued for several more minutes before the interview was brought to an end at 9.33 p.m.

At 9.55 the following morning, the interrogation continued where it had left off but now the altercation at the fair was forgotten completely as the interrogator made the final accusations.

'You were seen with a hockey stick hitting one of the West Indians outside. Do you deny that?'

'No comment!'

'It's quite important that you realise these injuries weren't all the cause of his death. He died as a result of the stab wound which was on his side towards the back. That is the wound you inflicted, so you killed him. Do you understand that?'

'No comment!'

'You can't put the blame on anybody else, can you?'

'No comment!'

'Can you tell me why, after the West Indian spoke to you and before you stabbed him in the side from behind, you didn't leave the café to prevent any harm coming to you?'

'No comment!'

The interrogator referred to a letter which had been received from John Davis, Talat's solicitor:

'Mr Davis submitted a letter to us yesterday in which he clearly indicated that you've given an account to him of what happened. Is that true? ... It seems you're fit enough to give an account to him but not us. I wonder why? Why? ... Is it because you can't face up to the fact that you haven't got the guts to give your account because you know you can't justify any of your actions during those two incidents. If you could, you'd tell us! Do you agree with that?'

'No comment!'

'In the letter, Mr Davis also wishes us to indicate whether we would be contemplating any charges against other persons for the assault and injuries caused to you. Is that something you want us to do, bearing in mind it's you he's acting for and from our point of view we'd like to know now? If we have no complaint we can't investigate or prosecute: more to the point, can you make up your own mind?'

The interview ended at 10.32 a.m. Ten minutes later it began again and Talat gave a list of the injuries which he had sustained. It finished a few minutes after that and this was the end of the interrogation of Talat Sarwar.

Later that same day, D.C. Wenman charged him with the offence of murder. He replied: 'I deny it!'

TEN

The Right To Silence

In the cases of Shabir Kayani – Superfly – and Talat Sarwar both exercised their right to silence. There is little doubt it was successfully adhered to in both instances because of the presence of their solicitor, John Davis. In the case of Talat Sarwar, the struggle for him to retain his silence and to have a solicitor present was hard fought.

It began immediately after the café incident when two police officers were despatched to the hospital. It was only on the insistence of doctors that they were prevented from interviewing Talat there and then. Having been denied that opportunity they took up guard outside his door with instructions to arrest him the moment he left hospital.

At the offices of Davis Walker & Co, as they continued in their chase for witnesses and information, it became abundantly clear that the police had only one suspect in mind and that was Talat. Superfly was obviously being considered as a culprit for a lesser charge and he wasn't to know for a further six months whether the police intended to prosecute or not.

John Davis contacted the hospital and arranged to visit Talat but the two policemen, part of a twenty-four-hour guard on Talat's room, denied him access.

At this point it would be useful to have some knowledge of the firm of solicitors representing Talat and in particular its principal John Davis. Their offices are in one of the very affluent little

Buckinghamshire towns known as the Chalfonts. It would be easy to imagine a repetition of the scene which exists in so many towns across the country, a firm doing a little conveyancing, a bit of commercial work and perhaps one partner handling run-of-the-mill criminal work.

In fact Davis Walker do all these things and also represent some very affluent clients in the Middle East. John Davis's office, with its original portrait of Sir Winston Churchill and paintings of World War Two fighter planes does not present the stereotyped picture of a committed radical. Neither does the Porsche parked outside.

But John Davis is an extremely experienced criminal lawyer, picking up major cases from nearby Heathrow Airport. He is also a person who is outraged by the inequalities of the criminal justice system. He describes the difficulties of trying to construct a defence case when, as is commonly the case, information is purposely withheld by police as: ' . . . like the Defence starting a race 200 metres behind, after the Prosecution is around the first bend and into the home straight!'

He has a dogged perseverance and a sense of what constitutes justice in pursuit of what he believes to be right. Perhaps just as importantly, he is not dependent upon maintaining a cosy relationship with pillars of the local community. He was to need all these qualities in this particular case.

Having been denied access to Talat by the police guards, John Davis persisted in his requests to visit his injured client and eventually the policemen sought advice from senior officers. The word came back that he could see Talat but only with a police officer present in the same room. Although this was in breach of the Police and Criminal Evidence Act he didn't make a huge fuss as the reason for wanting to see his client was simply to offer him advice, in the strongest terms, not to say anything.

It was here, right at the start of the investigation, that an inexperienced solicitor or one who was very closely linked with police in the local community, might have been reluctant to have pushed it as far as John Davis did.

In a similar way, hospital staff also showed great resilience in not giving in to police demands for access to the accused and in keeping his solicitors fully informed of his progress so that when he was released, they were present. They were also extremely cooperative in providing blood groupings and medical records of the accused.

Normally there is a close relationship between hospital staff and police because of the frequency with which they have contact. Their communication with Talat's solicitors in this instance ensured that he was accompanied during all interrogations and had the benefit of legal advice from beginning to end.

But the pressure was to continue. During the course of Talat's interrogation, John Davis was summoned to the offices of detective superintendent Childerley at High Wycombe who was in overall charge of the investigation and he and detective inspector Short let their views be known – very clearly.

They instructed John Davis to stop writing and faxing demands for information and told him that he would be supplied with information about forensic samples, post mortem, interviews and other items as and when they decided he was entitled to them. He was then asked, in the most patronising terms which implied complete lack of experience, whether he had ever conducted a murder investigation before. It can only be guessed what results such pressure might have had on someone lacking his experience.

John Davis's response was to challenge their assertion that he would receive information only at their behest and made it clear that he would continue with his demands because he was entitled to the information immediately.

The chilly atmosphere that had existed between them now became several degrees icier.

After Talat had been charged with murder, John Davis received a letter from the Crown Prosecution Service (CPS) warning him that he was in danger of being in breach of the code of practice established between the Law Society (the body which represents solicitors' interests) and the Prosecution. The warning revolved around a belief that a solicitor must not interview a prosecution witness without first notifying the CPS of his intentions. It was also expected that the police would be notified and invited to have an officer present during the interview.

The reason for this code is that unless there is an independent person present, the solicitor could be accused of trying to influence a person's evidence. The problem is that the policeman who normally attends is someone intimately involved in the case and may well be the person who took the original witness statement so can hardly be considered independent. This scarcely creates an atmosphere conducive to a witness changing their original statement or claiming that they've been pressurised, possibly by the policeman who is standing in the room looking at them.

There is frequently the fear that they will face prosecution by the police or be singled out and given a hard time afterwards – particularly if it's a small community and they're likely to come continually into contact with the policeman.

In the Talat case, the warning was unnecessary because of police behaviour. They had steadfastly refused to supply names and details of the people they had interviewed so Davis Walker could legitimately claim that they had no idea who were prosecution witnesses and could therefore interview anyone they liked without a policeman being present.

A code of practice such as this one is extremely worrying for justice. It appears to undermine the old principle that 'there is no property in a witness', a belief which established that a witness should be available to either side in any litigation to give evidence on what they have seen or heard.

Even more worrying was the suggestion put to John Davis that he was 'upsetting a number of people in high places'. The effect this might have on a local solicitor can be imagined when he has to deal with the police officers, court officials and prosecuting authorities on a regular basis. They may well ask themselves if it was worth jeopardising these relationships for the sake of one defendant? It's easy to see that some solicitors might deem it healthier to adopt a more cautious approach and wait for information to come to them rather than actively seek it out.

The problem with that, of course, is that by the time they receive what the police decide to give them, the prosecution case will have been put together and the defence won't even have started. There will be no opportunity to ask for such things as a second post mortem or to brief a defence forensic expert to examine the scene of the crime – something which was to be vitally important in this case.

This, then, was the atmosphere in which a solicitor was attempting to construct a defence for his client and there is absolutely no reason to believe that this case was exceptional. It was an atmosphere of threat, intimidation, obstruction and evasion. Nowhere was there any sense of an attempt to unearth the truth but rather a determination to prove the guilt of one man.

During Talat's interrogation, enormous pressure was put on him to break his silence. The caution given to an accused person is quite straightforward: 'You are not obliged to say anything unless you wish to do so but anything you do say will be taken down and may be used in evidence.'

At the heart of that caution is the presumption of innocence; an accused person is not obliged to prove his or her innocence and it is up to the prosecution to prove guilt. It lies at the heart of our criminal justice system but in this case as in so many others it was turned on its head by the interrogating officer.

'You see, when you are the central figure in such an incident, it is for you to convince me that your intention and action at the time was lawful, that you had a right to do what you did!'

He also tried every argument he could think of to try and drive a wedge between the defendant and his solicitor as well as continuing with a presumption of guilt: ' . . . this is a matter for you and not your solicitor. He is not answering the questions, you are, and it's you who's got to account for your actions on Saturday night.'

And it continued: 'Make a decision for yourself, be your own boss won't you. Your solicitor is to advise you and you don't have to listen!' And so it went on: 'You may have been told by your solicitor not to answer any questions ... but you don't have to accept that advice if you want to talk to us as it's not him that's possibly going to be charged with murder.'

The usual response to this type of approach by an experienced solicitor is to ask the police to repeat the caution. But of course the majority of people who seek the advice of a solicitor opt for someone from the duty solicitor list, someone they don't know, someone who may be constantly in and out of the police station, establishing quite close relationships with police officers and someone who may not be very experienced. In this type of case, badgering by the police can be extremely effective.

The choice that an accused can be faced with is a faltering and inexperienced solicitor on one side and a competent, experienced police officer on the other. The solicitor may well fail to stamp his authority on the situation, his advice might seem half-hearted and unconvincing and in the end the accused person is panicked into making a statement.

In the back of so many people's minds, particularly those who have never had any dealings with police other than to receive a parking fine, is a thought, a lurking doubt, a nagging irritation which sometimes finds voice. It usually boils down to a sentiment roughly along the following lines: 'Why, if the person is telling the truth and they didn't do anything wrong, don't they give their side of the story? After all, you can't do better than tell the truth!' That view presupposes a number of things.

Firstly, that it is all right for a guilty person to incriminate themselves, something which almost every written constitution in the world guards against. Once you accept the belief in self-incrimination it is an open invitation to the type of extreme pressure which led to the convictions of so many people recently acknowledged as having been falsely prosecuted.

Secondly, it presupposes that those who are doing the interviewing are searching for truth. All the evidence points to this being a completely false assumption. Usually what those doing the questioning are looking for is confirmation of something they have already decided. This couldn't have been more obvious in the Talat Sarwar case.

Despite the fact that a post mortem had been carried out only hours after Waite's death, the police seemed to be oblivious to its findings. Their first accusation was that Talat had been standing behind the door of the café and had stabbed Waite in the back. In their questioning of Superfly they intimated that the SOCOs believed that the fatal wound had been inflicted behind the counter when both Waite and Talat had fallen to the ground.

Eventually, however, it appeared that they had decided on a scenario in which Talat had stabbed Waite down near the window of the café not long after he had entered. Waite had then pursued Talat up to the top end of the café and had gone behind the counter before ending the attack and walking out of the café. All their questioning was aimed at extracting an admission to this effect. It's not difficult to imagine the scene if Talat had decided to answer their questions:

'So what did you do when Waite pushed you?'

'I put my hand up to stop him.'

'Which hand?'

'I think it was my left hand.'

'What do you mean, you "think" it was your left hand. Was it your left hand or was it your right?'

'I'm not sure. No, I'm pretty certain it was my left hand.'

'"Pretty certain", what does that mean? Was it your left or your right? Come on, you were there, surely you know the difference between your left and your right? So which was it?'

'I'm not sure, it all happened so quickly.'

'So now you're not sure, next you'll be telling us it was your foot. Come on, let's have the truth. Was it the left or right or was it Waite who tried to stop you because you had a knife in your right hand?'

'No, that's not true.'

'So how did he get a stab wound in the side, an injury that three people have said they saw you do? No one else fought with him, so how did it get there? Come on, you know!'

And so it would go on, creating a doubt here, an inconsistency there; playing on a lack of memory at one minute, provoking confusion at another; one policeman threatening and intimidating, another offering friendship. And at the end of it all, many hours and many interviews later, Talat Sarwar probably wouldn't have known the truth any longer.

His solicitor's advice to him not to answer questions was based on a very simple premise: 'We were still persisting with oral and written requests for information and were advising the defendant not to answer any questions because the picture was still very confused and he was very weak from his injuries. Whatever a defendant says in circumstances like this they are not necessarily going to be entirely accurate. They may be deficient in some detail which is then played upon by the prosecution in a way which is totally disproportionate to its importance but often of persuasive effect before juries.

'In addition, the defendant's instructions remained consistent from the very moment we first spoke to him, throughout the trial and afterwards, that he was unarmed and did not inflict any injuries on the deceased. Therefore there was very little for him to say beyond that.

'It might have been thought that he should have explained his own injuries but beyond recording that they existed we would not allow him to say how they were caused. This was the most difficult part of the interviews because of the great temptation to allow him to do so, particularly because if he later changed his instructions it would form the basis of a defence of "Self Defence". It was felt if he went into detail of the attack and got some matter wrong then again this could be used by a skilful prosecutor to show that his version of the attack was inconsistent with that of some other witness.'

The determination of police to persevere with their chosen scenario beggars belief as even on the evidence which they already had it was fairly obvious that it could not have happened that way.

A fight, with flailing arms, pushing and shoving, grappling and eventually a tussle which resulted in two men falling to the ground was what happened. Despite the numerous contradictory statements at least those elements were consistent. Before all this energetic exertion took place, Waite is supposed to have had a knife thrust into his stomach, a knife which penetrated both front and back stomach walls, had pierced his pancreas, opened up the duodenum, had transfixed the vena cava and had then sliced its way through three-quarters of the aorta, the great artery which carries blood from the heart.

With the exception of one lurid statement which claimed to see the wound and blood and Waite being helped out of the café by Pinnock, all other statements, including Pinnock's own, made no mention of Waite having any difficulty in walking from the premises. Yet he was supposed to have suffered such an extensive and fatal wound, had a fight which was full of exertion and then walked out apparently unharmed. That, at least, was the police version of events.

In fact, a pathologist was later to testify that a heart, in the excited state of Waite's, would pump out the whole of the body's blood supply in as little as two minutes.

Waite was still conscious when the ambulance arrived after several minutes and this was put down by the same pathologist to a slowing of blood loss due to the foetal position adopted by Waite as he lay in the road. Had he been stabbed prior to the fight as was claimed it is likely that he wouldn't have had any blood left to lose.

There were also eye-witnesses who spoke of Waite writhing in pain in the road, which seems to be the most likely and instant result of such a knife wound. It hardly seems likely that such pain would have suddenly afflicted Waite perhaps two minutes or longer after the injury – always supposing that he was still conscious.

No matter how thin the police version appears, it is that which they wanted Talat to confirm. Their whole questioning routine was to elicit information which would strengthen this version. He quite rightly refused. He exercised his right to silence which may well have ensured that he didn't become yet another example of miscarried justice.

But there is a move within the higher echelons of British justice and within the present Conservative government to end the right to silence. Such a move must be bitterly resisted because it would strike a blow at the very heart of a centuries-old right and would formalise a view already widely held, particularly within the police, that a person is guilty until they prove themselves innocent.

The right to silence has already been removed in the North of Ireland and it is the government's stated intention to do the same on the mainland. The recently retired Lord Chief Justice, Lord Lane, spoke out loud and clear about his desire to see the right to silence abolished. The Lord Chancellor, Lord Mackay, speaking to American lawyers and judges in Washington in February, 1989, made it very clear where he stands.

The excuse for such a dramatic and anti-democratic move is the same as that used to justify all the other profoundly reactionary judicial decisions taken in the North of Ireland – Diplock courts which sit without juries, the conviction of people on the evidence of super grasses, the use of internment, the introduction of the Prevention of Terrorism Act, the broadcasting ban on members of Sinn Fein even if they are democratically elected councillors or MPs and, of course, an end to the right to silence. That excuse is always the same: 'When faced with terrorism and violence there is no choice.'

In the past the government has stated that when the right to silence is abolished in the United Kingdom its operation will be along similar lines to those used in the North of Ireland. An accused will not be obliged to make a statement nor is there any suggestion that silence will be an offence. The prosecution still has to prove its case and the court has to be convinced beyond reasonable doubt. And of course, the fears that civil liberties will be infringed are quite understandable although misplaced.

Such bland assurances are disingenuous and are part of a consistent campaign to secure more convictions and not convict greater numbers of guilty people. While great soul-searching goes on in public over the seemingly endless parade of miscarriages of justice, almost every move by the administration in private increases the likelihood of more miscarriages happening.

The very first indication of the government's intentions to restrict the right to silence in the North of Ireland came from the then Secretary of State, Tom King. With impeccable timing, he announced it in the middle of a trial where I was representing three young people charged with conspiracy to murder him on his Wiltshire estate. Surprise, surprise, the three accused had exercised the right to silence.

The evidence against the three was purely circumstantial and revolved around articles in their possession – such as binoculars, money and car registration numbers.

The outcome was that they were found guilty and became known as the Winchester Three. However, the verdicts were overturned on Appeal because it was held that the jury would have been prejudiced by the introduction of that piece of legislation at that time.

The right to silence was another of the issues considered by the Royal Commission which followed the Confait case. A majority of the Commission's members firmly rejected any restrictions on it. They had considered proposals to restrict the right put forward by the Criminal Law Revision Committee as long ago as 1972 and it is these old, discredited proposals which are now being resurrected with a kiss of life called 'terrorism and violence' or 'hardened professional criminal', depending upon which appears to have the most credence at any given time.

The abolition of the right to silence has been a long time coming. It was first thought it would be undermined in 1990 but it didn't happen. Have no fear, the agenda hasn't changed and in the forefront are, of course, the police. Part of their argument is that the introduction of PACE has rendered the right obsolete. If only!

Under the Criminal Evidence (Northern Ireland) Order 1988, the very first interference for hundreds of years with the right to remain silent was introduced. It states that a court can draw inferences from an accused's failure to mention particular facts when questioned or charged in the following circumstances:

'Where, in any proceedings against a person for an offence, evidence is given that the accused –

(a) at any time before he was charged with the offence, on being questioned by a constable trying to discover whether or by whom the offence had been committed, failed to mention any fact relied on in his defence in those proceedings; or

(b) on being charged with the offence or officially informed that he might be prosecuted for it, failed to mention any such fact.'

It goes on:

'the court or jury, in determining whether the accused is guilty of the offence charged, may –

(i)   draw such inferences from the failure as appear proper;

(ii) on the basis of such inferences treat the failure as, or as capable of amounting to, corroboration of any evidence given against the accused in relation to which the failure is material.'

Picking the bones out of that legalese amounts to the following: if you don't tell a policeman where you were, what you were doing, what the stain was on your trousers, why you were out of breath, etc., etc., at the time he questions you, the court can place whatever inference on it they choose. Similarly, they can, if they choose, interpret your silence as corroboration of your guilt.

Of course the old caution would have to go and a new one will take its place. One that has been suggested is this:

'If there is any fact on which you intend to rely in your defence in court you are advised to mention it now. If you hold it back until you go to court, your evidence may be less likely to be believed and this may have a bad effect on your case in general. If you wish to mention any fact now and you would like it written down, this will be done.'

In the Talat Sarwar case the police, it seemed, had jumped the gun and believed that the right to silence had already gone:

'If you give an account now, it is an account which is fresh in your memory just like the witnesses who have been seen already. If a witness gives a statement to us some time after the incident, say a month or two months later, the accuracy of that statement will be in question. That criticism will be levelled at any statement you would make after such a delay.'

Can you imagine what a time they would have had armed with such a new and powerful caution? As a young man relatively inexperienced in the workings of police interrogators, Talat Sarwar showed enormous resilience in holding to his decision to say nothing. It seems unlikely that such a determination would have survived an ending of the right to silence.

It's very difficult to understand the reasoning behind wanting to end the right to silence. The excuse usually offered is that it will help to catch hard-bitten, professional criminals who exploit the right to their own advantage.

Sir Peter Imbert, the one-time commissioner of the Metropolitan Police, in 1987 launched in with his own view: 'The right to silence might have been designed by criminals for their special benefit and that of their professional advisers. It has done more to obscure the truth and facilitate crime than anything else this century.' Sentiments which have their origin in authoritarian pragmatist philosopher Jeremy Bentham.

Sir Peter Imbert is one of the highest-ranking and experienced policemen in the country. It would be reasonable to expect such public utterances to be supported with some research, some proof or at least some pretty convincing case histories – but none of it. And yet the facts are there, compiled by the Home Office following a study done between 1984 and 1986.

Of the 16,000 cases looked at, which covered the range of offences from fairly mild to very serious, only 3 per cent of those accused exercised the right to silence. Those who chose this path tended not to have long criminal records and the presence of a solicitor didn't materially affect the numbers opting to remain silent.

The Royal Commission of 1979 revealed statistics from a Brighton survey which showed that suspects opted for silence in 5 per cent of cases and a further 8 per cent were partly silent or evasive, which is not the same thing as remaining silent. When the survey was repeated in 1986 it came up with precisely the same results.

Recent research carried out for the latest Royal Commission, published in January 1993, covered 1000 cases involving six police stations in different parts of the country between 1986 and 1988. Its conclusion was that the abolition of the right to silence would not have a great impact on bringing the guilty to justice. They found a significant exercise of the right in only 5 per cent of the cases.

Anyone who has had reasonable experience of dealing with so-called professional criminals knows that these are the very last people who will be caught by ending the right. They are people well practised at offering alibis, who know precisely what the form is inside a police station and are neither intimidated nor panicked by the experience. It is the inexperienced who are the ones to stumble.

So that leaves a very disturbing question hanging in the air. Why do such senior policemen make such damaging assertions when none of the evidence supports them? I believe it is because they know with the right to silence gone they will secure more convictions based on confessions only. And the spiral of miscarriages will be given yet another twist.

A solicitor who has been involved in many of the major cases of the past decade and more, the Birmingham Six, Guildford Four, Maguire Seven, the Battersea Bomb Factory and Tottenham Three, who has spent endless hours inside police stations either trying to gain access to a client or sitting through interrogations with them, is Gareth Peirce. Perhaps no one is better qualified than she to talk about the importance of the right to silence and of the need to have a solicitor present at all interviews.

'Any interview, particularly after arrest, is traumatic. Arrest itself is traumatic but the interviews which follow present an environment which is unnecessarily hostile and it's that which is worrying. Can a person who is physically, mentally and emotionally disadvantaged present themselves in a way which does justice to them?

'They are generally interviewed in a room which tends to have no natural light but a flickering, unpleasant neon tube. Invariably there's no ventilation and the questioners are extremely close across a dirty table. They're stared at continually, they may not have their own clothes on, they may be cold but what they've just come from is worse. They have come from a cell which is like a Victorian public lavatory.

'They're in a situation where the one thing they want to do is get out of it and they may be tempted to think that by talking, by saying things, by short-changing explanations they might otherwise give in an extended way, they can get out quickly.

'As far as I'm aware no research has been done into the medical or psychological effects of detention in police cells, particularly extended detention under the PTA, but I believe it is extremely dangerous. There is a succession of examples of people who have had mental breakdowns as a result of the seven days' detention, including one I know who committed suicide as a direct consequence. We are purporting to investigate crimes in our society without any respect for our concept of a presumption of innocence or the right to silence.

'When a person is cautioned it's a declaration of war by the state upon the individual. It's saying we have reason to suspect you of a crime and thereafter you have no obligation, moral or in any other way, to assist us to prosecute you. That's what the caution is about. It's saying you have the right not to be your own executioner. It's an extremely important right and emphasises that rights belong to the individual and not to society, where society is always going to be strong and the individual is always going to be puny.

'I don't see any reason why a person who is under suspicion should not be interviewed in relaxed and pleasant circumstances in which they don't feel degraded and humiliated. There is no reason why reassurance shouldn't be given by the presence of a solicitor and by the knowledge that their family knows where they are and that they're safe. They should be able to have a cup of tea, get some fresh air if they feel they need it or take a break when they want to.

'Police have the power to detain people, to obtain from them evidence with which to prosecute and convict them which those people might not wish to give voluntarily and it is a coercive process. Whatever glosses of civilisation are put upon it, it still smacks of the rack and the thumbscrew.'

One accused person, arrested under the PTA, whom Gareth Peirce accompanied through the interrogation process and whom I later defended in court, was Eamon Wadley. He was a defendant in the case which came to be known as the Battersea Bomb Factory. The experiences he went through have marked him, perhaps permanently.

It was Christmas of 1988 when Eamon and his girlfriend Ulla returned home after a Christmas party. As they walked up the path to his flat, armed men leaped out of the dark and arrested them at gunpoint. They were told they were being arrested under the PTA and were driven off to Paddington Green police station, the usual venue for such arrests. They were kept in separate cells. Ulla was to be released after two days but it was to be much longer than this before Eamon saw his flat again.

It was twenty-four hours later when they were allowed to summon a solicitor and it wasn't until Gareth Peirce's arrival that Eamon Wadley knew the reason for his arrest. Some correspondence bearing his address had been found in a flat in Battersea where explosives had been discovered.

Eamon Wadley was in an extremely agitated and emotional state, being provided with Valium to help him calm down. It was in these circumstances that his interrogation took place, an interrogation which happened every day for seven consecutive days. For the first two days Eamon Wadley answered the questions which were put to him but when the same questions were repeated over and over and over again, on the advice of his solicitor he exercised the right to silence. But still the questions went on for a further five days.

It was ironic that during this period of detention the British government was censured by the European Court in Strasbourg which ruled that it was unjust and unfair to detain suspects for longer than four days. The government's response was not to release Eamon Wadley with apologies but to derogate from the European Convention. Having done that they continued with his detention for the full period of seven days allowed under the PTA, an Act which was then and still is in moral contravention of European standards of human rights.

At the end of his seven-day detention, Eamon Wadley was taken out of his cell: 'I was told that I was being released from the provisions of the PTA and I felt a huge surge of relief that at last it was all over. But instead of letting me go they handed me over into the custody of the custody sergeant and I was told that I was being charged with conspiracy to cause explosions and withholding information. Gareth explained that it carried a life sentence. At that point my legs gave way and I went to pieces. It was several months before I saw the outside again.'

Eamon Wadley has few doubts about what would have happened to him had he not had a solicitor present during his seven-day period of interrogation. 'I was dazed and confused and the questioning was so suggestive that I really believe they would have made me say something which wasn't true and I would have ended up like the Birmingham Six.'

So what happened to the Birmingham Six and their rights to a solicitor? Hughie Callaghan was arrested on a Friday night and within twenty-four hours had signed a confession. If he was told his rights they certainly weren't made clear to him:

'I knew nothing whatsoever, I didn't know a thing. I didn't even know I was allowed a solicitor.'

In fact he didn't see a solicitor until the Monday morning and the meeting lasted about two minutes, just long enough for him to sign the legal aid forms. The solicitor subsequently didn't return until the Thursday morning by which time he had been in custody nearly a week. Does he think that the presence of a solicitor during the interviews would have helped him?

'Oh yes, yes, yes, it would have made a big difference. They wouldn't have been able to do the things they done, the psychological stuff. When I signed that statement I was completely terrified of them people!'

Similarly with Billy Power, he 'confessed' within twenty-four hours but also didn't see a solicitor until the following Monday and even then no legal advice was given. His feelings as to the outcome had a solicitor been present during the interviews are very similar to Hughie Callaghan's.

'If a solicitor had been there the confession never would have happened. After I'd related to the police my movements that day, the questioning would have stopped there. I would have then been advised. The brutality would never have taken place, the threats would never have taken place and the terror they inflicted on me and the others never would have taken place – if I had access to a solicitor.'

In face of this criticism, both government and judiciary will almost certainly point immediately to the duty solicitor scheme and claim that everything is all right. Well it isn't! The duty solicitor scheme operates on a twenty-four-hour basis and theoretically offers free legal advice for people in custody. It is not working!

Police give suspects incomplete information about their rights and frequently it is the wrong information. Rather than reminding someone of their right to a solicitor they make the assumption that silence equates with not wanting one. They frequently don't mention that the advice on offer is free of charge and, even worse, they often fail to act when legal advice is asked for and don't bother to make a record of such requests. They employ a whole range of delaying tactics such as telling the suspect they will have a long wait for a solicitor so they'll get out quicker if they answer questions immediately. They also read a suspect's rights so fast that they can't possibly hear and understand what's being said. If the delaying tactics fail they then try to persuade suspects to cancel the request they've made.

Those are some of the initial hurdles suspects have to overcome before even beginning to receive the advice to which they're entitled. But that isn't the end of it. Few duty solicitors advise their clients to remain silent and sometimes they don't even bother to attend the police station themselves, simply sending along a clerk instead. In other cases solicitors simply give advice over the phone and attend less than two out of every three interrogations when they have been asked to give advice.

The basis for these allegations is research carried out by Birmingham law school and published by the Lord Chancellor's department. Solicitors' professional body, the Law Society, maintains that the main reason for these failures is insufficient funding which results in solicitors carrying out this type of work at a substantial loss.

This may well be true, in which case it is yet another example which gives the lie to the fine words of democracy, justice and rights which emanate on a daily basis from the higher echelons of the judiciary, government and the police. None of these concepts is worth a light unless there is a commitment to them, unless they are funded adequately and unless there is a will to monitor and defend them. It is my belief that none of these things is currently being done.

There are many things which the current Royal Commission must recommend if we are to reform the criminal justice system in a meaningful way. Perhaps the most important is that when anyone is detained or arrested they must have the automatic right of representation at that point. There should be no possibility of the police later being able to say that he or she didn't want to see a solicitor as they do at the moment.

There should be no option for a person to sign away their rights and they should have an automatic entitlement to see somebody. What a difference that entitlement would have made to the Birmingham Six and the Guildford Four and so many other people who have languished unnecessarily in prison for so many years. What a difference it would have made if they could have seen someone right from the start.

There is no provision in any legislation which allows this as of right. There are so many provisos and so much discretion allowed that, in the end, if the police don't want you to see a solicitor they won't let you see one. So, despite Royal Commissions and the Police and Criminal Evidence Act, very little has changed since the early seventies.

The power to delay access which the police currently have should be removed. Evidence of any kind which is obtained from a suspect, for whom access to a solicitor has been denied, should be inadmissible and should *not* be used in any trial. It should be considered in the same light as it would in the United States where it would be termed 'fruit of the poisoned tree' and would not be allowed under the exclusionary rules of evidence.

Coupled with this must go an absolute and unchallengable right to silence. Whatever attacks are mounted against it and whatever pressure is exerted by any administration, regardless of its political complexion, it must be resisted. In many ways the right to silence is the litmus test of a commitment to human rights. The very fact that it is currently under insidious and unrelenting attack speaks volumes about the state of Britain today.

ELEVEN

Remanded in Custody

Having been charged with the murder of Lloyd Waite, Talat Sarwar, who had no previous convictions, had his application for bail refused and was remanded in custody. He was not to see his home again for a further sixteen months.

Initially he was remanded to Winchester prison and for the first few weeks he was kept in the psychiatric wing where it was claimed he was under observation. There was no suggestion by the authorities that he had mental health problems, that he needed psychiatric treatment of any kind, that he was in danger of harming himself or attempting to take his own life. He was simply under observation.

Barely eighteen years old, Talat had for company a selection of psychiatrically disturbed convicted prisoners, some of whom had committed serious crimes and extreme acts of violence.

After being moved on from Winchester, the familiar and depressing merry-go-round began. It involves moves from one prison to another anywhere in the country, sometimes in the middle of the night, always without warning. It is the kind of treatment reserved for category A prisoners, into which group come so-called terrorists as well as those accused of murder.

The greater part of Talat's time in prison was spent in his cell, sometimes as long as twenty-three hours out of twenty-four, simply coming out to collect food and to take a short period of exercise in the yard.

Talat's parents originate from a very modest Asian background, have little in the way of money and his mother is elderly and in poor health. For her and for his father, visits across the country were both exhausting and financially ruinous so for much of the time they couldn't visit. Only during his period in Oxford jail, some twenty-five miles from High Wycombe, were they able to see Talat reasonably regularly.

It is hard to imagine what the strains of such a long period of incarceration, such isolation, must have been like for someone so young. In fact Talat was very philosophical about it. A non-drinker and non-smoker, he used his religion for support, sustaining himself with the Koran.

Remembering that those on remand in prison are still innocent, it is sometimes hard to fathom the attitudes of prison governors. In Talat Sarwar's case, one decided he should go on what is known as Rule 43, a type of segregation, mostly reserved for sex offenders, those in for child-related crimes and grasses. Prisoners never voluntarily elect for Rule 43 unless it is for their own safety.

Talat refused, knowing that when he returned from the specially segregated wing, whether at that prison or another one, it would be assumed by other prisoners that he was guilty of crimes in one of those three most reviled categories – that he was a 'nonce'. Had that happened, his life would have been made intolerable and his physical safety threatened.

Quite naturally he refused and as a consequence was placed in detention for a short period.

It would be nice to think that the judicial system keeps the thought constantly in mind that those on remand are not yet guilty. It would be nice to think that ... It wasn't until six months after Talat had first been remanded in custody that the prosecution served what is known as the 'committal bundle' on the defence. This consists of all the prosecution witnesses whose evidence they intend to rely on to support their case.

In some instances this evidence is very simple and straightforward, such as a policeman's statement listing all the forensic exhibits which were sent off for analysis, or the formal post mortem results of Dr West, the pathologist. If the defence accepts these as being non-controversial and they have no questions to ask about them, the written evidence is accepted and witnesses are not asked to attend court and give oral evidence.

The huge number of eye-witnesses to both the scene inside the café and what took place outside in the road would be included amongst the potential witnesses if the prosecution intended to rely upon them. The statements they made to police would be included in the committal bundle. If the prosecution don't intend to call witnesses that the police have interviewed then the statements those people made to the police may not be included in the bundle. In other words, some but not all the evidence which the police and prosecution had at their disposal is passed on to the defence.

In the prosecution bundle for Talat Sarwar's case there were numerous witness statements, statements which were included in the early chapters of this book, statements which said that witnesses had seen Talat Sarwar ask for a knife and then use it on Lloyd Waite. For various reasons it became obvious that the prosecution was not going to rely on any of these statements nor call any of the people who wrote them as witnesses. This meant that their case was essentially built around one witness only, Lewis Pinnock, the dead man's half-brother, a man with a history of violence, a man who had reason to lie about what he had seen, a man who could well have gone to the café intent on violence.

In view of what the defence now saw as a case with almost no substance to it, they made a submission of 'no case to answer'. Although this was turned down, the flimsiness of the prosecution would surely change the court's view on granting bail to the accused? That's what you would think! Despite applications which had gone as far as a Judge in Chambers in the High Court, the applications were refused.

One of the objections was that Talat might be at risk from retaliation by Waite's family. To counter this, a secret address was arranged in the Midlands, or it could have been arranged almost anywhere in the country if that's what was wanted. He would agree to the most stringent conditions of curfew, daily reporting regulations, a surrender of his passport and almost anything else in order to be released from prison.

It was all to no avail and Talat Sarwar remained in custody for a further ten months. Although he would eventually be found not guilty of the charge of murder, the total of sixteen months he served in prison, in conditions much worse than those experienced by convicted prisoners, was almost the equivalent of serving a five-year sentence as a convicted prisoner, with remission for good behaviour and early release on parole.

TWELVE

Emptying the Prisons

South Africa is not one of the most liberal countries in the world. If you're black then certainly it is one of the most oppressive, where your very colour virtually places you outside the protection of the law. Laws there are made to enshrine white people in power and to keep black people subservient.

Yet not so long ago in South Africa, Winnie Mandela and her body guards – the so-called Mandela United Football Team – were arraigned in court charged with kidnapping, assault and murder. She was convicted on four counts of kidnapping and four counts of being an accessory to assault and was sentenced to six years in prison. She immediately appealed the verdict.

Even in South Africa, possibly one of the last bastions of overt fascism in the world, Winnie Mandela walked out of court on bail despite the severity of the charges and the guilty verdict against her. That objectionable regime had proved, in this instance at least, that it had a greater belief in the presumption of innocence than the British judiciary.

We have a Bail Act which is supposed to ensure that there is a right to bail. But like so many other aspects of our criminal justice system that right is hedged in with so many provisos and so much discretion that in the end it is meaningless – unless of course you're a famous politician who's charged with commissioning a murder as was Jeremy Thorpe, or you run an organisation called Polly Peck or Guinness!

For the less prominent, the frequency with which bail is refused is an outrage and the conditions in which remanded prisoners are kept is an affront to a civilised society. The reality has been known for years but no one in the judiciary or the administration appears to be in the slightest bit concerned. A few pious words and a general utterance that 'something must be done about it' greets each new outrage and then everyone busily gets on with introducing new laws which ensure that even more people are remanded in custody.

Why does it happen? Because there is a pervasive presumption of guilt.

With the release of the Birmingham Six came a sense of relief that a dreadful wrong had been partially righted. But all six men were subjected to a type of treatment in prison, while still remand prisoners, that is shaming. And yet no further action is intended. You can hear the reasoning: 'Oh, but it's so long ago, the men involved have probably moved elsewhere or have retired and anyway, there's no proof.' Again the propensity to excuse, to bury, to divert attention takes precedence over action.

There is an assumption that such things could no longer happen, that they're a product of some dim and distant regime. The truth is that what happened to the Birmingham Six and many others could happen again today – does happen today. Silence by those in authority when cases of abuse like those of the Birmingham Six come to public attention can only be interpreted as an endorsement.

This is what happened to Hughie Callaghan, an innocent man in the eyes of the law at the time this happened and an innocent man in fact.

'We were taken from the police station to Winson Green prison on remand and walking into reception was just electric. There was a shout: "Here's the IRA bastards that done the bombings" and all hell let loose. Chairs went up in the air and it was just like a pub brawl.

'I was thrown on to a table then I was picked up, my head banged against a wall and then I was told: "Pick up the chair, you're knocking our furniture about!" The same happened to all the guys, we were kicked all over.

'They put us in a small room and made us lie down on a little bench. I said to Gerry Hunter: "They're going to kill us, they're just waiting to kill us off." Then I heard one of the screws shout; "Let's get the bath ready" and I thought it was to clean our wounds.' (All newly admitted prisoners have to take a bath or shower.) 'But we had to run to the bath, run a gauntlet, and we were kicked and punched all the way and then we were thrown in with our clothes on and our hair was pulled. When I got to the bath it was full of blood, the whole bath was full of blood and hair.

'They wouldn't let us sleep, they wouldn't let us look out of the windows and again we had to run a gauntlet of people every time we went out for our food. We were given routes we had to follow which meant we didn't see each other, couldn't talk to each other. But if in the confusion you turned the wrong way and bumped into one of the other six, you were beaten. I really thought we'd all be killed and if it wasn't through beatings then it would be with poison in our food or something like that.

'When the doctor came to examine me – I didn't know what was happening because I must have been spark out for a long time – he put the stethoscope on me and I'll never forget the look on his face. He looked at the hospital orderly and shook his head. The impression I got was that he meant no more beatings, that we couldn't take any more.'

But not all remand prisoners are held in local prisons with convicted prisoners, some have the dubious benefit of being remanded to institutions built especially for those who have not yet been convicted of any crime. Risley is one of them.

Risley Remand Centre sits in the flat, north Cheshire countryside, huge and commanding. Its nearest neighbours are barns and farmhouses and beyond the motorway road bridge lies Risley new town; further over to the west is Warrington. From the outside, to passing visitors with no business inside, Risley consists entirely of a concrete wall with a gate in it. This wall stretches upwards – twenty feet, thirty feet high, maybe more, and the top is surmounted with smooth, circular trunking – no grappling hooks will ever find a purchase here.

Someone who spent a great deal of time there is Wadi Williams, a forty-year-old black man. So disgusted was he with the place that eventually he became part of a protest movement in 1989 which led to the temporary closure of Risley. The media and the judiciary termed it a riot.

'Just the name of the place gives you a flavour of it – Grizzly Risley. It was horrendous; overcrowded, filthy, badly managed and cells that were originally built for one occupant had as many as three in them. There were even people sleeping on the landings. With these numbers of people using the facilities they simply couldn't cope and the plumbing was inadequate. The sluices, where you slop out your night's bucket, frequently blew back and flooded everywhere with faeces and urine.

'Essentially Risley is a concrete hell, a Dante's inferno. Those are the physical aspects but interwoven into that are the emotional factors. There is that appalling moment of remand when you know that your liberty has been taken from you and you know that this is the place you're going to have to live but for how long you don't know. I knew one man who'd been in for fourteen months and ten months isn't uncommon. If this happens it usually means the end of your job, your relationships and maybe even your home.

'A fifteen-minute visit is allowed five days a week and on Saturdays it's a closed visit, which means you sit with a glass panel between you and your visitor. This, of course, is the one day that most people have their visits because Risley serves a huge catchment area and most people can't get there during the week. On Sundays there are no visits. The effect for most people is that they travel long distances to spend only fifteen minutes in the most squalid surroundings.

'For convicted prisoners, waiting to be allocated to a prison, one travel warrant a month is allowed but for remand prisoners there are none whatsoever. There is no creche, no facilities for children and a prisoner is allowed no contact with his kids. You sit with a twenty-inch-wide ridge, a bit like a table, between you and your visitors, and if your kids try to crawl over it to come to you, to touch you, they're stopped. You can look at them but you can barely touch them. That is the most traumatic aspect of it all.

'Mostly it's the breadwinners who are inside and this simply cripples the family. Many of them just disintegrate even though a considerable number of prisoners are found innocent or they're given a fine and in other cases, when it comes to court, the police don't offer any evidence. You're kept inside for months and there isn't even a court case to show for it – you just walk free.

'Within Risley there are no facilities of any kind – no education, no leisure – and up to twenty-two hours a day are spent in your cell. In my cell, two people couldn't walk at the same time, couldn't even eat at the table together. The food was awful and the right to have your own food brought in or to receive food parcels was removed.

'The distance between where we collected our food and our cells where we had to eat it, was about a hundred, a hundred and thirty metres, which meant that we invariably had cold food. You had to walk back along corridors littered with dead and living cockroaches.

'The hospital was, in places, unfit for human habitation and it was considered a punishment to be sent there. I nursed two people suffering from acute withdrawal symptoms in our cell because they would rather that than go to the hospital.

'Then, of course there were the suicides – there were many suicides at Risley. After someone had been found it wasn't uncommon to hear a prison officer say something like: 'One down, so many hundred to go'. On one occasion a suicide was cut down and the distance from his cell to the hospital was about fifty metres. It took them fifteen minutes to get him there. They just didn't care.

'Being put on remand in a place like Risley is the most painful moment in anyone's life. You are taken from society and have to live in a cage. There is the loss of relationships, loss of liberty but most of all it's the cage and you can't get out. It's claustrophobic and panic sets in. That's the first thing you have to do – control your panic.

'I was aware that I could be shattered or I could resist – I had no other choices. When you are first received into the place you're put into the holding pen like animals. It was at that point that I was committed to a process of struggle.

'A new governor had tried to humanise the regime but the staff, who'd mostly trained under a different, more authoritarian system, wouldn't cooperate. So as fast as the governor tried to introduce change the POA (Prison Officers' Association) opposed him. The outcome was that rules changed according to who was on duty. Some screws weren't too bad but others were out-and-out fascists and you always knew when they were on duty because there would be a complete change in the whole atmosphere.

'Having decided that human beings, people who hadn't even been tried for any offence, couldn't live like this, I made it clear to staff that changes were necessary. There was only a small gym with just a few places and those places went to the screws' favourites so I started by challenging this. I then complained about the food and tried to reinstate the right to have our own food brought in at least once a day. I demanded greater access to washing facilities and more frequent laundry as we were allowed only one bath and one change of underwear a week. I also tried to get access to education.

'It wasn't that I started a revolt it was that history caught up with Risley. We simply started a protest and it wasn't our intention to take the roof off. The flash point came because the exercise yard was reduced to one-third its normal size and there wasn't enough room to exercise properly. We simply sat down in the exercise yard. Suddenly, we had the mufti (riot) squad on one side and dogs on the other so we did the only sensible thing and went inside and up to the fifth landing.

'One of the screws thought he could control it and was screaming, 'Get behind your fucking doors', but it was too late for that. He quickly ran off and pressed the riot bell. We didn't just stand and wait to be sorted out, we took positive action. We took the doors off, took control of the upper landing and the second wing and built ourselves into a defended position.

'We knew we had to make it public so that our grievances could be aired and to do that we guessed we would have to hold on for seventy-two hours in order for it to become a media issue. We just wanted the public to know. As soon as it ceased to be the number one item in the news we would give up.

'Once the protest started, the atmosphere inside the prison changed dramatically. There was no official leadership but we had mass assemblies and this unleashed an awesome sense of participation and democracy. Most of the decisions we reached were unanimous but when they weren't they were arrived at democratically. People were amazed to experience this unique feeling that they could participate in decision making. It empowered them.

'Of course the screws tried to get us down off the roof. They used hoses and thunder flashes and sent mufti squads in after us but none of it succeeded. We had made our demands clear and these were that we wanted a commitment to consider the time people are banged up on remand, not just in Risley but throughout the system; to consider the overcrowding in the system; to look at the appalling rates of suicide; and we wanted all the other dreadful abuses that I've mentioned looked into. Finally, they did agree to consider all our demands, the only thing they wouldn't agree to was our last request – for a meal to be served to us on the roof as a celebration.

'We knew we'd be dispersed to other prisons and that there'd be reception committees waiting to give us a good kicking. There are special prisons within the system which are like terror centres where the authorities send you if they feel you deserve a kicking. So we insisted on being photographed naked as evidence of our condition and it worked. We were right to be so cautious because those who bothered to have only the top half photographed or who left pieces of clothing in strategic places, had those strategic places kicked.

'The final decision to give up was taken at one of the main meetings. Having made the decision, we all stood in silence for one minute as a tribute to those who had recently died in the Hillsborough disaster, then we sang 'You'll never walk alone' and we came down.

'What happened at Risley had a profound impact on other prisoners and it's hardly surprising that Strangeways followed us.

'The way you're treated as remand prisoners within the prison system says that you are of no value, of no consequence and that you are guilty. Remand prisoners hold none of the levers of power and are expendable. Prison generally has nothing to do with rehabilitation and is not there to prevent crime but to unleash punishment. It is brutal and further alienates people who often are already alienated from society. When released, the community has to pick up the tab and some who come out are like volcanoes waiting to explode and it's the public who then pays the price. There is absolutely no strategy for rehabilitation.

'The only difference between a remand prisoner and a convicted prisoner is that as a remand prisoner you wear your own clothes. But you go in in handcuffs and you come out in handcuffs. Everything that happens to you while you are in there tells you that you are guilty and anyone visiting you couldn't possibly think that you were innocent. It even makes you believe yourself that you're guilty.'

It was into this type of environment that Talat Sarwar, an eighteen-year-old youth, was thrust – not for a day or two, not for a week, but for one year and four months.

Of course the Home Secretary will probably respond by saying that Risley has been rebuilt as part of the prison modernisation programme and will feign outrage that such criticisms should be levelled at his administration. It certainly has been rebuilt but not by design. It has been rebuilt partly because it had to be rebuilt as a result of the protest, partly as a result of the Dunbar report which was set up following the roof-top protest and highlighted the dreadful conditions in which men and youths had to live, and partly because of His Honour Judge Tumim's respected and constructive criticism as head of HM Prison Inspectorate.

In some cases the word 'youth' would more accurately be substituted with the word 'child' because our remand system regularly locks up fifteen-year-olds. One to hit the headlines in the most tragic manner was Jeffrey Horler who hanged himself only nineteen days before he was due to be released.

This took place at the young offenders' centre at Feltham in Middlesex and its governor, Joe Whitty, wasn't slow to apportion blame: 'I personally wish to say how abhorrent it is to have to deal with children – because that is what Jeffrey was, a child – in a penal setting and under the conditions in which I have to run Feltham for want of staff.

'It says nothing to the credit of the Home Office, local authorities or of society in general that we are still dealing with children, in this way.

It should be totally unacceptable in this age and it indicates that we are bankrupt of ideas and compassion in dealing with these admittedly very difficult but nevertheless very young and very vulnerable children.'

Jeffrey Horler died with a shirt tied to the bars of his cell window because he had been refused permission to attend his grandmother's funeral. It was considered that missing the funeral wouldn't have 'too great an effect on him' despite the fact that he was discovered sobbing in his cell after receiving news of her death. His mother couldn't visit and comfort him because she couldn't afford the fare to bring her the two hundred miles from her home.

Jeffrey was the third fifteen-year-old in two years to take his life in prison.

Another young man who recently killed himself was eighteen-year-old Tony Hook, remanded into custody for having unlawful sexual intercourse with his thirteen-year-old girlfriend. This wasn't a case of rape or of coercion but of an immature eighteen-year-old and a girl whom he obviously cared about and loved.

'May 4, 1990. Got remanded to Hindley. I cried all night. I am missing S like crazy. Can't stand being away from her. I love her more than anything.'

On his arrival at Hindley Remand Centre sufficient information came with him to mark him out as a possible suicide risk – that he had previously cut his wrists and taken an overdose. His probation officer had also told the authorities at Hindley that Tony could be at risk of suicide.

Without telling him, all mail between Tony and his girlfriend was intercepted and so his mental condition declined as he thought he had been abandoned. Eventually he was told:

'June 20, 1990. Today I have had a bastard of a day. Probation have told me that they stopped my letters to and from S. I am really depressed. I feel like topping myself. I love her like crazy. She'll always be in my heart.'

Two days later Tony was put into solitary confinement – '. . . for using threatening, abusive and insulting words to a prison officer'. He wrote in his diary: 'June 22, 1990. I got fourteen days loss of remission and seven days on the block but I don't care any more.'

Two days later he hanged himself with his shoe laces and some torn towelling while still in solitary. On the same night, Iain McKinlay also decided to end his own life with torn blankets. He was also eighteen and in the next cell to Tony Hook.

There is a huge class element at work in the sentencing policy of English justice and it is exemplified by the treatment received by seventeen-year-old Katherine Griffiths who spent infinitely longer in the squalid conditions of a closed prison than did Mr Saunders, who dabbled in City fraud. After conviction, Mr Saunders was whisked away almost immediately to the confines of an open prison. Ms Griffiths spent thirteen days in Holloway prison after admitting stealing a 24p bottle of milk.

Similarly, Lucy Kerr was sentenced to a six-month custodial sentence for allegedly fiddling the dole out of £62.

Anyone who attempts to justify this sickening abuse of human beings by pretending that understaffing or under-resourcing or special circumstances are responsible, is culpable. We have a barbaric remand system to which courts send people of all ages knowing what lies in store for them. It is not about individuals who fall through the safety net nor is it about the odd prison which falls below par, it is about an ethos. It is an ethos which must change if we are to claim membership of a civilised society.

The truth about the conditions into which people are remanded is known, has been known for years. Risley was no different but nothing was done. The glowing boil of repression was allowed to fester until it burst. Similar infections run through the blood of our penal system, from one end of the country to the other and will continue to erupt with great regularity. Politicians are transfixed by talk of 'slopping out' as though the introduction of a flushing toilet is all that's needed to transform a system based on inhumanity, oppression and abuse of human rights.

The outcome of the Risley protest was that of the fifty-four men who came down off the roof, forty-four were charged with riot. Wadi

Williams was in the first batch of twenty-two who pleaded not guilty. I was pleased to lead the defence.

In many ways this riot trial created legal history because not one of the accused denied the substance of the charges against them. They agreed that damage had been done, that barricades had been built and that they had ignored all orders to surrender and resisted all attempts to get them to come down. The defence we offered was a simple one: that the conditions in which they were forced to live were so extreme, so dehumanising and so far below the standards that should be expected in a civilised society that every action they took was justified.

The trial lasted one hundred and fifty-nine days, involved one hundred and thirty witnesses and forty hours of video-taped evidence. At the end of it the jury returned a verdict of 'not guilty' and all twenty-two men were acquitted. Subsequently the second batch of twenty-two were also acquitted.

Perhaps I'm naive but I would have imagined that any administration, in the face of an historic finding which said that prisoners have the right to protest when their conditions of incarceration are so poor, would have responded with humility and contrition. In fact what they did do was to introduce a brand new offence of 'prison riot'. Their reaction was one of: 'Well, we didn't get you this time but we will the next!' And so the sickness continues.

What is frequently overlooked is that although a person on remand is locked away, his or her defence has to be constructed and they must play an integral part in this. So what facilities does the remand system afford them? In Billy Power's case they were very few:

'Being remanded in custody is a terrible, terrible hindrance. You simply can't go anywhere or do anything and everything you do has to be through someone else. If you're not a criminal with experience of the system, you simply don't know the importance of getting to the right people and that's very frustrating.

'You have no access to the 'phone and have to write letters for everything but then your letters are censored so you're inhibited in what you can write. Anything I wrote in prison, screws would take it away so I couldn't even keep notes of meetings. Solicitors told me to write down all the things I remembered which might help with my defence, but I couldn't take the risk.

'When solicitors gave me the depositions of the police witnesses, the screws took them and held on to them for twenty-four hours. They were no doubt concocting their own stories to coincide with what the police had said.'

If you think that was too long ago to be relevant, consider Wadi Williams's experience some fifteen years later:

'Imagine the cramped and overcrowded conditions. Now imagine that you have to read through your depositions, pages and pages of information dealing with your trial. Imagine that you have to think and reflect on your defence and plan some approach. Then envisage two or three other people in the cell all trying to do the same thing. Add to that the sheer bedlam of the place and you can see that it is seriously impossible to prepare any case.

'And if you do struggle through that, the very mechanics of moving from prison to the courts every day is draining. You're up early in the morning – six or six-thirty. Remember you're only allowed one bath or shower a week so invariably when you do get into court you feel filthy, you are filthy. You have to go through the process of changing into other clothes, then the handcuffs, then the lock ups and then through the traffic in a pig bus – a series of tiny cells on wheels.

'You get to court and then you go through a whole process there of having the cuffs removed, more lock ups and you feel you've done a full day's work before you even set foot in the court. When you do, you feel exhausted, confused, disorientated and you have yet to deal with the court.

'All around you are people who've had a good night's sleep, they've started the day with a shower, they're properly dressed, properly fed and you're at a disadvantage before you've even opened your mouth. And at the end of the day you put the film on rewind and you go through it all again in reverse.'

Eamon Wadley, charged in the Battersea Bomb Factory case, was held in custody for three months despite the fact that he produced a string of character witnesses, including MPs, in his bail application. It wasn't until the committal proceedings that the conspiracy charge was dropped and bail was eventually granted but not on the normal conditions of guarantees – if the accused doesn't show up for trial the guarantors are asked to cough up to the tune of the amount they guarantee.

In Eamon's case the court wanted cash, £225,000 of it. Friends and relatives dashed around selling off insurance policies to raise the sum. The police claim was that he would escape to Ireland, even though he's a Londoner born and bred. When he emerged from prison his spirits were dashed at what he found.

'While I was inside the police held the key to my flat and wouldn't allow anyone to have it. Naturally I was concerned that it shouldn't be left empty but they assured me that it was under constant observation. When I went home on the day I was released I found it had virtually been demolished. It had been broken into, squatted and vandalised and anything of value had been stolen. Even photographs and little things of sentimental value had been taken and all my clothes. Also my job had gone. There's no compensation for any of this.

'Conditions of bail were that I signed on twice a day, at seven in the morning and at eight at night and that I lived with my parents. They are both old-age pensioners and live in a very small place. The last thing I wanted was to live like a child again. I was living in north London and having to sign on in south London and it was always a perpetual dash to get over there and back again. Sometimes I'd forget a pen and the police would be as obstructive as they could: "Well you'll have to go home and get one, won't you?" In addition to the signing on I was on a permanent eleven o'clock curfew.

'When Ulla and I decided to get married, they very kindly lifted the curfew for the wedding day but I still had to sign on at seven the next morning. When I got my job back they dropped the evening signing on but the curfew remained.'

For Eamon Wadley, these restrictions lasted for the best part of two years until he finally appeared in court:

'I was locked up again for two days while the jury was out considering their verdict and they finally came back at five o'clock on the

Friday evening. There were four charges against me and they had to read them out one by one. I was horrified at what might happen and I lost track of the charges being read. I could hear the loose change rattling in my pocket as I thought that it was now going to come to an end one way or the other.

'Then one by one came the verdicts . . . "not guilty", "not guilty", "not guilty", "not guilty!" I just burst into tears.'

He was acquitted of the charges against him. But that wasn't the end, there probably never will be an end for Eamon Wadley:

'I'm still a trades unionist and I'm still a socialist and I still believe in a united Ireland and I want to exercise my democratic rights but I can't! Why? Because I'm scared! I'm frightened to stand up for the Irish national anthem, I'm frightened to buy certain newspapers and I'm frightened to say anything at all about Northern Ireland because I'm scared it will eventually be brought up against me and so I say nothing. There are certain pubs that I would like to visit but I don't because Irish people go there. I used to watch the news avidly and now I avoid it because my heart stops beating when there's an incident. I automatically think "where was I when that happened?". I wonder if they're going to come and get me again, put me inside.'

I have quoted at length from both Wadi Williams and Eamon Wadley because no one could more eloquently communicate the reality of a remand in custody. For an outsider's perspective I will settle for the European Committee for the Prevention of Torture and Inhuman or Degrading Treatment or Punishment, set up by the Council of Europe. They conducted research at three English prisons, Wandsworth and Brixton in London and Armley in Leeds, and reported in 1991. Their conclusion? That certain aspects of these regimes are inhuman and degrading.

The British government's response was largely dismissive but perhaps that's to be expected when even its one sacred cow of prison reform – to install flush lavatories by 1994 – was rubbished. Building short wooden gates around a w.c. in a tiny cell shared by three men offered 'only a modicum of privacy'. It would only be acceptable if the cells reverted to single occupancy and even then it would be 'like living in a toilet'.

Of course there is no suggestion that these cells will revert to single occupancy.

The report is critical of many other aspects of prison life including the infrequency with which bedding is laundered, the lack of drying facilities for eating utensils and cups, the lack of ventilation and the abysmal lack of any activities. 'It came as something of a shock to members of the delegation to find, in 1990, grown men sitting on ancient wooden chairs, sewing mail bags by hand with crude metal implements.' They felt that most of the work on offer was dull and repetitive and did not develop skills and the average wage of £3.95 a week offered no hope of saving.

Perhaps their strongest comment was on the practice of housing three men in cells built for one. Their view was that this should end 'immediately'. The government's response was, at best, equivocal but when it came to a recommendation to lay down prescribed limits on the numbers of people in every jail there was no equivocation: 'Prisons have an absolute obligation to hold accused and sentenced persons committed by the courts.' In other words: 'We will continue to send people to prison in their droves and the prisons will bang them up without arguing!'

It is precisely this policy which has led to Armley housing 1200 people when it was built for 600. And the authorities' answer? To reintroduce prison hulks which could be moored in estuaries close to where overcrowding is the greatest. This revelation came in a leaked document to the *Guardian*. It was from the Prison Board's Estate Management Committee for consideration by the Home Office.

In spite of the appalling regimes experienced by most remand prisoners, conditions which led to 'rioting' at Risley, it was these very people that the hulks are designed to serve. 'It is understood that floating facilities would be used to house remands because the limited regimes they could provide would be inadequate for sentenced prisoners.' Yet again it is a policy of giving the innocent the worst.

And if that isn't enough, there are estimated to be some one thousand remand prisoners held in police cells where there are no facilities of any kind, no association, no education, no leisure – just

unrelieved, unremitting boredom. Doesn't anyone in the prison service
and Home Office learn anything from history?

The disturbances at Strangeways, and six other prisons following
in quick succession, created perhaps the most concentrated look at
prisons for many years and as a result of what happened there, Lord
Justice Woolf was charged with producing a report on prison conditions.
This he duly did and it made 204 recommendations. The government
boasts proudly that it rejected only six of them.

Built in 1868, Strangeways was the largest prison in Britain and like
all prisons it has a certificate which identifies the maximum number of
prisoners which should be incarcerated in it. It is termed the CNA, the
certified normal accommodation. At the time of the protest, Strangeways
contained twice its normal CNA!

As at Risley, the outcome was a full-scale protest which began
in the chapel and quickly spread to the rest of the prison with
inmates eventually occupying part of the prison, taking to the roof and
barricading themselves in. The scenes dominated television and press
reporting for days.

The irony of the Woolf report's findings and recommendations is
that government doesn't dispute them, it simply says it can't afford
to implement them. This is then taken as sufficient excuse to wash
its hands of the problem and seek the cure through a cosmetic policy
of privatisation. It's quite amazing that government ministers can avoid
expenditure when confronted by huge social problems but spend thousands of millions of pounds to save face in supporting an overvalued
currency and a failed economic policy.

But of course there is an answer to this dreadful overcrowding
and it is an answer which serves justice rather than trampling all over
it. The remedy is already in existence and has been for hundreds of
years except that we pay only lip service to it. I'm talking, of course,
about Habeas Corpus, that mark of civilisation which every schoolchild
learns about but can never remember how to spell. That's what should
guide us, a principle based entirely on the presumption of innocence
but which has become a toothless wonder.

We should start by granting bail as of right unless someone has previously committed a bail offence such as absconding, breaking the conditions of bail or has committed offences while on bail. Those should be the only reasons for refusing bail.

It is difficult not to return continually to this one point but it is the cornerstone of all that is written in this book; it is the fount from which all other changes spring and that is the presumption of innocence. The moment we begin to move away from that basic concept, usually because it suits an administration, it is ordinary people who pay the price. The lessons of history are that such a move does not produce better justice but opens the door to injustice and abuse.

What should have happened in the case of the Birmingham Six or in a future case similar to it? They accompanied the police to the police station quite voluntarily and should not have been held there overnight. They should have been allowed to go home and come back the next day.

That will be seen as a fairly remarkable proposition and I can hear them now in the corridors of power saying, 'But they'll all get away!' But that's because they have assumed they're guilty. That is where the implementation of Habeas Corpus becomes almost a litmus test of what this system is really about. If it was implemented it would unclog our prisons overnight.

We have a far greater passion for remanding people to prison and handing out custodial sentences than almost any other country in Europe. Almost one third of the prison population at any one time is on remand. These people have the worst regime of all, the least facilities and are kept locked in their cells for the longest periods. The official excuse is that with a shifting population it's very difficult to plan education and leisure and, in any case, they're not there for long enough to make it worth worrying about. That, of course, is rubbish.

We have one of the worst regimes in Europe and what does the British government do? It simply refuses to implement European minimum standards. The argument is that not all facilities are bad and some offer much better conditions than those laid down in the minimum standards. The pretence is that to comply would reduce the overall standards. Of course it's an argument that a child could see through but that's been their reaction to date. And they're still resisting despite cross-party support and despite a demand from numerous other organisations, such as that representing prison governors. So, the next step in my reform package is an automatic right to bail and consequently an immediate reduction in the prison population.

THIRTEEN

Enter the Scientists

The case of Talat Sarwar, at this stage, was not a level playing field as far as the defence was concerned. Following the killing of Lloyd Waite, police had flooded into the International Café, they had supplied some 135 exhibits for analysis by Home Office forensic scientists at the Aldermaston laboratories, they had had as much time as they desired to examine the interior of the café and the road immediately outside, and they had pulled in dozens of witnesses from the surrounding area.

The defence? Through their contacts with the local community they had managed to speak to some witnesses but then only under harassment and pressure from police and the Crown Prosecution Service. Through prompt and effective action they had been able to support and advise the accused but again under pressure.

The defence felt that two immediate courses of action needed to be taken. The first was to conduct another post mortem and the second was to provide their own forensic evidence in an attempt to determine what had taken place inside the café. Neither decision is an easy one to implement when an accused person is being represented on legal aid – but more about that later.

Racial divisions had been opened up between the black and Asian communities in High Wycombe with the death of Lloyd Waite. The tension was heightened by the defence's request for a second post mortem, which meant that Waite's body could not be released for burial.

Owing to the case load of pathologists, the time taken to arrange a post mortem can be months. During this wait, the deceased's relatives are unable to grieve properly and the interminable waiting can exercise tempers. There is no facility for murder cases to jump the queue and receive more prompt attention.

The prosecution immediately objected to the defence request, offering the usual complaint that the doctor who performed the original post mortem, Dr Iain West, was an eminent pathologist and therefore there was no need for a second opinion. His independent and unbiased opinion should be good enough for anyone!

The defence insisted and on 4 May, after a comparatively short wait, a Dr Heath re-examined the remains of Lloyd Waite. One of the principal reasons for insisting on a second post mortem was because of a simple statement included in Dr West's original report. In this statement he said that he had been shown by the police: ' . . . a very helpful video of the scene of the murder'.

The role of a pathologist is to examine the body and determine the physical cause of death. He is not obliged to speculate, piece together evidence or set the death in any context. There was absolutely no reason why he should have been shown a video of the scene, a video which no doubt was accompanied by a police explanation of their theory. No matter how independent Dr West was, no matter how unimpeachable his integrity, there was a fear that he could be innocently influenced by what he had seen and been told.

In the event, Dr Heath's examination was not markedly different from Dr West's except that he noted Waite had recently eaten. This offered a strong challenge to Pinnock's assertion that he believed Waite had gone to Desborough Road in order to buy food from the Caribbean Kitchen. Dr Heath's viewing of the body and the fatal wound, however, was to have an important bearing on the case.

By the time the defence had managed to locate an independent forensic scientist and arrange for him to have access to the café, seven days had elapsed. It was only Superfly's inherent good nature which had ensured the café was kept closed. However, his girlfriend, Susan Ray, had already gone in armed with hot water, disinfectant and cloths and had cleaned it up. Any objects of interest (except, of course, for the bent knife, which they had missed) had been removed by the police SOCOs so it was uncertain what, if anything, the scientist would find.

The man they managed to contact was Russell Stockdale from Newbury and he, together with Lynda Davis, John's wife and a member of the practice, visited the International Café and walked straight into a storm in the form of Lloyd Waite's family. With a combination of diplomacy, tact and firmness, Lynda Davis stood up to them and controlled the situation.

Fortunately the scene didn't develop beyond wagging fingers, shouts and threats but the family refused to leave. In the end Superfly called the police who cleared the café. The irony of the situation didn't escape the defence duo but it was under these rather bizarre circumstances that they had to try and piece together their case to prove the innocence of Talat Sarwar. They searched the café and found blood stains which the police had missed, including those on the underside of a stool which were consistent with the stool having been used for defensive purposes.

Once the hysteria was gone, Russell Stockdale set about seeing what he could find and, surprisingly, he found quite a lot. Searching in the darker recesses and corners of the café he came across tiny traces of splattered blood on a variety of surfaces – the walls, pool tables, fruit machines and chairs. He carefully collected these samples, took a number of photographs and a series of detailed measurements.

What he had was far from a complete forensic picture of the happenings inside the International Café. The rest of the picture lay in the samples which were in the hands of the prosecution – perhaps the Crown Prosecution Service, the police or the Home Office at Aldermaston, no one knew for sure. To prepare a meaningful report it was vital for Russell Stockdale to gain access to these exhibits.

The defence's request to the CPS for access to them wasn't exactly refused but it certainly wasn't acceded to. In strictly non-legal terminology you could be forgiven for describing what followed as 'the run around'.

The first request was met with the parry that any decision to release the exhibits was entirely in the hands of the police and had nothing to do with the CPS. But when the police were approached they stoutly maintained that they couldn't release the exhibits because such a decision lay entirely in the hands of the CPS. So, back to the CPS. As far as they were concerned the matter was one over which the police had complete authority and it was nothing to do with them.

The defence kept pushing the CPS and eventually received the information, which was obviously delivered as a final dismissal to this irritating country solicitors' practice, that the exhibits were no longer in police custody but were at Aldermaston. The analysis had not yet been completed and wouldn't be for a further three months.

Their parting shot was to say they couldn't understand the defence's worries because even the police hadn't yet received any reports on the forensic evidence. Why didn't they just stop worrying because when the CPS eventually received something in writing they would pass a copy on to Davis Walker.

What concerned Russell Stockdale was the fear that the longer the police took in providing access to the blood samples in particular, the greater the danger that they would have deteriorated. Without examining them in good condition he couldn't even begin to draw any conclusions. He didn't even have the basic information as to which blood groups were supposed to be present in the café and who had what grouping. It was seen as crucial to the defence case to establish whether it was just Talat's blood which was in the café, whether there was any blood from Lloyd Waite, from Lewis Pinnock or from any other person.

What lay behind this concern was some very simple reasoning which even the prosecution agreed with, that Talat Sarwar could be the murderer only if the fatal wound had been inflicted inside the café. Anywhere else, such as immediately outside the café or in the road, and Talat was innocent as there was absolutely no evidence whatsoever which placed him outside the café during the battle of the pool cues. Establishing whose blood was present inside the café could contribute to this. For instance, if only Talat's blood was found then it was unlikely, although not conclusive, that he had stabbed Waite. If blood from an unknown, unidentified third party was found then it could be that he was the guilty person.

As is the case with anyone held on remand, frequent court hearings are held to reconsider the position. At each one of these remand hearings the defence made requests for access to exhibits. Each time the prosecution responded by saying that because of the time needed to carry out an examination the defence must be patient. Aldermaston was very busy and they couldn't be expected to change their routine for this one case.

With every refusal, the defence's concern grew until eventually the totally unprecedented decision was taken to apply for a witness summons against the director general of the Home Office laboratories at Aldermaston. It meant that he would be obliged to appear before the examining magistrates at High Wycombe to explain why the samples had not been provided to the defence or, at the very least, why Russell Stockdale had not been granted access to them at Aldermaston. The subpoena winged its way towards Aldermaston and landed on the director general's desk. This course of events is so unusual that it could be compared with the mountain coming to Mohammed.

The shock waves travelled far and wide but the response was instantaneous. The vital information which the defence had been seeking for weeks was made immediately available and the director general was saved an embarrassing appearance in High Wycombe magistrates' court. But that wasn't the end of the matter.

The branch prosecutor for the CPS leaped into the fray and issued a public statement accusing John Davis personally of having misled the court when 'he persuaded' them – the magistrates – to issue the witness summons. So incensed was he that he threatened to refer the matter to the Law Society, the solicitors' governing body.

It's interesting to speculate what the reasons of the prosecutor were for issuing such a personal attack and for making such a threat, particularly when he was so obviously and utterly wrong. One would have thought that a man who spends his life sifting evidence would check basic facts.

The facts were that John Davis had not made the application. After long and independent consideration of the problem and after continuous refusals to release vital information, it was Counsel which had decided that an application should be pursued.

When this was made known, the local chief prosecuting solicitor wrote an apology to John Davis on behalf of the CPS and withdrew the allegation unreservedly. Meanwhile, Talat Sarwar was sitting in a prison cell somewhere in Britain, unable to receive visits because he was too far from home and spending twenty-three hours a day locked up as a category A prisoner.

But Russell Stockdale was now able to continue with his examination and prepare a report on his findings. It's hard to understand how the police arrived at their original theory that Talat had waited behind the door and had stabbed Waite in the back as he entered. If the post mortem hadn't dismissed that idea as a non-starter then certainly Dr Stockdale's findings should have done.

He was able to establish that the blood which was splattered around the café belonged to Talat. By conducting a series of tests at his Newbury laboratories he was able to show that the pattern of the blood and the shapes of the splashes he had found were totally consistent with someone with a cut hand retreating, casting his arms around him in an attempt to ward off an attack. It was what became known as the 'flying blood' evidence. Talat, of course, did have a cut hand as Dr Beechey-Newman's report at High Wycombe general hospital verified. He described it in the following way: 'The wound to his finger was also relatively minor … and had not severed nerves, tendons or vessels.' A 'relatively minor wound' had caused quite a mess.

But Talat wasn't the only person to have a cut hand as the post mortems on Lloyd Waite confirmed. In fact both his hands were cut and neither of them could be described as 'relatively minor'. In the original report, written by Dr West, Waite's injuries were described in the following detail:

'Left arm; superficial combined stab and cutting wound on the outside of the left wrist (thumb side). It cut through the skin and subcutaneous tissues and extended down to the surfaces of the wrist bones for one-and-a-quarter inches. From the end of the wound to the back of the wrist ran two superficial cuts. The first was half-an-inch in length and the second one-and-a-quarter inches in length.

'Right arm; there was a T-shaped deep incised wound on the back outside front of the right hand. The wound was composed of a one-and-a-half inch linear incised wound … on the back of the hand. The leg of the T … curved around the thumb for a distance of three-and-three-quarter inches to terminate at the ball of the thumb. The wound involved skin, subcutaneous tissue and muscle and involved a stabbing component over the ball of the thumb.'

Dr West went on to sum up his findings with the words: 'There were cutting wounds on both of the deceased's hands. These were entirely in keeping with defensive injuries with the deceased attempting to block blows from a knife.'

What these technical descriptions were actually saying was that Lloyd Waite's left wrist had been cut through to the bone. There were two further cuts on the wrist. On his right hand was a cut nearly four inches long which sliced through the base of the thumb. There were also other, or at least another, cut on the same hand. Several cuts in total, at least two of them extremely deep. It looked fairly obvious that whoever stabbed Lloyd Waite had had several attempts at it. It was also fairly obvious that Waite's hands would have been bleeding profusely.

Even compared with the disputed witness statements of people who were in the café and who subsequently denied the truth of what they were supposed to have said; even compared with Pinnock's own dubious statement, no one had proposed a scenario in which Waite's attacker had stabbed at him several times. No one had spoken of Waite attempting to ward off blows or of trying to grab the knife blade with his bare hands, which is the implication of Dr West's report.

Pinnock claimed, and even this claim was to be disputed and discredited in court, that Waite had been stabbed in a much more straightforward, even furtive manner:

'As we moved, so did the Asian and I saw he had a knife which had a short blade, about four inches or so in length. I saw the Asian stab Lloyd in the right side and almost immediately Lloyd reached into his right trouser pocket and pulled out his brown lock knife. He flicked the knife in the air and the blade shot out and he went after him. The Asian dropped his knife as he ran and I picked it up as I followed Lloyd.'

There was no suggestion from Pinnock that there had been more than one attempt at stabbing, no suggestion that Waite had tried to block the blows and no suggestion that his hands had been badly cut. And just to prove that it didn't happen later in the fight, he claimed to have picked up the knife which Talat was supposed to have been wielding and had tossed it away out of harm's way.

If Waite had sustained these severe cuts to his hands right at the beginning of the fight it is more than a little surprising that traces of his blood were not distributed around the café. It may have made a different pattern to Talat's and the 'splash' shape of the droplets might have been different but it is reasonable to believe his blood would have been widespread, possibly even more widespread than Talat's. Russell Stockdale didn't find that.

One of the prosecution's exhibits was Talat's leather bomber jacket and there were a number of slash marks down the front of it and near the neck, but these had not been commented on by the Home Office forensic scientist. Again the defence felt this confirmed Talat's own story and that of several witnesses, that he was attacked by Waite and Pinnock and retreated backwards up the café towards the counter. The downwards stabbing movements from Waite's knife eventually cutting his neck. The cuts to his jacket, according to the Home Office report, were more consistent with a razor slash than a knife but however they were caused, the defence were convinced that Waite had been the aggressor and Talat the victim.

If any further proof was necessary it came in the form of the post mortem in which Dr West had clearly indicated that the stab wound which killed Waite had almost completely severed his aorta, the main blood vessel from the heart. How long the fight lasted could only be speculation but an aorta as damaged as Waite's would allow the whole of the body's blood to be lost in about two minutes if the injured person was in an excited state. Everyone, including Pinnock, agreed that Waite was in a very excited state and was very physically active in pursuing Talat.

For the prosecution theory to stand up it required that Waite, so badly stabbed that his aorta was almost severed, showed no signs of feeling any pain or discomfort, that he was able to conduct an aggressive fight without losing consciousness or even appearing to be dizzy when he must have lost most of his blood and that he walked unaided and seemingly unhurt from the café.

That the wound was painful is beyond doubt because just a little while later Waite was seen lying in the road, doubled over obviously in very great distress. So the big question facing the defence was, if he wasn't stabbed inside the café, where was he stabbed? There was not one witness so far who could supply the answer to that question.

Apart from hoping to unearth evidence which would prove the innocence of Talat, the defence were equally keen not to allow the whole weight of authority in matters forensic to rest with the Home Office scientists. This was why they looked upon Russell Stockdale's contribution as vital. As it transpired, they were very wise to do so.

In the preparation of a court case, not everything flows in a logical, ordered and coherent manner. For instance, the witness statements collected by the police and with which I started this book are completely unknown to the defence until a committal bundle is served on them. In this bundle are all the statements which the prosecution might or might not rely upon. Because a statement is included doesn't necessarily mean that that witness will be called at the trial. Similarly, there might well be witnesses whom the police have interviewed but whose statements are not included in the bundle.

This is an extremely controversial area of the law and what is described as 'non disclosure' runs as a fairly common theme throughout some of the recently acknowledged cases of miscarriage. It was to be an element in this case, also.

With forensic evidence, the defence is supplied with the Home Office scientist's report but any inconsistencies cannot be explored until the trial or, in some cases, the committal which can take the form of a trial and at which a decision is taken as to whether there is actually a case to answer.

The Home Office scientist who carried out the investigation into this case was Anthony Peabody, a man with a string of letters after his name – BSc, MSc, PhD, Chartered Biologist, Member of the Institute of Biology. While his evidence was not to be subjected to the critical analysis of another scientist, namely Russell Stockdale, until the committal proceedings, I have included the main findings here because it makes more sense of the whole forensic lottery.

It isn't hard to imagine how a man such as Anthony Peabody is presented to a jury by the prosecution. An almost infinite number of qualifications, a full-time, professional, highly regarded scientist with years of experience whose words fall only marginally short of being enshrined in tablets of stone. Juries love these scientists and are inclined to treat them as they would a priest – unless, of course, they're challenged by other scientists of stature.

Apart from Talat's jacket, which had not appeared in Dr Peabody's original statement, there were several other areas of concern. He had examined the three knives which had come to light at or near the scene, including the one which was found under Lloyd Waite's body and was thought to belong to him. The other knives were the bent kitchen knife found by Susan Ray and a rusty knife found in a culvert at the scene and probably nothing to do with this case. He had not, however, carried out any tests on the blood found on the knife thought to belong to Waite. The other two knives had no blood on them.

Surprisingly, none of the knives had been tested to see if they could have caused any of the cuts to the various pieces of clothing in this case, none had been tested to see if they could have been the murder weapon and none of them had been tested for finger prints. Even when the bloodied knife was released to Russell Stockdale it had still not been tested for fingerprints and he felt unable to conduct his own tests on the blood for fear of accusations of tampering with evidence.

Dr Peabody's summary of his findings included identifying blood which could have come from Waite on Pinnock's shoe – nothing untoward in this as Pinnock had been with Waite in the road. Blood which could have come from Waite was found on a wooden doorframe inside the café and on the knife which was found outside the café in the road. Considering how many people were supposed to have beaten Waite while he was in the road, it doesn't stretch the imagination to visualise people with bloodied hands after wielding pool cues touching the door frame or football game on their return.

Blood which could have come from Talat was found on the fridge/ freezer and cash till inside the café, a fairly modest finding in comparison with Russell Stockdale's discovery – and that after the café had been cleaned. No blood from Pinnock was found inside the café but blood from Waite was found in one place on the inside lining of Talat Sarwar's jacket.

Had the defence not employed an independent scientist that is probably where Dr Peabody's contribution would have ended. In his statement were two points which could have caused concern for the defence: the fact that Waite's blood was found on the football game and on a wooden door post inside the café and on the inside of Talat's jacket.

In fact there appeared to have been little control over the handling of exhibits, including blood-soaked items of clothing. There was absolutely no guarantee that there had not been contamination by items of clothing touching one another, by officers transferring blood from one item to another with their hands or by the people inside the café returning with blood on their hands, feet or pool cues. In fact there was absolutely nothing in the evidence which could cause damage to the defence case but equally, there was nothing of merit which would help Talat. With further questioning the reason became apparent. Dr Peabody acknowledged that:

'I have not been to the scene of the alleged incident nor have I seen any photographs. We sometimes visit the scene of a crime but very often we do not.

'I do not know how extensive the blood stains were in the café.

'I do not know what the blood stains looked like at the time they were found.

'I cannot say how the blood stains arose on the football game or door.

'I could not say that a blood stain arose as a result of a person bleeding directly on the game or the door. I have not seen it. In those circumstances it would not be possible for me to say how the blood got there.

'I cannot say, or tell you, how the blood came to be or was found by the police officers. I have not been to the scene or seen the blood.'

Dr Peabody had not visited the scene of the murder at all and therefore had no idea where the examples he had examined had come from other than what he had been told by the police. He had no idea how the blood had got on to the surfaces in the first place, whether it was original or secondary transfer. He had taken no photographs and no measurements. Was the blood on the doorframe and football game smeary as if it had come from someone's hand or was it profuse and pooled or in droplets as though someone had bled directly on to those surfaces? Dr Peabody didn't know!

Had Russell Stockdale been able to examine the scene before it had been cleaned up, the defence might have had some more valuable answers. But, compared to the normal run of events, they were extremely lucky and extremely unusual in having an independent scientist to inspect the scene at all.

The traditional view is that the defence doesn't need their own expert because it is possible to rely entirely on the competence, integrity and independence of the Home Office forensic scientist. Anyone who is persistent enough to push for their own expert can be treated with resentment.

The experience of Davis Walker is that if a defence tries to do anything which is active or inventive, there is a reaction from the establishment. It isn't a question of the CPS lacking independence but the fact that they feel they have to champion the police cause. It isn't that they are actively trying to prevent the defence from having information but they operate on a belief that the police, from the highest-ranking officer to the lowest, is telling the complete truth about everything.

On the basis of this thinking, they assume that a Home Office forensic scientist, whether called by the defence or the prosecution, will have the same degree of independence, objectivity, ability and integrity. The majority of defence solicitors themselves often fall into the same trap of believing there is no need for their own scientist.

So, when a solicitor attempts to exert his or her independence, the reaction isn't particularly favourable. The supposed search for truth takes second place to conformity and an unspoken instruction not to rock the boat. As in the case of John Davis, when threats are made of complaint to the professional body, there is an intimidating effect which encourages people not to stick their necks out. When he began to hear rumours that his own senior professional colleagues thought he was being over zealous, he understood why cases are rarely defended this strenuously. Is one defendant worth it all? Fortunately, he felt his defendant was worth it.

FOURTEEN

Aiding the Accused

The market town of Newbury in Berkshire is now almost encircled by motorways but it is still a quietish, country town and a centre for the agricultural interests of the surrounding rural area. Boots, Tesco and Dixons are paralleled by livestock feed merchants, veterinary suppliers and purveyors of green wellies.

Not far from the town centre is a tranquil, unprepossessing, residential road, the type of road where Neighbourhood Watch stickers proliferate and the gardens are neat. A crunching gravel path, flanked by privet hedges, finds its way between two houses, opening out into the back garden of one of them. Facing you is a small, new, single-storied extension which looks as though it could be a granny flat. It is, in fact, the offices and laboratories of Forensic Access and a home to one half of all the properly trained, independent forensic scientists in the country – all three of them. It was two until recently.

It is from here that Russell Stockdale and his partner Angela Gallop operate as independent forensic scientists at the disposal of defence lawyers. Police and prosecution have the services of some seven hundred scientists to call on with few constraints in terms of availability, the time they're able to devote to a case and costs.

The distribution of government forensic scientists is four to five hundred in the service of the Home Office and a further two hundred or so at the Metropolitan Police laboratories. Both Russell Stockdale and Angela Gallop know how the situation works because they were both once senior Home Office scientists. In fact, it was disillusionment with the forensic service which caused them to leave, set up independently and become what is known in court parlance as 'expert witnesses'.

In their opinion there is a massive imbalance between the weight that Home Office forensic evidence provides for the defence and that which it provides for the prosecution. As a consequence, the scales are tipped heavily against a defendant. 'The prosecution holds all the trumps.' This is exacerbated because of the lack of controls over independent expert witnesses who often claim to be experts but rarely are. For anyone without a scientific background it is often hard to determine who are the good guys and who are the pretenders. Increasingly often, the system itself stands in the way of your making the correct choice.

The essential injustice of the situation struck Russell Stockdale and Angela Gallop when, as Home Office employees, they were continually required to show around the laboratories so-called defence experts who simply didn't know what they were talking about. Angela Gallop was far from happy with the situation:

'One of these "experts" didn't even know how to use a microscope. Defence expert witnesses are frequently scientists who have decided that being an expert witness is a nice little side-line, a nice little earner, but have had absolutely no training in forensic science. As a consequence, defendants are being badly served.

'There is no regulation and anyone with a scientific background can place an advertisement in the legal journals claiming that they are experts. I've actually heard one admit in court that he was an 'enthusiastic amateur'. I've heard another claim as his experience to have examined fifty-seven fibre samples. We would expect to do that in one case and over the years have examined tens of thousands of examples. In this particular case he was looking only at the Home Office scientist's findings and had not even done his own research.

'There is only one source of trained forensic scientists and that is the Home Office but we are all specialists following one of four forensic disciplines. Often when a scientist leaves to become an independent, expert witness, he or she suddenly becomes an expert in every area. That of course cannot be right.

'There are huge problems and my personal concern was for the poor deal which defendants were and still are getting. The defence misses vital shortcomings in prosecution evidence because they simply don't have the knowledge or the experience to know when something is being fudged over.

'The other side of it which disillusioned us was the way in which we were expected to give evidence in court. Because you are a Home Office expert no one bothers to draw the evidence out properly. The defence doesn't know how to and the prosecution isn't interested in doing so. If you feel that the evidence you have been asked to present could be misleading and you try to expand on it, you are cut off by the prosecution in mid-sentence.

'Frequently we have left the court feeling that we didn't get the balance right and by that I mean that the case wasn't presented fairly.'

The truth is that scientists rarely disagree on the facts but when it comes to interpretation of the facts – that's a very different story. When Home Office scientists begin work on a case they are provided with very little background information by the police. They usually have to rely on a brief summary written by one of the officers involved in the case and who may already have firm ideas about who is the guilty party. He will lead the scientists in the direction he wants them to go.

A typical example of how this might prejudice a scientific investigation is the classic attempt to prove a connection by analysing fibres. A scientist can say that, yes, the fibres found on the victim's jacket were the same as those in the accused's sweater. What the scientist can't prove and won't be asked to prove is whether a policeman first handled one item of clothing and then the other and by so doing transferred fibres quite innocently. The police won't provide that information and the scientist won't be expected to seek it out. It is also highly unlikely that the prosecution scientist will be asked to report how common the fibre is and what other sources might produce it. It could well be a very common fibre and the victim himself may have a piece of clothing containing those fibres.

Angela Gallop believes that a forensic scientist cannot give a clear picture of the value or the shortcomings of scientific evidence unless the scientist carrying out the tests is something of a detective:

'Now that I'm part of the defence team I don't just want to be given the Home Office findings, I need to know the background to them. I want to know what tests they've done, negative as well as positive. I need to be able to read all the information surrounding a case. I need to see all the prosecution's witness statements and those of the defence. Having done that I can then place all the scientific findings into a context and sometimes that gives you unexpected answers. You can sometimes suddenly see how an exhibit became accidentally contaminated or how someone might have inadvertently handled a piece of evidence.

'The forensic scientist who works for the police receives very little of this background information and no matter how well intentioned he or she might be, they cannot place the evidence in context. From the defendant's perspective, it's vital that someone qualified has a good look at any scientific evidence which is offered against them. Unfortunately it rarely happens. It's also important to have a second qualified person to analyse a scientist's evidence and perhaps put forward other possibilities as frequently a scientist giving evidence can become intransigent in front of a court. They will obstinately defend a position which, to another expert, is obviously untenable. It's as though their whole competence is being challenged.'

Russell Stockdale was involved in just such a case where supposedly incontrovertible evidence of guilt was offered by the police in a rape case. It was considered particularly damning because it involved the new god of forensic science – DNA fingerprinting.

The only evidence against the accused was a semen stain on a sheet in the bed where the rape was supposed to have happened. With genetic fingerprinting it was established that the semen almost certainly belonged to the accused because the chances of it belonging to anyone else was one in several million. That would have appeared to be that!

On microscopic inspection, Russell Stockdale established that the semen stain contained only semen and no vaginal material of any kind and nothing else which indicated that sexual intercourse had taken place. On investigating all the background information he established that the accused had been sleeping in the bed for two weeks prior to the alleged rape and the presence of the semen could be easily explained. When his report was served on the prosecution they immediately dropped the case. Without a scientific input on the part of the defence it is highly likely that the man would have been found guilty.

The use of scientists by the prosecution isn't quite as impartial as we're led to believe and, according to Angela Gallop, the Home Office can be very selective in the evidence it presents:

'In the case of a mask used in a robbery they can make statements like: "A hair similar to the defendant's was found in the mask." They might omit to say that four other hairs, all of different types, were also found. Or they may say something like: "No hairs belonging to the accused were found." The implication is that it was his mask but they couldn't find any hairs in it. In truth, if the mask cannot be linked to the accused it shouldn't even be raised in evidence. They might also omit to say that there were a whole selection of hairs from different people in it. We have learned to recognise what we term "weasel words" in Home Office reports when we see them.'

Evidence based on hair analysis can be very misleading. There is not just one type of hair on each head; each head contains several different types of hair. There is frequently an overlap and two people with seemingly different hair may each contain some of the same type. An explanation of this ambiguity may well be missing when the prosecution's case is presented in court. Is it conspiracy or carelessness on the part of scientists? Angela Gallop doesn't think it's either.

'I know from my own experience that no pressure is put on Home Office scientists to be selective or to report in a particular way. The problem is that we constantly work with the police, we are often directed by them and we become caught up with them in the search to find the criminal. It's difficult to expect people who hunt with the hounds to give the kiss of life to the hare when it's caught.

'I spent over a year assisting with the search for the Yorkshire Ripper and I could not have presented evidence for him satisfactorily. Two advocates are required in our court rooms and I have no doubt that there should be two scientific perspectives also.

'In support of this, many people quote the Scottish system where two opinions are required but in my view this works no better than the English system. All the Scottish system does is to ensure that the evidence put forward is scientifically correct. If one scientist says a sample of blood is Group O, the other must agree. Each scientist will do exactly the same tests in exactly the same way and, surprise, surprise, they will come up with exactly the same results. As a consequence our work for the defence in Scotland is just as effective as it is in England.'

One of the ways in which the present system fails is the brevity of scientific reports. The reason why only the main points of an investigation are included, we are told, is to avoid confusion. Yet this in itself can be very confusing. One of the excuses used is that evidence has to be simplified in order that a jury can understand it. Such simplification and the absence of an independent scientist to challenge the evidence almost certainly led to the conviction and imprisonment of Jacqueline Fletcher.

She was jailed for life for the murder of her six-week-old son, Glen, by drowning, in October 1984. Ms Fletcher wasn't arrested until four years later and the only evidence against her was a confession she supposedly made to police. Despite the fact that she was described as of 'borderline intelligence' (whatever that means), and was therefore a 'vulnerable person' under the rules of PACE, the rules governing interviews with vulnerable people were completely ignored.

At her trial, the pathologist, Dr Peter Andrews, an expert witness, stood in the witness box and described the baby's lungs as being 'waterlogged'. Hardly surprising, the jury assumed this to be evidence of drowning and returned a verdict of guilty. The defence never saw fit to ask Dr Andrews to explain what he meant and he never saw the need to clarify his statement despite the gravity of the charge and the obvious implications of his evidence.

In fact there was no 'water' whatsoever in baby Glen's lungs and what Dr Andrews meant to say, what he should have said, what he should have been challenged into saying was that the baby's lungs were 'bodily-fluid-logged'. That imprecise description contributed to Ms Fletcher serving four years of a life sentence before being released on appeal in 1992 – another in the continuing toll of miscarriages. In fact the original verdict on Glen was finally upheld as having been accurate; that he had died a cot death.

In Angela Gallop's experience such simplistic, badly phrased and incorrect simplifications are unnecessary for juries:

'If juries don't understand the evidence they are given it is simply because it hasn't been presented to them properly. They are eminently capable of interpreting scientific evidence. We are very keen on what we call the "whoosh" approach. You can give a very long and detailed scientific explanation of what happens when petrol is ignited but nothing can describe it as well as the word "whoosh". This is a form of simplification but it is a description which no one could confuse.

'One of the reasons why scientific evidence is poorly presented in court is because of the prosecution's attitude towards it. It was a rarity for us to have a pre-trial conference with prosecuting counsel. We simply stood in the witness box and were asked questions without any indication of where they wanted the evidence to go. They simply wanted bald statements which fitted in with their presumption of guilt.

'Now that we work for the defence, it is a matter of course to discuss our findings with defence counsel and properly plan the presentation of evidence in a way which juries understand and which fairly represents the interests of the accused.'

It is quite horrific that in this day and age, with all the examples of failure as proof, we still don't have a national forensic service for defendants. In 1991, the government suddenly announced that it was going to open up the Home Office forensic laboratories to defence scientists. This sudden appearance of generosity was not based on any re-investigation or re-analysis of the situation but because it was under tremendous pressure from the continuous failures of justice.

Opening up the laboratories does nothing to redress the forensic bias in favour of the prosecution, it doesn't place a single additional independent scientist at the disposal of the defence, it does nothing to examine or control those claiming to be 'expert witnesses', it does nothing to improve the loose criteria for admitting scientific evidence and it does nothing to advance inter-verifiability – that is, it is still impossible for one scientist to verify what another scientist is doing.

It also does nothing to improve the knowledge of barristers who have to examine and cross-examine scientific witnesses.

Barristers are rarely qualified in scientific matters and there has traditionally been a long-term resistance to engage in what many of them see to be 'gobbledygook' and it is much the same for judges. In order to understand scientific evidence it is vital that lawyers receive some training in scientific principles and methods.

It is only in very recent years that scientists have been required to attend court and give evidence in person. When I began my career at the Bar it was considered sufficient for their statements to be read out in court. They were presented as incontrovertible fact and should a lawyer have the temerity to challenge it or call for a second opinion, the judge would be distinctly unhappy. The attitude would be: 'Why do you need a second opinion to prove that two plus two equals four?', particularly if the cost was to be passed on to legal aid.

On cross-examination, it often transpired that these 'incontrovertible' statements referred to tests carried out by someone other than the person who claimed responsibility, that the tests were not specific to the substance being tested for and that notes on the procedures used were not available. While we have moved slightly further forward in the last decade or two, many of the same attitudes remain.

It must be that courts take on the responsibility of setting scientific standards and no evidence should be admitted unless it meets these standards. There must be access to the defence for double checking and the tests must be carried out only by accredited scientists. The methods used in tests must satisfy the criteria for that specific subject and we must be absolutely clear about what is and isn't science. For example, is face mapping, where the structure of someone's face is recreated from a poor photographic image, a genuine science with measurable success?

And just as important as all these things is the need to reform the legal aid system to prevent individual and anonymous employees from making value judgements about when and if a second opinion should be provided under legal aid.

Another constant theme which runs through cases of miscarriage is poor record keeping and the proper protection of forensic evidence. In one of my cases, the Home Office scientist produced a test tube which supposedly contained a vital piece of evidence – a fragment of glass. He shook the test tube to indicate its presence but no matter how much he shook it not a sound emanated from that test tube. Not surprising, because the glass had gone.

In the very disturbing case of Stefan Kiszko, sentenced for child murder, the one piece of scientific evidence which could have proved his innocence was never produced in court. When this dreadful miscarriage came to light after sixteen years and he was acquitted, the vital piece of evidence had been lost. In this case it didn't interfere with the Appeal Court's verdict and the quashing of his conviction – but it certainly could have.

Despite the lessons which have emerged from the Birmingham Six, Guildford Four, Maguire Seven and many other cases, we are still left with a forensic system to which the defence has little or no access, over which there is no effective independent check nor quality control. Despite the large number of cases in which the forensic expert Dr Clifft was involved and which subsequently had to be overturned, there is absolutely nothing to prevent these miscarriages from occurring again. So long as the courts deify Home Office forensic experts, the miscarriages will continue.

Dr Clifft didn't lie and he didn't present false evidence but the results of some of the cases in which he gave evidence were much the same as if he had lied. What he did was to obscure certain findings in his scientific reports, and it was ultimately established that he had suppressed evidence about the blood group of a victim which would have nullified his evidence about the blood group of a defendant found on the victim; that there was no support for his claim to distinguish various forms of seminal and vaginal staining and that his evidence about fibres had been 'meaningless'.

The attitude of the CPS and the judiciary, and many other people for that matter, to scientific evidence is that it is clear and unarguable. 'You can't argue with fact'. But in the law as elsewhere, one person's fact is another's fancy. This attitude is condemning innocent people to prison for want of a proper defence and the problem starts at the very beginning with the granting of legal aid.

In the International Café murder the Legal Aid Board did not want to sanction the use of Russell Stockdale because eminent Home Office scientists were handling the case. Not only did Russell Stockdale find things which had been missed by the Home Office experts and the police, he provided the only physical evidence that Talat Sarwar had been the victim of an attack.

Legal aid did not want to pay for a second post mortem because the first had been carried out by an eminent pathologist, Dr West. In the end they funded it to the tune of £500 even though the standard charge is £750. The second pathologist did make a small contribution to the defence effort by establishing that the deceased had recently eaten but his real worth was in supporting a defence theory as to the possible manner in which Waite died. When the theory was put to Dr West he vehemently denied the possibility. Without the second opinion, which was to swing other scientific opinion behind the defence, there may have been a different verdict.

As a deterrent to solicitors, who they think might abuse the right to make such requests, the Legal Aid Board will frequently only pay for a second post mortem if it finds something which the first post mortem missed.

That may seem an unreasonable attitude but it is only one of an increasing number of restrictive approaches to the use of expert witnesses and in particular forensic scientists by the Legal Aid Board. These are important and worrying decisions because the vast majority of people accused of criminal offences in this country depend entirely on legal aid to mount their defence.

In the rape case referred to earlier, the attitude of the Legal Aid Board was unbending. They refused point blank to fund an independent scientist because the main plank of the police evidence was a DNA profile of the accused man. In their opinion this amounted to 'overwhelming evidence' and it simply wasn't worth the cost of a second opinion.

So certain of his innocence were they that the accused man's family clubbed together, begged and borrowed sufficient money to pay for the second opinion themselves. Although quite poor, their determination to find the money proved his innocence. There are many accused people who don't have families to fight for them and have no option but to accept the rulings handed down by the Legal Aid Board.

The scientific community already knows that DNA profiling is not the clear cut evidence it was once thought to be. Those commercial organisations responsible for marketing its testing like to portray it as infallible but in fact it can be flawed. As with blood grouping, there are grey areas.

None of this has deterred the Legal Aid Board who now hold the opinion that if the police are offering DNA profiling as evidence there has to be a very strong defence case for them to fund a second opinion. In one city this attitude has become so hardened that they simply won't pay for a second opinion where DNA is involved, despite the precedents.

Another way in which legal aid restricts the rights of defendants to protect themselves is by controlling the amount of money available for an independent scientist. They frequently lay down instructions as to who can and who can't be used. They may stipulate the use of a local 'expert' and this often drives the defence into the arms of the 'enthusiastic amateurs' or the non-specialists.

Just recently, Angela Gallop was asked by the solicitor representing a man accused of murder by strangling, to attend the scene of crime.

He felt that biological evidence might be vital in proving his client's innocence. The Legal Aid Board refused to sanction the request and insisted the solicitor use a local analytical chemist. How much does an analytical chemist know about biology?

One thing is certain, these are decisions taken solely on the basis of cost containment and have nothing to do with justice. But there are other hurdles thrown up by legal aid all, it seems, designed to test the resilience, commitment and patience of those who defend and depend for their livelihood on the payments meted out by the government through the Legal Aid Board.

It is common practice for defence lawyers and independent scientists to have to wait for a year or more before being paid. There is only one source of training for forensic scientists and that is either in the Home Office or in the Metropolitan police. Almost nowhere else can provide the breadth of experience and certainly nowhere else can offer practice at scenes of crime. The independent sector is therefore totally dependent on these scientists, with all the protections and benefits of civil service employment, coming out into the wider world and taking their chances with legal aid. They also know they will have to wait at least a year before receiving their first payment on completion of their first job. Hardly encouraging is it?

But legal aid's whole method of operation seems designed to deter lawyers from handling legal aid cases. Every change which is introduced seems designed to cut incomes, place obstacles in the way of justice and reduce the scope to mount a proper defence.

There is no doubt that the government's attitude to justice is motivated almost entirely by cost. The Lord Chancellor, Lord Mackay, said as much in a recent interview when he exclaimed that the 80 per cent increase of legal aid which has taken place in the decade since 1982 simply cannot be allowed to continue. What he completely ignored was an almost parallel percentage increase in crime over the same period. More crime means more people to attend in prison, more people wrongly accused, more people to defend. Unless, because of increasing crime, the state is prepared to completely jettison a belief in innocence until proved guilty and deny every accused person the right to be defended, then obviously costs will increase as crime increases. It is a sad indictment of our society that the *only* 'growth' industry is crime.

Current proposals on legal aid funding to solicitors will, it is estimated, reduce their incomes by between 30 and 50 per cent. The implementation of these changes has been delayed so at the time of writing it is government intention to go ahead in the face of the most outspoken and angry resistance ever seen by criminal law solicitors.

The context within which these fee reductions takes place is disturbing. The twenty-four-hour duty solicitor scheme, the first line of defence for those arrested, is already under threat. The number of solicitors prepared to participate in the scheme, and particularly young solicitors, is constantly declining. In just six years, Portsmouth has lost 25 per cent; Wakefield nearly 50 per cent; Cardiff 30 per cent; Northampton 50 per cent; Norwich 40 per cent; Huntingdon 45 per cent; Manchester 20 per cent; and so on across the country.

At the heart of the Lord Chancellor's proposals is a scheme which will replace solicitors' hourly rates of pay with fixed fees, almost regardless of the time spent on a case. The Lord Chancellor claims that these changes will speed up payments to solicitors, control government expenditure and of course – the old shibboleth trotted out for every cost-cutting exercise – they will improve efficiency.

Criminal law solicitors disagree and are so angry that they have threatened to withdraw from the twenty-four-hour duty solicitor scheme. Alastair Logan, who represented the Maguire Seven and two of the Guildford Four, maintains: 'To impose a scheme which would have the effect of depriving the defendant of skilled, professional and properly remunerated legal advice and representation can only be destructive and retrograde!

'The Lord Chancellor's proposed refusal to pay anything for listening to tapes of police interviews with suspects would encourage police to fabricate summaries of interviews. A high proportion of successful defences have been based on discrepancies between what the defendant said on the tape and what the police summary indicated he said.'

Danny Simpson, solicitor of Mark Braithwaite, one of the Tottenham Three, estimated the changes would reduce the income of his practice by up to 50 per cent: 'We will have two choices – either we will do all our work badly, spending less time on each case and employing unqualified staff to whom we pay a pittance to prepare our cases, or we will go bankrupt. We won't be around to help people like Mark Braithwaite or Winston Silcott or the Guildford Four because we won't exist at all.'

Mike Fisher, who represented Paul Hill of the Guildford Four, added his weight to the protests: 'Lawyers in their thousands will cease to practise criminal law. The proposals are a recipe for further injustice cases – I would say it's inevitable!'

Robert Winstanley, a Law Society spokesperson, supported this view: 'Two of the key factors which have been identified as contributing significantly to miscarriages of justice are the imbalance of resources between prosecution and defence and the absence of timely and effective advice to a suspect under arrest at a police station.

'In effect this is capping the resources available to the defence which is outrageous when you think that it's not happening to the prosecution.'

Lord Mackay's response to this barrage of criticism was at best disingenuous and at worst a piece of highly political and cynical manoeuvring. He began by saying: 'I am not introducing standard fees as a cost-cutting measure', but he quickly moved on to criticise the Law Society for soliciting the opinions of those involved in some of the recent miscarriage cases, as though there were something reprehensible about the opinions of those who are at the forefront of this country's failing criminal justice system. He added:

'I wonder what possible relevance these cases can have to the debate on standard fees for routine cases in the magistrates' courts. Some more cynical than I might suggest that it is an attempt to promote your financial interests by reference to well-known cases which are in no way connected with this present issue.'

His comment on money almost directly parallels Kenneth Clarke's view of doctors in their opposition to the government's NHS changes – that they were 'feeling for their wallets'. But his dismissal of the views of experienced solicitors because of their concern for 'routine cases' is equally disturbing. It is tantamount to saying that miscarriage of justice in routine cases is of no real concern. But that is precisely where the rot begins.

The public tend to believe that lawyers fees are, generally speaking, excessive and I have a certain sympathy with that view. But one area in which they are not excessive is legal aid work and that is precisely why fewer and fewer solicitors want to do it. To every one of the great institutions of this country this government's response has been the same – to look first at how to cut funding and only then to consider how that institution is meeting the needs of British people. Their approach to the law is no different.

The war between the Lord Chancellor and solicitors was not concluded at the time of writing but even if solicitors win this battle they won't win the war. Government will simply approach the problem by a different, perhaps more subtle route but in the end the spending on justice will be reduced or, at best, capped. And a further reduction in the numbers eligible to receive legal aid might be one of the ways in which they do it.

Since 1981, the number of people entitled to claim legal aid has dropped by 14 million. Eleven years ago it was available to 80 per cent of the population but now the proportion has fallen to less than 50 per cent. Higher incomes and a more affluent society which can afford to pay for its own litigation are the reasons given but the high costs which can be involved in court cases makes a nonsense of this assertion. While this reduction in eligibility applies largely to civil actions, the criminal side has also been drastically affected. Take the case of Clare Newton.

At the age of twenty-three and with a BA Honours degree in psychology and sociology she came to London from Sunderland to take up a job as a psychiatric care worker. In a search for work, her brother, Lee, also came down from the north and joined her. Neither knew London but, one evening in 1991, they went to a local benefit gig for the poll tax campaign at Chats Palace in Hackney. Clare says she is not political and went solely for the music.

Towards the end of the evening there was something of a fight which was quickly ended but, as they left Chats Palace, the road outside was swarming with police. They called in at a chip shop and while they were waiting to be served they saw people running past chased by police dogs and others being struck with batons.

As they came out of the shop with their chips, the road was still swarming with police and people being violently arrested. Directly in front of them was a man on the ground with four policemen sitting on him: 'I was very frightened and tried to get out of the way, to get around them, and so I walked out into the road. I suddenly realised that I had lost my brother and was worried because he didn't even know the way back to my flat.

'I began to look around and couldn't see him anywhere but then I heard his voice, looked in that direction and saw him in the back of a police van with three policemen. The police say I then ran across the road, jumped into the back of the van, grabbed my brother and tried to drag him out. What I really did was to walk over to the van and ask them why he was there.

'No one replied so I asked again and then one of the police in the van said he could go and my brother began to get out on to the road. With that, a W.P.C. in the van said that he'd been arrested and couldn't go, so he got back into the van again without any trouble.

'I asked them why he'd been arrested and was eventually told it was for obstructing the highway. The W.P.C. added that if I didn't go away I'd also be arrested. With that, three policemen grabbed me by my arms and legs and threw me into the back of the van.'

They were driven to Hackney police station and Clare was locked up in a cell with another girl and at 2.30 a.m. was charged with obstructing the police. She tried to remember police numbers but was too confused. When she asked what were her rights, the reply was that she didn't have any rights. Some friends of the girl she was with came into the station to find her and were arrested for supposedly being drunk and disorderly.

After fourteen hours in custody, Clare and her brother were taken to Highbury magistrates' court. It was read out to the magistrates that when arrested Clare had replied: 'I'm going to Trafalgar Square tomorrow to demonstrate against the poll tax.' In fact she hadn't made any reply at all. She was remanded on bail with a condition that she did not attend any political gatherings. Her brother was remanded to Sunderland so that he had instantly to abandon his search for work and go home.

While at Highbury Court, just before she went in front of the magistrates, she had a very short interview with a duty solicitor and filled in an application form for legal aid. On leaving the court she returned to Hackney police station to ask for her charge sheet which no one had bothered to give her. The desk sergeant replied that he had given it to her but she was too drunk to remember.

Clare Newton had no criminal record, in fact she had never been inside a police station before. She was detained for fourteen hours. This, presumably, is one of Lord Mackay's 'routine cases'.

For the moment, forget that Hackney police are facing an unprecedented number of civil actions for assault, false imprisonment and malicious prosecution; forget that some of these cases have already come to court and have gone in favour of the plaintiff (Gary Stretch, brutally beaten in a pub by a group of off-duty policemen; and seventy-three year old Marie Burke, awarded £50,000 compensation for all three counts); forget that Scotland Yard is conducting Operation Jackpot in Hackney, the biggest investigation into corruption in the Metropolitan police since Operation Countryman; and forget that seven Hackney policemen have been transferred to other stations following allegations of drug dealing.

Forget all that and just imagine the outrage, anger and desire for justice you would feel if you were Clare Newton. A routine case to Lord Mackay but a unique, worrying and very unroutine case to Clare Newton.

Clare earns about £160 a week – a good deal short of the average national wage and a long way short of the London average wage. Thanks to the introduction of student loans at the expense of grants, she left university with an outstanding loan of £700 and an overdraft of £600, which she still owed at the time of the incident. Before her appearance at Old Street court to face the charge of obstruction, she received a letter from the solicitor who had seen her at Highbury court to tell her she was eligible for legal aid but, because of her financial status, her contribution to the costs would be £589!

Clare had two choices – to defend herself or to plead guilty. Fortunately for her, however, the community of Hackney has responded to the concerns about the standard of policing in the borough by forming a self-help group called the Hackney Community Defence Association and they were able to support and advise her and prepare her to conduct her defence. In the event, however, they were able to find the services of both a solicitor and a barrister who were prepared to work for nothing to represent some of those involved in the Chats Palace incident.

The case was heard by a bench of three lay magistrates. The outcome? A conditional discharge, which is not particularly punitive but it is a finding of guilt which is on her record and will remain with her for many years. Clare Newton was left to come to terms with her feelings of outrage.

These then are the kind of conditions under which ordinary people are expected to defend themselves. The prospect of legal aid is being placed further and further out of reach. Even as I write, a new requirement has been issued – just another little turn of the screw, another means of excluding a few more applicants, another device which will deter solicitors from wanting to handle criminal defence work paid for out of legal aid.

This latest instruction doesn't mince its words. It says that before being granted legal aid, applicants who are in employment must produce thirteen weekly or three monthly payslips. Applicants on social security have to produce evidence of the receipt of benefit in the form of a notification of the award or an order book. It goes on to say that there has to be a real danger of a custodial sentence being imposed and states: 'Having regard to present and future sentencing policy, this danger is likely to become more remote.' Legal aid orders cannot be backdated: 'It follows that no order will be issued until all the necessary information has been supplied and the grant has been approved.' It also allows for a review of a case at the end so that if a person's financial status has improved they can be asked to make a contribution even though no such condition was attached at the outset. If accused fail to keep up any contribution order which has been made (their contribution to the costs): ' . . . the grant of legal aid may be

revoked and recalcitrant payers may find themselves unrepresented.'
It concludes with the words; 'It should be appreciated that in certain
cases legal aid will no longer be granted as freely as hitherto!'

From a solicitor's perspective (and from the perspective of anyone
else who cares about justice) this is a very worrying development.
Few people in custody have their social security books or numbers
on them. Very few people keep their payslips and many are dismissed
from employment as a result of the crimes they're supposed to have
committed and will find it impossible to get confirmation from their
employers. It is also impossible for a solicitor to determine in advance
if a custodial sentence is likely to be imposed in a border-line case.

At the moment, legal aid is granted from the date of the submission
of the application so these new rulings beg the question of how many
solicitors will now be prepared to work for nothing. It could take months
for all the information to be supplied, if at all.

So what part did legal aid play in the defence of Talat Sarwar?
Initially, Talat's defence team had to take a financial risk and this
they were prepared to do because they knew the local Asian community. Legal aid is available for a solicitor to offer advice to a detainee
in the police station or for appearances in court but only for those
clearly defined functions. The cost of preparing a defence, interviewing
witnesses and the myriad other instant actions which are needed for a
good defence are not covered by legal aid unless and until the person
has been charged and appears before the magistrates. As legal aid isn't
retrospective, some of those initial costs had to be borne by the defence.

The standard fee available for a post mortem is about £500 but it is
almost impossible to get anyone to do it for less than £750. Immediately
there's an in-built, little disincentive to solicitors to request one and if
they do request one they may well have to subsidise it. To begin with,
the Legal Aid Board would not sanction the use of Russell Stockdale
so he was appointed on chance – a chance that the defence would have
to cover the cost of his fees. As it transpired, his fees were not fully
covered and the argument between Talat's solicitors and the Legal Aid
Board continues to this day – nearly three years after the event.

Talat's defence team firmly believe that fees are reduced to those solicitors who are very diligent in their work in order to act as a disincentive to 'sticking your neck out'. The attitude, they claim, is that the system will take care of defendants without the need of a great deal of work on their behalf. Where the evidence is 'strongly' against them, all this work is a waste of time and designed solely to line the pockets of solicitors.

When the case is finished, as in all cases, the complicated file and accounts are submitted to the Lord Chancellor's taxation department where they're checked and payment is authorised or not, as the case may be. In Talat Sarwar's case, and in many, many other cases, a civil servant with no legal experience decreed that many of the disbursements were unnecessarily incurred, particularly some forensic costs, and refused to pay them.

The battle for payment continues despite the trial judge asking Counsel to convey to the defence solicitors his belief that they were extremely dedicated and thorough and that the early intervention of a forensic scientist had been vitally important to the outcome of the trial.

This is the kind of complication with which defence solicitors live on a daily basis. The belief of many of them is that there is pressure not to defend people too vigorously in cases where the evidence is 'clear cut'. It is another aspect of the criminal justice system which is predicated on a presumption of guilt.

The next two changes which I would advocate are therefore obvious. There must be established a properly funded, controlled and monitored independent forensic science service which is available to the defence as of right. This must be matched by a legal aid fund which has at its heart a fundamental belief in the right of all citizens to a proper defence regardless of cost. Just like the NHS, in criminal cases it should be available free and without question with all costs deferred against taxation. For those who say that this will not be cheap then my response is simple – justice does not come cheap. However, the move towards a criminal justice system which is geared to cost saving, which writes off certain members of our society and engenders a deep feeling of injustice also has a cost. And that is a cost we cannot afford.

FIFTEEN

A Proper Investigation

The theme which runs through most miscarriages of justice is clear and constant. It is the failure of the police to conduct a proper investigation. The case of the Birmingham Six was riddled with discrepancies but just to take one of them: the accused men were supposed to have entered the two pubs to leave their bombs and yet it wasn't even considered necessary to conduct an identity parade to see if anyone recognised them.

In the case of the Guildford Four, it was physically impossible for Gerry Conlon to have travelled from London to Guildford in the time he was supposed to have done. Either no one spotted this discrepancy or if they did they were not concerned about it. And so it goes on.

Any serious consideration of the British criminal justice system must go further than bland reassurances, trotting out yet again the old cliché that 'it's only the odd rotten apple that's at fault', and then proceed to tinker around the edges. There are fundamental flaws which have to be tackled and some of these I've outlined. Perhaps the single most important change must be to remove the responsibility for investigating crimes from the police and place it in the hands of an independent authority. In other words, we are back to the *juge d'instruction*.

He or she should deal with all crime except run-of-the-mill administrative offences. They should not only supervise and monitor all the activities of the police who are handling a crime but they should be responsible for initiating lines of enquiry and supervising the way these are pursued. They should be responsible for the manner in which an accused is interrogated. They should be the ones who guarantee that an accused's legal rights are not infringed: their right to silence; their right to legal access; their right to accuracy in the recording of detail and the safe-keeping of evidence concerned with the offence; and their right not to be physically or psychologically abused.

So how would Catherine Samet, the *juge d'instruction* from Senlis have handled the Talat Sarwar case? Her method of investigating is probably best summed up by her attitude to a murder case which she recently observed in which I was defending. It was a case in which the accused burst into a crowded room where people were sitting around the dining table eating and someone died. By the time the case came to court it was fifteen months old and witness after witness stood in the dock and recounted what they had seen. I then cross-examined in an attempt to see if their stories were consistent or if there was something else they may have overlooked. In essence I was testing the reliability of their different memories. There were huge differences in the recall they had.

Catherine Samet found this whole procedure quite extraordinary. She was astounded that so much importance should be placed on the ability of people to remember events that had happened so long ago. Most of them had seen the scene of the crime only once, on the fateful evening, and had never returned.

A French investigator sets a great deal of store by reconstruction and that is what she would have done in my murder case and in the case of Talat Sarwar. The procedure would have been much the same for both and it would have been carried out as soon after the incidents as possible. In the case of the International Café, after having taken statements from all those who were present, both inside the café and outside, she would have digested their content. Following that she would have brought together all the witnesses and the accused (if in fact he had yet been accused under her system) and reconstructed the crime.

She would not have been concerned with how long it took, how many different aspects of it needed to be reconstructed and how seemingly inconsequential the role of some witnesses appeared to be. The arrival of Lewis Pinnock and Lloyd Waite (obviously using a stand-in) outside the café, their conversation at the door before entering, their aggressive search to identify Talat inside the café, the fight which travelled from one end of the room to the other and the exit of the two West Indian men from the café would have been brought back to life. Similarly, outside the café, the shadowy Asian men who were seen disappearing in a car, the outraged pool-cue and hockey-stick-carrying cafégoers and the passing witnesses would have all been resurrected.

One person's memory would have been tested against another's and the hope would be that one person's recall would spark off someone else's. Even our own police know the power of reconstruction in triggering memories, which is why they frequently use the device in abduction or disappearance cases.

At the café, once satisfied that reconstruction had gone as far as it usefully could, the *juge* would then have taken a further statement from every person involved. If she thought it necessary she would take yet a third statement, perhaps a month later, just to see if the intervening time span had produced anything further. During the course of this theatre it is highly unlikely that Talat Sarwar would have been held on remand.

For forensic evidence she would have the right to use anyone in the country she believed to be best for the job. It might well be that she would choose the internationally recognised forensic laboratory in Paris, supervised by Madame Ridereaux but it could be any professor or doctor from any university or commercial organisation – the choice would be hers. Her power and resources in conducting an investigation are almost limitless. For example, she can obtain second or even third scientific opinions and the respective work can be monitored and checked by her at all stages. She can direct the police in anyway she chooses and interrogate witnesses and suspects as and when she chooses. There are no financial restrictions on her spending powers and she can travel where she wants, order whatever medical or psychological investigations she chooses.

She can either conduct all interviews herself or she can instruct the police to do so, with the proceedings strictly controlled by a criminal proceedings code.

The normal venue to conduct an interview is her office, in the presence of her clerk, a policeman for security reasons and, if they choose, the person's lawyer. Apart from these other bodies the interview would normally be a one-to-one but the *juge* is quite at liberty to organise face-to-face confrontations between witnesses or an accused and his or her accuser or anything else she thinks might provoke a useful reaction.

For those weaned on British investigations – and that means police investigations – it is difficult to grasp the concept that in France the search is not simply to find the guilty person but to establish the truth. In pursuit of this, it is highly unlikely that Lewis Pinnock would have been excused investigation considering the aggressive nature of his visit to the International Café. She would have considered all the evidence and not just that which pointed to Talat Sarwar.

When the evidence points towards a witness's culpability, the *juge* must immediately charge them with the offence and the witness becomes an accused but the presumption of innocence still applies. The accused will be told on what basis he or she is being charged, that they can either speak or remain silent and that they can be represented by a lawyer of their choosing or one will be appointed and paid for out of legal aid.

From that moment on, the accused's lawyer will have absolutely free access to the case, will be able to attend all subsequent interrogations and can request new investigations. They also have access at will to the accused and the right to request particular expert witnesses, second opinions and anything else which they believe will help the search for truth. In reality, French lawyers hardly ever exercise this right which says something either about the impartiality of the *juge* or the quality of French lawyers. But the theory remains absolute; evidence which points at innocence is investigated just as thoroughly as evidence pointing to guilt.

When compared with the parsimonious, penny-pinching almost amateurish way in which British defence lawyers are forced to conduct investigations, the almost unlimited resources of the *juge* are vitally important. But even more important is the underlying ethos of the *juge d'instruction*. Catherine Samet explains:

'The investigations which we carry out are aimed at discovering the truth, which is never a simple task owing to the complexity of human psychology.

'There is no one method of investigating a crime as each case is different. But there is one constant and that is to be an unprejudiced judge. Because of this our strategy specifically avoids targeting and concentrates on a search for evidence which is one reason why we tend to favour reconstructions.

'We are not obliged to obtain confessions but on the other hand we would not ignore one even though we would not rely on that alone. It is interesting that a confession amounts to a plea of guilty and there is no such concept in French law. We concentrate on material evidence – the facts – and the personalities and histories of those involved. We need to establish motive and then responsibility.

'We see the time in police custody – the *garde à vue* – as important. It is a period when people are held at a police station prior to being charged and without legal representation. It puts pressure on them but it can only be allowed because it is done with the knowledge of a judge and we know where the person is being held and by whom and it is with our authority. In the first instance it can be only for twenty-four hours and then, if I choose to sanction it, for a further twenty-four hours. The police have no power to continue holding someone.'

When a case has finally been put together, everything pertaining to it, every statement, every piece of evidence, every test (whether positive or negative) and every instruction will be held together in a dossier. This is the full and total case against the accused and a copy of it will automatically be presented to the defence lawyers even though they will have been allowed free access to the dossier throughout the investigation.

This method of investigating has several advantages over our own. The whereabouts of the accused is always known and their detention is strictly controlled which reduces the chances of police brutality, the threat of brutality and of their fabricating evidence. It investigates a crime rather than simply attempting to nail someone for it. It provides a level playing field for prosecution and defence. There are checks all along the way. Our own Crown Prosecution Service is precisely what the name states, a prosecuting service and is not there to search for truth or to test the veracity of evidence, although it might occasionally throw out no-hope cases.

With so much work carried out before the case even gets to court, it's hardly surprising that those cases which are tried at the *Cour d'Assises* largely result in a guilty verdict – over 90 per cent compared to our own Crown Court trials which result in a 50 per cent guilty rate. There is absolutely no evidence to show that French verdicts are arrived at falsely or that the presumption of innocence is jettisoned as a result of the system or that French judges are more inclined to convict the innocent. It is almost certainly a result of good, exhaustive and committed investigative work which isn't based on a presumption of guilt and targeting.

Having praised the system of *juge d'instruction*, I feel the period of *garde à vue* is clearly the Achilles' heel of the system, where a person can be held for up to forty-eight hours at the police station. Considerable police malpractice may occur at this stage and is why a *juge* is not a substitute for a code of conduct controlling the police and enshrining absolute and fundamental rights during the period of detention. The *juge* must, however, have the right and the facilities to enter any police station at any time for any crime in order to ensure the code is being adhered to.

While the *juge* can place as much or as little importance as she chooses on a confession and would normally look for material evidence, I would formalise the use of confessions. They would be admissible only if made in the presence of the person's lawyer and then it would have to be repeated in front of a *juge* within twenty-four hours. Without these qualifications a confession could not be used in evidence.

Perhaps the single biggest defect in the French system is the liberal use of custody to hold people on remand. Because of reconstructions and the more leisurely pace of the investigation, accused people can spend long periods in prison awaiting trial. This is unacceptable and I would apply precisely the same conditions for bail which I outlined earlier – that bail should be an automatic right unless the accused has previously committed a bail offence such as absconding or has offended while on bail. As I have said before, this is the litmus test of a presumption of innocence.

The police will immediately say that everyone who is guilty will disappear and this is of course nonsense. The vast majority of those who are accused of crimes simply don't have the resources to go anywhere and even long-term criminals have a habit of frequenting the same old haunts. Without their 'manor' they appear to have no sense of being. Ironically, the very people who do have the resources and contacts to organise disappearing tricks, the whitecollar offenders involved in such crimes as fraud, are the very ones who are always granted bail and even they very rarely abscond.

It is important to stress that I am not advocating the whole-sale adoption of the French criminal justice system. Once the *juge d'instruction* has finished her investigation and the case goes forward for trial, that is where I end my interest in France. I believe that at the trial the inquisitorial system should be jettisoned and we should retain our own adversarial system. I believe this will provide the final check against mistakes and failures which might have happened further back down the line. There is nothing better than a strong and reasoned challenge to explore any defects in evidence.

I think we can look to the United States as well as France to improve our quality of justice. In the case of the Birmingham Six, they would have had protection under the Fourth Amendment and police would not have been allowed to detain them simply because they happened to be travelling from Birmingham to Belfast at the time they were. Such is the US citizen's view of liberty that if this incident had taken place in the US it is highly unlikely that the six would have accompanied the police voluntarily in the first place.

Inside the police station they would have had additional protection under the Sixth Amendment. Questioning could not move on from the simple niceties of name, address, age, etc., without police reading them their rights, including the right to a lawyer. Had a US lawyer been present they would almost certainly have advised them not to provide a sample for analysis on the basis that the whole operation was nothing more than a fishing expedition and there was no evidence against the men.

Had police ignored the men's refusal and taken samples anyway, this would again have been an infringement of the Fourth Amendment which gives the right to be free from unreasonable searches and seizures, including the body. If police had wanted to take the samples legally they would have had to have gone before a judge and request a signed order. To do this police would have to show probable cause that the men had committed the offence; there would have to be a clear indication of what they expected to find on them and why; and police would have to show that the tests they intended to use had been deemed reliable in the past. The application would have failed on all three criteria.

If the swabs had been taken against the men's will, their attorney would immediately have asked for an exclusionary procedure to have the evidence excluded from the case. If an accused's constitutional rights are infringed the police are, in a sense, punished and the evidence is not allowed to be entered in the case.

The so-called confessions made by the Six would also have been covered under US law. If someone's rights are abused in interrogation by coercion or threats of physical violence, or their rights (referred to as the Miranda warnings) are not read to them, the remedy would be an exclusion of the statement.

Arielle Jarret is a criminal defence attorney operating in New York's Manhattan and has watched the Birmingham Six case with interest:

'If I had been involved with this case, right from the outset I would have been looking for witnesses to substantiate the whereabouts of my clients. Let's assume the men couldn't afford to pay me privately and I had been appointed by the court under legal aid. Under the US court's terms I can use whatever experts I need and in this case I would definitely make a request – and it would be granted automatically – for the services of private investigators.

'They would try and trace the movements of the Six and see if they could find any witnesses to substantiate their story. They would go to what was left of the bars and talk to the staff and customers and see if there was anyone, perhaps people carrying bags, who might have been suspect. Although we don't have any burden of proof to find the guilty it is nice to bring to court the perpetrators if you can.

'I would also have appointed a forensic scientist, almost certainly an explosives expert, who would be entitled to test any of the material left on the swabs investigated by Dr Frank Skuse, the Home Office scientist used by the police. Depending on how early in the case I was involved, I would want them to be there when the prosecution is carrying out its tests.

'Looking at the case as a whole, I think these defendants' rights were violated right from the outset. Whether or not they went to Morecambe by consent, their detention became too long, they were held without sufficient cause and every piece of evidence that resulted from their illegal detention could have been suppressed. We call that "fruit of the poisonous tree". The tree had been poisoned by police conduct and the fruit from it would not have been allowed in evidence.'

SIXTEEN

The Committal

A little over six months after the incident in which Lloyd Waite died, Talat Sarwar's defence team prepared to face the first court – a magistrates' court at which the committal proceedings were to be held – in their attempts to prove his innocence. So far they had not seen any of the prosecution's papers, they had no indication as to who was to be called as witnesses so were not absolutely sure what the case against Talat contained. From their own interviews and expert witnesses they were certain that the evidence against him was threadbare.

Almost from the time Talat was charged it appeared that High Wycombe police had done little else in the way of investigating the facts surrounding the International Café incident. As far as they were concerned they had their man. It required a certain amount of faith to sustain that belief.

Talat, the police maintained, had stabbed Waite soon after he had entered the café. What they had to support this contention was the statement of Waite's half-brother Lewis Pinnock. There were some other witnesses who were inside the café who had originally claimed to have seen Talat stab Waite but had subsequently tried to withdraw these allegations. What would happen in court with these witnesses was anyone's guess.

There was a post mortem report which implied that Waite would have had to be superhuman to carry out the actions attributed to him if the police theory was correct.

There was prosecution scientific evidence which showed very little indeed – that some blood from Talat and some from Waite had been found inside the café but they didn't know how it got where it was found. They had not managed to establish which of the three knives was the murder weapon, they had no fingerprints and very little else. On the other hand, the defence scientific evidence appeared to have much more to offer – that Talat's blood was all over the café and evidence could be offered as to how it had got there. It pointed to him as having been the victim and Waite the assailant. Waite's blood appeared in only three places and no one was sure how it got there which, again, didn't seem consistent with him having been stabbed where and when the police maintained he had been.

The defence felt fairly confident; in fact they felt so confident that they opted for an old style committal. At these proceedings they would conduct a proper defence rather than simply going through the formalities, reserving their evidence for a higher court.

Committal proceedings are held in magistrates' courts to determine if there really is a case to answer. The court can dismiss the case there and then or it can be sent for trial to a higher court.

There are two ways of conducting a committal – 'old style' or 'new style', also known as a 'paper committal'. The latter is something of a formality where little evidence is presented other than on paper and witnesses don't appear in court. The reason for a defence opting for a new style committal is that committals are usually heard by magistrates who, as a matter of course, tend to send cases to a higher court. Because of the perfunctory nature of the proceedings the defence can avoid tipping the prosecution off as to the line they intend following.

An old style committal is a valuable opportunity to test the strength of the prosecution case by calling their main witness. Because of the lack of evidence against Talat Sarwar, the defence decided to opt for an old style committal in the belief that they could show the evidence against Talat to be so fundamentally flawed and inconsistent that he would not be placed in jeopardy of a trial and that the charge would be dismissed there and then with the proceedings brought to an end.

One big difference between a committal and a trial in a Crown

Court is that a solicitor can appear in person and represent his client rather than being forced to hand the case over to a barrister. Such is the arrogance of some barristers that solicitors are often accused of opting for old style committals in order to increase their earnings from a case. The fact that they may be better able to represent the interests of their client doesn't appear to occur to the critics.

At the time the defence took this decision they thought the case would be heard by a stipendiary magistrate – a professional, paid lawyer. When the case came up, however, the stipendiary magistrate was not sitting and it was heard by a bench of three lay magistrates – untrained, 'leading' members of the community who administer law in a part-time capacity. The change was not greeted with enthusiasm by the defence. The prosecution had taken well over six months to prepare their case and finally presented the papers not long before the committal on 12 and 13 October. The defence were served with the prosecution bundle and for the first time were able to determine the strength of the prosecution case. It was a big, bulging, lever-arch file of statements but on close examination there was very little of substance contained in it. Many of them were the contradictory and not directly enlightening statements with which I began this book.

The heart of the prosecution's case was the statement by Lloyd Waite's half-brother Lewis Pinnock in which he claimed to have seen Talat Sarwar stab at his brother. It also transpired that Pinnock had originally been charged with kidnapping Suk Sukhpal Sandhu but because of the Asian community's fear of reprisals they were reluctant to give evidence. At his trial Pinnock was acquitted.

The charges accused Talat of the 'malicious wounding of Jason Waite on Friday, 21 April, contrary to Section 18 of the Offences Against the Person Act, 1861' as well as the murder of Lloyd Waite on Saturday, 22 April. Much to everyone's surprise, Shabir Kayani, Superfly, had been dragged into the proceedings, accused of 'Violent Disorder contrary to Section 2(1) of the Public Order Act, 1986' by attacking Pinnock with a hockey stick. No one else was charged with any offence, not even Pinnock, who had certainly not gone to the International Café with the intention of having a quiet chat.

It didn't take a Sherlock Holmes to work out what could possibly lie behind the particular nature of these charges. By linking together the charge of malicious wounding with that of murder, it could be seen as a very transparent attempt to prove that Talat owned a knife. If it could be established that he owned a knife then the jury would be half way to believing that he was guilty of the stabbing on the following evening.

Superfly's testimony had been consistent and unbending from the very beginning – Talat was totally innocent, had not stabbed Waite and had himself been the victim of a vicious assault by Waite. With a charge of violence against him this testimony might appear to be less than watertight. Pinnock was the star witness and it wouldn't do to have him, virtually the only witness, with accusations of violence against him.

The prosecution's case was very much as the defence had anticipated. Working their way through the prosecution bundle, however, with very little time to consider all its contents, they came across a witness statement which had been given to the police just one day after the killing of Waite. It was buried on page 118 of the 202-page bundle and was made by a twelve-year-old boy called Michael Anthony. It was not apparent that the police had conducted any enquiries into the scene which he had reported seeing outside the café. His statement read as follows:

'I was standing with my mother on the same side of the road and in front of the Caribbean Kitchen waiting to meet my grandmother who was playing bingo. After we had been standing there for a couple of minutes two people appeared from near to the corner of the road. I didn't see exactly where they came from but I saw that they were fighting.

'The first to emerge was a West Indian and he was struggling with a Pakistani. The Pakistani was behind him and grabbed hold of the West Indian by putting his arm around him. The two of them then wrestled with each other and the Pakistani threw the West Indian to the ground.

'The West Indian was in his early twenties, he was about five feet ten inches tall and of medium build. I think he had short hair and he was wearing a dark track-suit-type top with a hood. I know this because when I first saw him emerge and just before the fighting started he put the hood up over his head.

'On falling to the floor he lay in the middle of the road about fifteen yards from where we were standing and as he did so, the Pakistani who had been wrestling with him was standing over him and was kicking him, mainly in the stomach.

'The person I saw kicking the West Indian I would describe as being a Pakistani male about twenty years of age. He was about five feet eleven inches tall, of slim build and had fairly short hair.

'He had been kicking the West Indian for a few seconds when I saw about six other Pakistanis appear from near the road I have already mentioned. They ran towards the West Indian and at least four of them were carrying sticks which appeared to have broken ends. They gathered round the man on the floor and those armed with the sticks began hitting him with them all over his body and on his head.

'As this was happening, another ten or so Pakistanis appeared in the road and this group went over to a white-coloured car which was parked in a lay-by opposite the road junction. Two of the group opened the door and dragged another West Indian out from it. He was pushed to the floor and he was also hit with sticks and kicked.

'As this was happening, the majority of the group then started to smash the windows of the car. I remember that the West Indian who had been dragged from the car was still being hit as he lay on the road but I didn't notice what was happening to the first of the West Indians.

'At this point my mother and I became very frightened and we ran into the bingo hall.'

The defence believed that this very clear and lucid statement from a young boy, only twelve years old, was actually a testimony to the killing of Lloyd Waite. It raised a scenario which no other witness had referred to and it described a fight in which close contact between two men was made, close enough for a knife to have been used.

The man described as a Pakistani looked nothing like Talat Sarwar – he was tall, Talat was short; he had short hair, Talat's was long; the fight had taken place outside the café where, the prosecution had already agreed, Talat could not have inflicted the wound. When Michael Anthony had first seen Lloyd Waite in that reasonably well-lit street, Waite must have just exited from the café (the entrance is recessed and doesn't look like the entrance to a commercial establishment) and had been putting up the hood of his track suit top, hardly the action of a man who had just been stabbed. Following the scuffle, Waite had fallen to the ground and had stayed there, a much more likely response to having had his aorta virtually severed.

The case for Talat Sarwar was beginning to look promising. What Talat's solicitors had to decide was whether to raise this evidence in support of Talat and by so doing put the prosecution on notice of their intended defence. If the case then went beyond the committal stage, the prosecution could attempt to counter this evidence in some way. A first and obvious ploy would be to challenge the reliability of a twelve-year-old boy but there could well be other ways of minimising the relevance of what he had claimed to see. They decided to risk this and use the statement.

And so the case went to court. The first defence move was to register a complaint that the defendant should be tried on two totally different charges at the same time. The prejudicial nature of this, they claimed, was obvious. The magistrates declined to separate the two charges.

Surprisingly, the eye-witnesses who claimed to have seen Talat with a knife in the café, and to have seen him stab Waite, appeared in court. However, they refused to give evidence on behalf of the prosecution. They were quite adamant that the only way they could be induced to give evidence at all was if they could have access to the first statements they claimed to have made. These were statements which labelled Waite as the aggressor and in no way implicated Talat in Waite's death. Perhaps not surprisingly, these statements had never appeared in the prosecution's evidence.

A great deal of consternation ran through the prosecution's ranks and the proceedings were adjourned for an hour while it was determined whether these witnesses would be called for the prosecution or not.

They repeated that they were prepared to give evidence but would have to say that it was untrue that they had seen the defendant with a knife at any stage of the café incident. They would insist that they had been forced to say this. One of them was quite explicit about what he would say; that he had been detained in the police station even though the police were aware that he had recently been the subject of a violent attack and had lost one of his kidneys. 'I was climbing up the wall with discomfort and would have said anything to get out of the police station.' As a consequence, the only witness who was prepared to give evidence as to the fight itself was Lewis Pinnock.

When it came to Pinnock's evidence-in-chief, the evidence being presented in support of their case by the prosecution, it was inconsistent and frequently contradicted his original statement.

His claim that they had accidentally finished up outside the International Café in the search for food was destroyed by medical evidence that Waite had not long eaten and by the statement given to police by Waite himself when interviewed about the kidnapping on the day before he died. P.C. Rush wrote: 'Lloyd Waite stated that they had visited the café in Desborough Road and 58 Mill End Road in search of Jason Waite's assailant.' Having already been there the previous evening, Pinnock knew precisely where they were going and almost certainly why.

Pinnock had also stated that he and Waite had previously had a quick snack at Waite's house and yet Waite's mother confirmed that they had all sat down to a family meal not long before the two men left on their journey to the International Café.

When they pulled up outside the café, Pinnock left the car headlights on and the keys in the ignition but claims he switched the engine off. An eye-witness disagrees. Either way, these are not the actions of someone innocently visiting a café.

It would have been impossible for him to know that he was outside the International Café unless he had previously been there as there is nothing to identify it as a café – no signs, no advertisements, nothing. In fact it looks like a house. Yet he stated that after Waite had got out of the car he, Pinnock, suddenly realised that Waite was following up on the previous evening's enquiries. He had absolutely no reason to believe that if what he was saying was true.

He claimed that had they been looking for trouble he would have been 'tooled up' and had back-up outside. The implication being that he did carry a knife when necessary and was no stranger when it came to looking for trouble.

He maintained that he stayed inside the doorway, holding the door open with his foot. This accorded with what eye-witnesses said; that he barred the exit making sure that no one could make a dash for it.

Pinnock maintained that, having looked in the café for Talat and failed to find him, he was encouraging Waite to leave, which he was about to do when he was stabbed. There seemed little logic to a slightly built, seventeen-year-old launching an attack on a powerfully built, aggressive, known hard-man at a point when the danger appeared to be over. Such an attack could only provoke instant retaliation.

The prosecution maintained that Talat had approached Waite from the rear but Pinnock insisted that he saw him stab Waite in the right side at which point Waite pulled his own knife. However, in his deposition he had said: 'I had hold of Lloyd's arm and Talat came from the other side and I saw him as he was about to push the knife into Lloyd and I pushed him away from him. He was going to stab him on the left side above the waist. I had taken hold of Lloyd's arm ... I saw what was about to happen and I pulled Lloyd away from it. I pulled Lloyd on to me and I did not see whether he had actually stabbed Lloyd or not at that stage.'

In his notes of interview he had said something similar: 'He came up to Lloyd and it looked like he stabbed Lloyd in the side here (indicating the left midriff).' When asked if he had actually seen the knife go in he replied, 'No, I can't say I did. I saw the guy lunge forward.'

Pinnock also claimed to have tossed one of the knives away where no one could reach it. Such a statement, coming from a man who had already admitted that he would go 'tooled up' if he thought there was going to be trouble, didn't sound very convincing. Here he was, in the middle of a knife fight in which his half-brother was involved and he supposedly threw away a knife. His previous convictions for violence rather belied his altruism.

As he and Waite were exiting from the café he says he saw Waite's knife on the ground and picked it up to avoid leaving fingerprint evidence and to reduce the number of weapons available to the opposition. He was then struck on the head and dropped the knife yet Waite's knife was found outside the café, in the road under Waite's own body. The defence assumed the knife Pinnock dropped was his own. Also, concern about leaving a fingerprinted weapon lying around hardly smacked of innocence.

It appeared that Pinnock had to justify his and Waite's presence at the café and reasons of chance were the best he could offer. He also had to justify Waite's use of a knife and what better than an unprovoked attack by someone else with a knife? The fact that his various descriptions of the attack were inconsistent didn't help Pinnock's position. He also had to justify his own role in the affair and that of innocent bystander was far from convincing.

In his deposition he denied ever carrying a knife and yet when questioned in court he said: 'The only knife I ever carry is in my tool box and that is a Stanley knife. I never carry any other weapons.' That assertion was made despite having been already convicted of using weapons in a fight at Aylesbury. But the mention of a Stanley knife was interesting.

Dr Peabody, one of the prosecution's expert witnesses, gave evidence of several cuts to Talat's leather bomber jacket which he thought had possibly been made with either a Stanley knife or a razor blade. In Talat's statement, which we have not yet covered, he mentions that Pinnock attacked him with a silver, flashing knife which could neatly fit the description of a Stanley knife.

When asked whether Waite showed any signs of weakening after the alleged stabbing, Pinnock replied that he was in a rage and that he wasn't weakening. Asked if Waite had made any comment during the fight about having been stabbed Pinnock said that he hadn't: 'No, there wasn't anything said!'

The defence were slightly amazed that none of the items found at the scene had been fingerprinted and the results compared with Pinnock's prints, something which could well have shown him to be more involved than he claimed. They were also amazed that, despite numerous letters to the police which had remained unanswered, Pinnock had never been charged with anything – not with attempted murder nor even unlawful violence. As a result of the committal hearing they began to realise why – not only was Pinnock the police's star witness, he was their only witness to the stabbing as they had conceived it, the inconsistencies of his evidence and his own part in the events notwithstanding.

Dr Peabody was able to add little to his statement but the defence felt that having Russell Stockdale present in court was a useful reminder to the doctor that they could not be fooled by science. He summarised his own evidence: 'My evidence cannot specifically assist the Court to the point where I am able to say what happened inside or outside that café that night by reference to my forensic analysis. I cannot say that the defendant stabbed Lloyd Waite or that Waite stabbed the defendant. I do not know that. If someone cut themselves on their own knife I would not expect to find any different qualities of blood in the body in terms of my analysis. I would not know if the blood was from the hands or anywhere else.'

The proposition that Waite could have cut his own hand, to some degree or other, and this would account for traces of his blood inside the café, was not really advanced. Witnesses spoke of him producing the knife from his pocket already open and a cut could have been caused as he slid his hand into his pocket to retrieve it. But no one was really to know.

The only two 'live' witnesses – those who appeared in person – were Peabody and Pinnock. All the other evidence was called from witness statements.

One of the statements was by Alexander Till who claimed to have seen two black men running from the café towards a white car pursued by a group of Asians. Obviously at this stage, Waite was still in no obvious trouble or discomfort from the proceedings inside the café. He wasn't staggering, he wasn't clutching himself and he didn't fall to the ground until he was attacked in the road. Till gave no evidence against Talat.

John Newell's statement said that, prior to entering the café, two West Indian men had walked across the road together and spoken to some Asians standing outside the café. It was not the scene which Pinnock had described. He also gave no evidence against Talat. Neither did Karen Ray, who spoke of seeing someone resembling Superfly ushering people back into the café – although she was never asked to attend an identity parade. In fact no one involved in the whole affair was ever asked to attend an identity parade in order to help clarify whom they had and hadn't seen.

The statement of twelve-year-old Michael Anthony was next which told what he had seen outside the café – Waite in a tussle with an unidentified Asian. The defence were particularly interested in his statement that ' . . . the Pakistani was behind him and grabbed hold by putting his arm around him . . .'

This, they felt, fitted the facts that Waite was apparently not injured in the café and was able to continue a fight, was able to run but was then caught and stabbed from behind. With a man standing behind him, the blade of the knife would almost certainly have travelled in an upwards direction, particularly as the assailant was taller than Waite. And that is how the wound was described in his post mortem.

Knowing that the case might still go forward for trial at the Crown Court, the defence were hesitant to put forward the proposition that Waite's wounds, including those to his hands and wrist, were fully consistent with having been stabbed from behind.

This final piece of the jigsaw brought to an end the committal proceedings. Any fears that the defence might have had that the prosecution were able to mount a convincing case against Talat Sarwar were completely unjustified. In fact the opposite was true. The prosecution had offered no compelling evidence to show Talat's guilt and some of the evidence they did offer reflected to his benefit.

Talat Sarwar's version of the events was contained in his statement which was read to the court: 'I had my foot on the ledge at the front of the café and my back to the door, quite close to it so that when it opened I would be behind it. The door opened quite suddenly and quite fast and Waite and Pinnock walked in. Waite had an expression on his face which indicated that he was looking for trouble. However, I didn't realise that they were looking for me.

'Waite walked in and Pinnock had his foot in the door. Waite walked straight over to Saeed who was standing next to me and asked him if he knew who Talat was. Saeed said he didn't know but Waite wanted him to point me out. Waite was saying "when I find him I'm going to kill him!"

'I was a bit scared, though I didn't see he had a knife at this time. I got the impression he was trying to work himself up and he seemed to be getting more and more angry. I should add that Pinnock was also asking who I was and was not playing the passive role he pretends. He was also saying that Talat Sarwar had cut Waite's son and he was going to cut Talat.

'Waite walked up to the West Indians near the kitchen and asked them if they knew me but they said they didn't. He came back towards the door, got his knife out and threatened Ateeqe. He was holding the knife by his right leg. Pinnock came fully into the café and said, "Forget it, they're not going to tell you."

'I couldn't run as I was more or less facing them. I just hoped that they would go away. I was trying not to look at them although I was sweating by this time. I was near the door but couldn't get out as Pinnock was in the way.

'After Ateeqe, Waite grabbed another boy and although he said he didn't know me he looked straight at me. Waite followed his stare and must have seen the expression on my face. He came over to me and said, "You're Talat, aren't you?" I was so scared although I was trying to remain calm and I said it wasn't me. He was swearing at me and he said, "Don't lie to me, I know it's you!"

'I was really frightened and I had to run somewhere and I thought of the front door but by the time I'd grabbed the handle, opened the door and stepped back, they would have had me and probably stabbed me. Waite pounced on me and I then noticed that Pinnock had a knife as well, a silver one.

'I tried to run to the back of the café. My one concern was to get away as I realised that Waite meant to do me harm. I ran between the pool tables and had a scuffle with Waite who had caught up with me. At this point Pinnock also joined in the attack. He was slashing at me with a knife and I was flailing my arms about. I avoided him and I was trying to avoid contact with Waite as he had a knife and I was backing away the whole time. I thought he was going to kill me.

'Pinnock then came as well slashing and I kicked him in the stomach and he stepped back. I think he was the one who slashed my finger.

'I then managed to break away, ran to the back kitchen area and picked up a chair to defend myself. Waite was running at me with his knife and was definitely out to stab me. He wasn't just slashing at me this time, he was going for the stab. I remember someone trying to pull him off and I think it was his brother. He was either trying to stop him from stabbing me or trying to get in front of him so he could stab me.

'However, Waite didn't back off and lunged towards me with his knife and I fell backwards. I didn't feel the stab but I began to feel slightly dazed. By this time they had backed off. I had been shouting for help from the moment he attacked me shouting "Get him off" to anyone who would listen. I can remember Superfly shouting, "Don't kill him, don't kill him!"

'I would estimate that from the start of the fight to the moment they left the café was between three and five minutes. Although I didn't realise at first that I'd been stabbed, Waite stopped attacking me as Pinnock pulled him backwards. I can't remember what he said but I got the impression that he had seen I was injured and wanted to get out of the café. I fell back and they retreated.

'As far as I can remember, Waite seemed perfectly normal and not injured in any way. He was upright and he was still spoiling for a fight as Pinnock was taking him out of the café. The last thing in my mind was to chase after them as I felt dizzy and faint and my only thought was to get to the hospital and get treatment.

'I stayed in the café and it seemed as though everyone else was leaving me virtually alone in there. I realised I had to get out but I hesitated in case they were waiting for me outside. However, I staggered out of the café and met Suklain and Arif and they took me to the hospital in their car.'

In summary, the only evidence against Talat was Pinnock's and even this was far from reliable. Pinnock had shown himself to be a little less than truthful and even he could offer no convincing proof that Talat had stabbed Lloyd Waite. One of the prosecution witnesses, Michael Anthony, had even provided the one missing link and that was an alternative stabbing scenario. There really did not appear to be a case against Talat Sarwar and accordingly the defence made a submission of no case to answer.

The three lay magistrates adjourned and what, in the magistrates' court, would normally be a routine consideration and rejection of the defence submission that there was 'no case' for Talat to answer began to look more promising. Perhaps they were going to accept the submission and allow Talat his freedom. The adjournment went on and on until an hour and a half later the magistrates filed back into court and gave their decision. They had decided that Talat Sarwar did have a case to answer and he was committed for trial at the Crown Court.

With such a flimsy, weak case against him, the defence immediately entered an application for bail and felt sure that now, after more than six months in custody, Talat would be released. The Court refused the application and Talat was remanded back into custody. Although virtually no evidence at all was offered against Superfly, he too was committed for trial. The time was 8.30 p.m. and British justice had completed the first step in its proceedings.

SEVENTEEN

History Rules, OK

In 1361, the system of trial by magistrates first started. It wasn't quite the same then as it is now and the person who acted as judge and jury tended to be the local squire. On second thoughts, perhaps things haven't changed much at all.

The current idea is that people are tried by representatives of their own community. These representatives are not professional lawyers and their principal occupations may well be that of butcher, baker and candlestick-maker. Any community is comprised of many different sections and, theoretically, the lay magistrature reflects this.

Anyone can put their name forward to become a magistrate so long as they have two reasonably respectable referees. In practice it is usually magistrates themselves who put forward the names of others to follow in their footsteps. Once that is done the whole process then begins to move into slightly more obscure territory.

Of course, being a British institution, there has to be an advisory committee and, naturally, no committee is complete without a sub-committee so there is an advisory sub-committee.

Members of the sub-committee are recommended by the previous chairperson of the sub-committee and the chairperson is appointed by the Lord Chancellor and the Lord Chancellor, of course, is a political appointment. Anyone who wants to be or who has been invited to be a magistrate will be interviewed by the sub-committee and recommendations as to who should get the job are made to the committee by the sub-committee. Is that clear? In fact it sounds a little like a self-perpetuating circle which also precisely reflects the way the higher judiciary are appointed.

Applicants are judged on their lack of bias (I'm not quite sure what criterion is used to assess bias), their occupation - if there are already several farmers on the bench then another one may not stand much of a chance – and on 'their ability to fit in with the existing bench', whatever that means.

Having been appointed, a magistrate has to undertake to sit for at least twenty-six half-day sessions annually. It would take a fairly understanding employer to sanction that number of absences from work. There is no pay, but a financial loss allowance, subsistence and a travel allowance are all available.

Initial training amounts to a few evening sessions over a period of a week or two and then three afternoons observing. After that, you join two other colleagues on the bench and judge 90 per cent of all the court cases heard in England and Wales.

There is always one professional lawyer in court to advise the bench and that is the Justice's Clerk, appointed by the magistrates themselves. Both the Lord Chancellor, Lord Mackay, and I want to reform the magistrates' courts.

Lord Mackay's proposals have a familiar ring to them. He wants to streamline the number of committees and rationalise the areas served by a court, reduce the size of committees and have the court's performance monitored by an inspectorate. Staff will be paid by performance and committees will be encouraged to tender for support services in the private sector. Justice's Clerks will be subject to screening before appointment, given fixed-term contracts and have their pay related to performance. And in a wonderful touch of new realism, courts will be funded on the basis of how many cases they handle and their success in collecting fines.

It's hardly surprising that the response of the Magistrates' Association is to demand guarantees of independence; the Justice's Clerks' Society expresses fears of political manipulation and the Bar Council reckons the courts will become canned-pea factories. With all the shortcomings of British justice, this is the best that can be offered. It will not prevent one future miscarriage and will not advance the prospects of better justice one iota.

My reforms are very different from Lord Mackay's. I would abolish the magistrates' courts altogether, whether lay magistrates or solitary stipendiary magistrates. The fairest form of trial is in front of a jury and I suggest that unless it is a purely administrative offence such as parking, rubbish tipping, licensing or something similar, all cases should be tried by juries. If it is a plea of guilty, then there should be a fast-stream dealing only with pleas. If an offence is contested, whatever its nature, then that also should be put before a jury. There should also be strict time limits for contested cases which, if not met by the Crown, should lead to dismissal for want of prosecution.

The immediate cry will go up that we can't afford such a system and my response is simple – justice doesn't come cheap. Ask someone who has languished in prison for sixteen years, falsely convicted, whether justice should be properly funded!

The reality of my suggestion is not problematic. The vast majority of cases which appear before magistrates are pleas of guilty and magistrates' main role is to consider requests for mitigation. But my principal consideration is not to justify my proposed changes on the basis of administrative ease or financial prudency, we've had too much of that. My concern is to propose a system which will improve the quality of justice which people can expect from the courts of this country.

The involvement of the magistrates' court in the Talat Sarwar case is a prime example. They were asked to sever the charges on the grounds that the Friday night incident would prejudice his trial for murder. They refused. At the old style committal they were asked to find there was no case to answer and despite the threadbare nature of the prosecution's evidence they refused. Following this they were asked to grant bail and again refused. Through numerous court appearances they did nothing to prompt the prosecution into releasing vital forensic evidence to the defence. Throughout the case their role was that of a cypher and made no contribution to the eventual and obvious outcome.

Even in the earlier case I referred to, that of Clare Newton and the Chats Palace incident, their role was entirely predictable, that of believing the police and disbelieving the accused. A young care worker with no previous convictions, a stranger to the city, is kept in custody overnight on a minor offence in very dubious circumstances, is denied legal aid (a decision in the hands of the magistrates) and then found guilty of obstruction. That is a miscarriage of justice and is the type of miscarriage which happens daily in our magistrates' courts. For most people affected, the scale of the miscarriage is insufficient for them to make a fuss and so they reluctantly accept it.

Like in so many other areas of the law, the miners' strike acted as a catalyst in the magistrates' courts and tore away the veneer of impartiality. Nottinghamshire was the area where much of the picketing took place in an attempt to persuade the miners there to join the strike. Many of those arrested appeared at Mansfield magistrates' court where it was standard practice to grant bail, but on condition: that the accused is 'not to visit any premises or place for the purpose of picketing or demonstrating in connection with the current trade dispute between the National Union of Mineworkers and the National Coal Board other than peacefully to picket or demonstrate at your usual place of employment.'

These conditions were supplied on a printed piece of paper and stapled to the bail form. When large numbers of miners were brought before the court these 'usual conditions' were applied routinely in almost every single case. The organisation Liberty maintains that the process was such a production line that the Lord Chief Justice suggested tactfully that it might be better if the Clerk of the Court didn't actually attach the 'usual conditions' to the bail form until after the defendant's application for unconditional bail had been heard. He didn't want the court to be seen to prejudge people. The outcome was no different but the niceties of justice were upheld.

The effect of this exercise was to have a huge impact on the ability of miners to engage in secondary picketing and some would say that was the purpose of it. However, secondary picketing is a civil matter not a criminal one and there is no provision in the Bail Act which allows the court to use bail to prevent a breach of the civil law. But the magistrates were either willing or ignorant parties to this abuse and in either case it is not a very reassuring example of the unbiased administration of the law.

At the end of the strike, some twelve thousand miners had been found guilty of various offences, the vast majority of them offences which relied entirely on the words of a policeman – obstruction, threatening behaviour, breach of the peace, actions likely to result in a breach of the peace and so on. Virtually overnight, extremely law-abiding and hard-working members of the community are supposed to have transformed themselves into criminals. That is a quite extraordinary and unbelievable occurrence. Juxtaposed with that is the fact that not one policeman faced any charge whatsoever during the whole of that twelve-month period or since.

Whatever the selection process for magistrates the end result is that the largest sector of our criminal justice system is administered by amateur, virtually untrained men and women who are predominantly affluent, conservative and middle class. What is worse, they act as both judge and jury.

It is a poor system of justice and it is getting worse as the whole concept of jury trials comes under increasing attack. Every few years new attempts are made to weaken the role played by jury trials and it is always the same people responsible; the higher judiciary, the higher echelons of the police and cabinet ministers, with the agenda first being floated by back benchers. Of course, there is always an excuse for removing yet another offence from the list of those tried before a jury.

In the case of Northern Ireland, they have done away with them altogether for many serious offences which are now heard in the Diplock courts by a judge without a jury. The reason given is that jurors can be intimidated. The same excuse was put forward in an attempt to abolish juries in mainland Britain for trials of serious crime such as armed robbery.

With Clive Ponting, accused under the Official Secrets Act, outrage was generated in the establishment when a jury returned a not guilty verdict after having virtually been directed to find him guilty by the judge. The result was not to enquire into the political motivation of putting Ponting on trial but to label the jury 'perverse' and suggest that future trials of a similar nature should not be put before a jury. This was also the reaction recently when Randle and Pottle were acquitted after having confessed to helping George Blake escape from prison some sixteen years ago.

When members of the establishment are rebuffed by ordinary men and women of the jury, their anger is so great that it is almost palpable. The commitment of these leading members of society to jury trials is often only as strong as the jury's willingness to bring in the verdicts the establishment deems necessary. Once a jury begins to go its own way, there's trouble.

Another category of crime which is under threat of losing its jury trial is that of fraud cases. It was claimed that they were so complex that juries couldn't understand them and a panel of three judges would be much better.

Interestingly, one of the most complex fraud trials in history recently ended and the jurors were complimented by the trial judge for the role they played and were thanked 'for the quite remarkable care, attention and patience you have shown'. Immediately the call went up again to remove fraud trials from juries but the tack was changed. The reason now given is that it is unfair to take up so much of jurors' time in these long trials!

In a complete reversal of the establishment's normal position, the Bar Council produced a report saying: 'Past experience has shown that juries have consistently produced verdicts which are sensible, responsible and entirely just.' It then added: 'Important fraud trials have ended up being tried by unsuitable judges with the result that unnecessary difficulties have been caused for the juries.' In short, the report was saying that it wasn't the juries which needed to be changed but the judges!

All my experience and instincts tell me that the ultimate aim of the establishment is to dispense with jury trials entirely. Their main problem, however, is that every time they attempt to knock another complete category of offences off the list there is an outcry. Because they can't succeed in the public arena, every time a new criminal justice bill comes through they adopt a piecemeal approach, knocking off the list a few more offences that can be tried by a jury, giving them over to magistrates to deal with. The excuse is always one of cost saving and these erosions, like all others, should be forcefully resisted by all those who care about justice.

There are also calculated attempts to weaken juries in the hope that they'll bring in the verdicts required. For almost as long as juries have existed, defendants have had the right to challenge jurors as a safeguard against the administration stacking the jury against the defendant. The prosecution has exactly the same right to object to jurors it doesn't like. In 1990, that right was removed entirely from defendants so they now have to accept whatever jury is put in front of them. The prosecution has not been similarly penalised and, should they ever choose to exercise the right, they can object to as many jurors as they please. This goes hand in hand with the intention of ending the right to silence.

It's important to be aware that when this type of change is introduced or when new legislation is enacted which confers draconian powers on the police (as with the Public Order Act), no change is noticed immediately. But these powers are the 'SMART' weapons of judicial warfare and they sit there waiting for the day when they're needed. When that day comes, they will be dusted off and used without hesitation.

The origins of the present jury system date back to the Magna Carta and the role of juror provides one of the few ways in which ordinary citizens can exercise genuine democracy. It is the right of people to be tried by their peers, by people who are in touch with the realities of life, who nearly always bring with them common sense and a sense of justice. Jury trials do fail sometimes, as in the case of the Birmingham Six and others, but I would suggest that the failure is not the jury's but the system which has produced the material on which they are convicted. The jury is as good as the information laid before it and the manner in which it is directed by judges.

Jury trials are a precious institution and must be preserved as the ultimate and most powerful safeguard against an overweening legislature and judiciary and the corruption of officers of law enforcement. As in the

Ponting case, juries will be put under pressure when the state sees its interests threatened but that is nothing new. On the exterior of the Old Bailey in London is a plaque commemorating the trial of William Penn in the 1600s on charges of seditious libel. To encourage the right verdict the jury was locked up without food. They refused to be intimidated and acquitted Penn, as a result of which they were fined. I have no doubt that under similar pressure the result would be no different today.

Just as the origins of jury trial are lost in the mists of history, so is the structure of our legal profession but this defies even the most basic logic. At the lower levels there is a complete chasm between the different types of lawyer. The first point of contact for the general public is a solicitor, usually sited somewhere in the High Street and qualified to carry out the day-to-day legal requirements that most of us need at some time or other – making a will, conveyancing a house, sending a strongly worded letter. They are also the first call for those in trouble with the law.

It is the solicitor who attends the police station when someone is first detained and it is he or she who then does all the leg work and goes on to prepare the case for the defence. They take the statements, they track down the missing witnesses, they look for the corroboration. During the course of their preparatory work they may well brief a barrister, perhaps a Queen's Counsel, who can offer advice but essentially it is the solicitor who is the front line of defence. The solicitor can then represent his or her client in the magistrates' court. If it is a comparatively minor offence the case might be dealt with there but for more serious offences, as in the case of Talat Sarwar, it will be sent for trial at a higher court.

Although John Davis had been involved in defending Talat from the beginning and was an experienced advocate, the rules which existed at that time prevented him from taking the case through to its completion. That wasn't in the interests of Talat Sarwar and it wasn't in the interests of justice.

Until recently, to all intents and purposes, solicitors could not represent their clients in these higher courts, that role being reserved for barristers. It was therefore necessary to instruct a barrister and hand to them the case for the defence. Similar rules applied to the prosecution.

Having been briefed and taken up the case, often only days before the trial, it is then the barrister's role to present the case in court in the best possible way, to cross-examine prosecution witnesses and to act as an advocate for the accused.

This division amongst lawyers is almost unique in the English-speaking world and owes far more to tradition than it does to common sense. Trying to explain our system to someone like Arielle Jarret, the New York defence attorney, is like attempting to explain quantum physics to an innumerate.

In any legal system some people specialise, so in the US there are those lawyers who do the spade work and little else and others who litigate and present the case in court. The main difference with their system is that any lawyer can undertake any elements of a lawyer's work they choose. The decision is theirs.

In 1990, the Lord Chancellor produced a White Paper on intended changes to the legal profession, part of which would have effectively brought about 'fusion' in the legal profession and eradicated many of the differences between solicitors and barristers. He recommended the introduction of multidisciplinary practices which would include other professions such as architects; he advocated direct access to barristers without the need to go through a solicitor; and he proposed rights of audience for solicitors in higher courts. Although I agree totally with the policy I disagreed with his reasons, which were all about cost saving. There are far more important reasons than that for fusion.

The Lord Chief Justice, at that time Lord Lane, went to the barricades and spoke in the House of Lords against the Lord Chancellor's proposals as they affected the judiciary. There were warnings of oppression, the spirit of Hitler was invoked and in a quite extraordinary series of outbursts the independence of the Bar judiciary was defended as though the Mongol hordes threatened. A string of miscarriages, evidence of police assaults, forgery and perjury, proof of our courts' inability to dispense justice had not prompted any public misgivings of the kind displayed by the present Lord Chief Justice in his Dimbleby Lecture in 1992.

Since that time, however, there have been some changes. Solicitors do now have rights of audience in higher courts. The right is hedged with restrictions on the length of service, experience and status (whether in private practice or employed – perhaps by a large company such as ICI). But there is still no fusion.

As a barrister, I am the advocate who represents the interests of an accused person in court. In that role, however, I am not allowed to interview witnesses, I can't go out in the field, see people and talk to them. I have to make judgements second- or third-hand on what other people tell me someone is like, what their weaknesses are and what faults they have. I am forbidden to advise witnesses on the best way to present their evidence. Although things vary from state to state, essentially it is totally different in the US and Arielle Jarret and most other US lawyers find our system incomprehensible: 'It's crazy! How can you possibly know what type of witness you're going to have on the stand? Nearly all of my witnesses in just about every case I handle have never been in a court room before, let alone been on the witness stand. I have to prepare them for this. It isn't that I want them to make anything up but they have information inside them, sometimes vital information, and I want to be sure they're capable of producing it in court.

'The prosecutor's job is to cross-examine and basically try to discredit them. He'll try and make it sound like they're lying and I have to prepare them for that, warn them what it's going to be like and show them the type of questions they might be asked. The prosecutor does exactly the same with his witnesses.

'I control the case from beginning to end and I start by trying to establish some relationship with my client. I will be the only lawyer they deal with. It's up to me to interview all the potential witnesses and to appoint forensic scientists, forensic psychiatrists, interpreters or whatever expert witnesses are needed. In a homicide there are few restrictions on who you can and can't use.

'If the crime scene was really crucial to the case, I would have a crime scene expert appointed to take photographs, measure, make a model if necessary – it's not a big deal getting permission for experts to attend the scene. Even if you have to go to court because the police are obstructive it only takes a day.

'An essential element in the early stages is a private investigator. They're the ones who track down the witnesses and they are good at it. There's no spending limits but all their travel and expenses have to be authorised in advance.

'If the accused is held in custody they can ring me at any time of day or night, there are no restrictions, and they have access to a legal library within the prison. When I visit them, our conversations are strictly private.

'Right from the start of an investigation I am thinking of the witnesses and how to get essential points into evidence. Frequently I will go out with the PIs to interviews and prepare witnesses for the case. I have to be absolutely certain of their credibility and their creditworthiness in terms of the evidence they'll give. It's very important to rehearse them and prepare them for attempts to undermine their evidence.

'For instance, because they're nervous, young people tend to smirk and smile and I'll coach them so they don't do it. I'm looking at the strengths and weaknesses of a case on a daily basis.

'In the meantime, the prosecution will be preparing their case and they have to disclose all the statements and evidence that are submitted to them. In the Birmingham Six case, the results of the tests on the two men on the Liverpool ferry would have to be disclosed to us; it's what's called exculpatory material. To conceal it would constitute prosecution misconduct.

'Of course, not everyone in the US is a good trial lawyer but not all barristers are good trial lawyers either and that's their only job. But to be presented with a brief just a little while before you have to represent someone in court is, I honestly believe, not in their interests. Having two professions makes no sense and the way some barristers handle their briefs, with no commitment and no interest, I actually think constitutes malpractice.'

Strong words but often justified. The so called 'cab rank' system which operates for barristers, in which they are not supposed to refuse any legal aid case no matter how poorly paid, ensures representation but not quality. There are too many barristers who are more interested in the fee which goes with the brief than in the brief itself. Advising the defendant to plead guilty disposes of the case in the quickest possible time and allows them to pick up another brief and its fee.

All this has to change and the way to bring it about is with a fused profession as in the US. The entrenched position of the Bar Council may represent the interests of their members but may not represent the best interests of the people of Britain.

EIGHTEEN

The Trial

After committal on 13 October 1989, allowing for the normal time delay before a case reaches trial, it was anticipated that Talat Sarwar would finally stand trial shortly after Christmas, probably in February, 1990. By this time, however, he would have been in custody for almost one year. The defence had tried everything they could to have bail granted but without success.

So archaic is our judicial system that it isn't a straightforward matter of a case automatically being entered on a court list and then waiting its turn for trial. That would be much too simple. There are different types of judge, some of whom are authorised to try serious offences such as murder, rape, kidnapping and treason, and some who aren't. Then there are particular preferences to contend with, as to who is going to try a murder. The International Café case ran into all these obstacles.

It should have been put down for trial in Aylesbury Crown Court before a judge qualified to deal with murders. However, this didn't happen and the case was transferred to Reading to come up before a red judge. Unfortunately his list filled up so he released it to the presiding judge. The presiding judge found he could not do it so he released it to the original judge but, having done that, he later took it back again. Some time later, however, it came winging back to the original judge yet again.

Unfortunately it wasn't listed and delay followed delay and time slipped away. Whether this was because they wanted to start the next session off with a murder and hold on to the case for that purpose, we don't know. Had they done so, Talat, on trial for his life's freedom, would have had the honour of appearing in court only to be instantly arraigned and taken back down to the cells. Why? Because at the opening of a new session, judges are inclined to invite their friends into the court to experience the pomp and splendour. The accused makes a fleeting visit before the judge and the High Sheriff and the court officers, all done up in fancy dress, troop off to church and then lunch.

In one sense it was lucky for Talat that this didn't happen but in another it was a tragedy because the course that the trial took subsequently wasted even more time. The judge at Reading eventually decided he couldn't try the case and handed it back to Aylesbury. But he refused it and Regina v Talat Mahmood Sarwar and Mohammed Shabir Kayani was sent back again to Reading.

The case did come to court in February but only for a pre-trial review and a plea and directions hearing in which Talat's defence applied to have the two charges against him severed on the grounds that it would be extremely prejudicial to him to be tried for both the Friday night and Saturday night incidents in the same court case. The application was dismissed speedily by a High Court judge in a manner that the defence describe as 'a thoroughly bad-tempered review' and no comment was made by the judge about the length of time Talat had been in custody.

Following this decision defence solicitors wanted to take their objections to the dismissal of the severance further but their QC insisted that nothing further could be done. They disagreed with him but rather than force a division in the defence team, acceded to his view.

Again the delays mounted and the defence registered more protests about the effect this was having on their client and on the witnesses who were supposed to recollect events which had happened over a year ago. It was felt that each delay must diminish their usefulness as witnesses.

It transpired that the judge at Reading couldn't, in fact, handle the case after all because his list was full and so back it went to H.H. Judge Verney at Aylesbury. Finally, a pre-trial review was held at the beginning of July.

At this review, H.H. Judge Verney specifically requested that Talat be brought before him as he wished to express his grave concern at the length of time he had been kept waiting to come to trial. Talat appeared and was told by the judge that what had happened was unforgivable and that it was the worst example of delay he had ever experienced during the whole of his career. He then remanded Talat back into custody! The trial was to be H.H. Judge Verney's last before his appointment as Recorder of London and his handling of it was impeccable at all stages.

Various provisional dates for the trial were then discussed and eventually 14 July was chosen with an estimated one week's duration.

This placed the defence in something of a quandary for having repeatedly pushed for a trial date, they could hardly reject it now, even though it allowed only ten days to complete their case. That was to be only one of their worries.

The QC who had been instructed a year earlier and had been involved throughout this long and tortuous case had, when he took the brief, told the defence solicitors that he would be available in July but not in September or October. It looked as though the timing of the trial fitted in perfectly. It didn't!

He suddenly announced that despite his acceptance of the brief and the fact that he had agreed to being available in July, he had been offered the biggest case of his career beginning in September. He had known this from the beginning but had decided that he needed a holiday and time to prepare himself. As a consequence he would not now be handling the Talat Sarwar case.

Such a decision was in breach of the Bar Council's code of practice but Davis Walker & Co decided not to register a complaint in case it dissuaded other barristers from accepting their instructions. However, they now had a client who had been in prison for well over a year, an extremely good case and no counsel to represent his interests in court. Under the legal laws of the land, John Davis could not undertake that role because he is a solicitor and only a barrister has rights of audience in a Crown Court.

A replacement Queen's Counsel was found and instructed just seven days before the opening of the trial.

Despite advice from the original counsel that nothing further could be done to sever the indictment, H.H. Judge Verney, took an entirely different view and reopened the issue. He maintained that his reading of the papers indicated that it would be highly prejudicial to try the two matters together and, despite what had been said in a previous court, he was going to sever the indictment. What was really surprising was that the prosecution agreed with him and offered no objections despite their previous intransigence.

This was the same prosecution which had objected to severance before another judge and it made nonsense of the advice offered by the defence's own QC that there was nothing more which could be done. The stated policy of all prosecutions in England and Wales is simply to prosecute the evidence and to let the jury decide. It is not part of their ethos, they say, to win at any cost. In this case, however, it looked as though they had been giving themselves the very best chance of securing a conviction.

At this stage of the proceedings in determining a young man's guilt or innocence, you might be forgiven for thinking that justice can be contrary. In fact, the blindfolded person dangling the scales in one hand, in which facts are carefully weighed before the sword held in the other hand is used, may not be the right visual image at all. In the case of Talat Sarwar and many others, a bowler-hatted bookie shouting 'five-to-four the field' might be more appropriate. The case was taking on all the aspects of a lottery.

The central plank of the defence case was that Talat Sarwar was unarmed, that he was the victim and Waite was the aggressor and there was no evidence to prove Talat's guilt. It was up to the prosecution to prove him guilty and not for the defence to prove him innocent. That is the theory of British justice but it does help to persuade juries if you can prove the accused person innocent.

The defence felt the one way in which they could do that was to follow the theory that Waite had died outside the café. The eye-witness who provided evidence of it was the twelve-year-old Michael Anthony.

But here they were in a quandary. They had already tipped the prosecution off that they believed Michael Anthony had witnessed the actual killing. If they were to try and strengthen their case by interviewing him in an attempt to extract more detail, it would have to be in front of a policeman as the boy was a prosecution witness. Experience told them that conducting an interview under such circumstances was inclined to push a witness further towards the police perspective. They decided against it.

The fact remained that he was the only witness who had seen anything outside the café that could have been a stabbing. Not only could it have been a stabbing but the relative position of the two men involved and the direction in which the knife would have been thrust fitted almost perfectly with the post mortem report. It was very likely that despite his obvious intelligence and self-assurance, the prosecution would cast doubt upon the reliability of a twelve-year-old witness. But it was worth a try.

In most criminal cases, the police take a huge number of statements from numerous witnesses. Some of them are considered to be of importance and eventually form part of the prosecution's case. Others are deemed to be of no significance – or of no significance in progressing the police case – and are not relied on to form part of the evidence. As a consequence, prior to the Judith Ward decision, copies of these 'reject' or 'unused' statements were often not given to the defence. Many of the statements with which I began this book were considered by the police to be of no importance and although they may have contributed to our understanding of what went on inside the International Café, the defence were completely ignorant of them.

However, there is a well-established rule (which isn't always adhered to) under the Attorney General's guidelines that any material relevant to the background and circumstances of the offence not relied upon by the prosecution should be provided to the defence. The defence in this case, as in many others, have a standard practice of asking for this material and did so at repeated and regular intervals throughout the fifteen months of the wait. They were initially ignored and then told that none existed.

On the first day of the trial, Talat Sarwar took his place in the dock. The new Queen's Counsel for the defence spoke to the prosecution for the first time and requested that any undisclosed material should be provided to the defence. The Counsel leading the prosecution agreed to the request and directed that any such material should immediately be handed over.

To those not used to the workings of the law it must seem incredible, perhaps even outrageous, that a defence team working with so many of the odds stacked against them, for very little money and with few resources, should have to wait until the first day of the trial for information which might assist their case. But that is the way it often transpires. And so it was in this case.

The trial was underway, the prosecution was calling its first witnesses to give their evidence in chief and possibly, just possibly, vital information to the defence might have been about to surface in the court for those sharp enough to pick up on it. And where was the defence? Certainly the solicitor was at the back of the court with one eye on the proceedings and the other on the two-hundred-plus pages of witness statements which had just been presented to him.

The late disclosure meant the defence had to read all this in the middle of the trial, look for something which might be relevant and attempt to relate one witness statement to another at the same time as trying to listen to what was being said in court.

Amongst the statements were those that threw a little more light on the fight inside the café. There was confirmation that Waite was armed, there was more than one statement which showed him to be the aggressor, there was evidence that Pinnock was also carrying a knife and there were eye-witnesses to say that Waite had his knife out at an earlier stage than anyone had previously thought and not as a response to actions by Talat Sarwar. It was concealed in his hand by the side of his leg. But important as all this new information was, it was not the most significant. That was the statement which supported the twelve-year-old boy, Anthony Michael's eye-witness account. It was made by his mother.

It was not the prosecution's intention to call Mrs Anthony as a witness but they were intending to call Michael and, as luck would have it, Mrs Anthony was en route to the court with her son.

The newly appointed defence QC had arrived in court with a very different perspective on how the case should be conducted from that of the defence solicitors, particularly with regard to how Pinnock should be discredited in cross-examination and the need for either Michael Anthony or his mother to be called as witnesses. A huge division opened up in the defence team and the defence solicitors, that evening, felt obliged to produce a one-hundred page briefing document as to how they felt the case should be conducted. Fortunately Talat knew nothing of all this.

So convinced were the solicitors that Pinnock's inconsistencies were important that they had previously tried to obtain a transcript of the trial in which he had stood accused of kidnapping the Asian boy, Suk, in an attempt to discover Talat's whereabouts. Although Pinnock had been acquitted in that case, they wanted to check the statements he had made under oath against his statements in this case. Incredibly, the cost of obtaining the transcripts was put at £3000 and, in any case, they couldn't be prepared in time.

So, although that was another avenue which was closed, Mrs Anthony was due in court and was subsequently called as a witness. Her testimony was interesting. Not only did she support all that Michael had said in his statement but provided even more crucial evidence. She described the fight outside the café in similar terms to her son – the taller Asian grappling with the West Indian from behind with his arm around him. But she also thought she recalled the West Indian shouting out, 'Oh no, oh no'.

This was entirely consistent with the defence theory that Waite had been stabbed from behind, outside the café by the tall Asian. The wounds to Waite's hands were also entirely consistent with an attack from behind. In fact, it was felt that the type of cuts he had on his hands were more likely to have been caused by his fending off a knife from his stomach, a knife which was being wielded by a man behind him, attempting to pull it inwards and upwards. His right hand was almost severed at the top whereas defensive wounds sustained in warding off an attack from the front would almost certainly have resulted in cuts to his fingers and palms – exactly like the cut sustained by Talat Sarwar on his hand.

It seemed quite extraordinary that the police and prosecution, having had access to both Michael Anthony's statement and his mother's, had never initiated any enquiries into what they had seen. Even more extraordinary, the defence had tipped the prosecution off at the old style committal that they were interested in this 'alternative scenario' for the murder but again no further attention had been paid to it by the prosecution.

What was now needed was the scientific and medical confirmation that the wounds inflicted on Waite were consistent with this type of attack.

Professor Gresham TD, MD, ScD, FRCPATH was the man called by the defence and he was asked to consider the reports of both post mortems as well as the new possible scenario for the killing. He agreed that Waite could have died in exactly the manner outlined by the defence. He also felt that the wounds to his hands were consistent with this type of attack. But he had rather a difficult time in the witness box when prosecuting counsel threw doubt on his judgement. He raised the testimony he had given in a previous trial where he concluded that a man who had died of gunshot wounds had committed suicide when the cause had been murder. Despite protestations that gunshot wounds were particularly difficult to analyse so precisely, some of the conviction had gone from his testimony. But it went on.

He maintained that Waite could not have been killed in the manner outlined by the prosecution because had the stabbing taken place where and when they said it did, he would have been unconscious before leaving the café. He maintained that Waite would have lost consciousness in about one minute. He estimated that, in an excited state, his heart would have been working at approximately one hundred beats a minute and in that time would have pumped out two-thirds of the body's entire blood content.

But there was another reason why Waite's death could not have been caused in the manner outlined by the prosecution on the basis of Pinnock's testimony. The way in which Pinnock described pulling Waite away from the path of the knife was simply not consistent with the angle of the thrust and with the wound described by Dr West in his post mortem report.

He believed that Waite's own knife, the one found under his body, could have been the cause of the stab wound to the stomach. Any discrepancy between the width of the knife blade and the width of the hole in Waite's clothing could be accounted for by his movement on the knife blade.

The handle of the knife carried a metal ring and Professor Gresham thought that this could have been responsible for the bruising to Waite's ribcage.

What had been obvious almost from the very start of this case, that Talat Sarwar had not killed Lloyd Waite, was now on the point of receiving official confirmation. In fact, the jury returned a verdict of not guilty in the case of Talat Sarwar and Shabir 'Superfly' Kayani was acquitted of affray without even needing to give evidence on his own behalf.

Immediately following the verdict, Talat then stood trial for the charge of malicious wounding at the Booker fair. He had already made a brief written statement:

'On Friday, 21 April I went to the Booker fair. We had been there about an hour when I saw some West Indians standing by the side of the dodgems, spitting at my friends. I told them not to do it and one of them apologised, saying, "No hard feelings". He was the one actually spitting.

'The next thing I knew, another one came up to me and started arguing and trying to look big. Then about twenty of them surrounded me. I told them I didn't want any trouble and started to walk down the steps when one of them pulled me back. I saw him produce a screwdriver and I thought he was going to stab me. I was carrying a Stanley knife for protection and took this out and waved it towards them to frighten them away. I then ran. I don't believe I cut him but I don't know.'

Judge Verney indicated that he thought it appropriate that the charge of malicious wounding should be withdrawn and the defendant, if he was so advised by his defence, should plead guilty to grievous bodily harm. Talat could not face another trial whatever his defence thought and as he would be out on bail was fearful of being attacked. He pleaded guilty and was immediately released as any sentence was academic in view of the time he had already been in prison. Until this point he had a clean record.

He walked out of the courtroom door after fifteen months in prison and was immediately put on a plane to Pakistan by his family for his own safety.

And so ended the case of Talat Sarwar, a triumph for justice!

NINETEEN

Reforming the Courts

The non-disclosure of evidence – the holding back of information which might assist the defence – is an affront to any concept of justice. Why is it done? Some would argue that it is cock-up rather than conspiracy but others wouldn't be so charitable. The examples are too frequent, too profound and the consequences too alarming for every investigating policeman, every forensic scientist and every prosecutor not to be aware of the importance of disclosing all the information they have at their disposal. And yet there is still a reluctance and a dragging of feet in this area.

In the case of Talat Sarwar, undisclosed evidence in the form of witness statements was released on the first day of his trial, fifteen months after the incident of which he was accused and every request for access to it had been ignored. Those statements had been in the hands of the police for almost the whole of that period. In the end, it wasn't a constitutional right which led to their release but simply the good nature of the prosecuting counsel who instructed that it should be done. It's hardly surprising that when the defence thanked him for his intervention he replied: 'If word got around that I was fair, it wouldn't do my practice any good at all!'

Running through some examples of non-disclosure which have recently come to light graphically outlines what is likely to be the outcome of this practice. Take Stefan Kiszko again.

Mr Kiszko had an alibi in the case of the murder of Lesley Molseed, that he had been visiting his father's grave together with his mother and aunt. Being members of his family, these witnesses were not considered very reliable. There is some dispute about why and with whose authority they did it but his defence, headed by Mr David Waddington (later to become Home Secretary and then a Lord) offered an alternative plea; that he, Stefan Kiszko, was not guilty of murder but guilty of manslaughter.

Kiszko was said to have a mental age of a twelve-year-old, suffered from anaemia and was sexually immature. He had been undergoing a course of testosterone injections which, the defence was to claim, might have affected his behaviour. The jury didn't believe it and found him guilty.

Although this case says as much about the quality of defence as it does about the prosecution, the fact remained that undeniable evidence of Stefan Kiszko's innocence was in the hands of the prosecution at the time of his trial but it was not produced in court. Semen was gathered from the scene of the murder, taken from the girl's clothing and there was no doubt that it belonged to the murderer. The crucial point was that it contained spermatozoa and therefore could not have come from Stefan as he was infertile. This fact was almost certainly known to the Lancashire police as semen samples were taken from the accused for the purpose of cross-referencing.

It took sixteen years for this injustice to be corrected, by which time the original semen sample from the scene had been lost. In the event it did not affect the outcome of the appeal. The murder investigation was reopened and Lancashire police are currently enquiring into why the evidence was not made available at the trial!

The Birmingham Six case is another classic example of selective evidence being put forward in court. At the original trial, besides the disputed confessions, there was scientific evidence against three of the six. The crux of the prosecution case rested on swab tests for explosives which were carried out on the six at Morecambe police station. Dr Frank Skuse was called out in the middle of the night and swabbed the hands of five of the men at the police station using a chemical process known as the Griess Test – a colour test. Strictly speaking it is only a presumptive field test requiring confirmation by more sensitive and precise tests at a laboratory. But Dr Skuse was to claim that the conditions under which he operated made it specific for nitroglycerine. He reported positive findings for the swabs from the right hands of Power and Hill.

As Billy Power recalled, the atmosphere in the police station changed instantly and from being six people helping police with their enquiries they became the Birmingham bombers and the brutality began, eventually leading to supposed confessions.

When the case came to court, enormous emphasis was placed on the forensic tests which were carried out on the swabs to prove that the men had been handling explosives. What was not disclosed to the court was that two other men were swabbed that night on a ferry from Liverpool to Belfast and they showed positive results. The scientist who carried out the examination employed the Griess Test and was based at the same laboratory as Dr Skuse. He discovered that adhesive tape the two men had been handling was itself capable of providing a positive reaction to the test. They were able to prove their innocence, that they had not been anywhere near explosives, and were allowed to go on their way. Had the court known these results it would have lent considerable support to the defence expert whose evidence was marginalised by the judge.

In fact it took the best part of sixteen years for the reliability of the Griess Test to be challenged firstly by *World in Action* experiments carried out by Dr Caddy to demonstrate how other surfaces including playing cards could produce positive results and finally by Dr Lloyd discovering that soap was yet another substance capable of producing similar results. The latter is of great significance where the scientist might either wash his hands or the bowls used for testing in soap between the swabbing of each suspect.

What is more disturbing is that the Liverpool test results were not even revealed in 1988 during the first fresh evidence appeal in front of Lord Lane. Yet one month before the appeal police had been taking statements from the scientist so no one can claim the matter had been forgotten.

The Maguire Seven equally have reason to deplore the practice of withholding information and in their case it again involved evidence of their having handled explosives. They were convicted on the word of scientists from the Royal Armament Research and Development Establishment (RARDE) who, it was claimed, provided the necessary proof of their contamination prior to their arrests in December 1974.

The hand and fingernail swabs from six were said to reveal the presence of nitroglycerine and, in the case of Annie Maguire, a similar claim merely related to a disposable plastic glove which she used for housework, owing to a skin condition from which she suffered.

It was suggested that a possible source of contamination could be a particular brand of heart tablets – Sustac tablets – which were in the house and were regularly used.

When the case came for trial in 1976 there were a number of important scientific issues for the jury. One, the specificity of the TLC (Thin Layer Chromatography) test for Ng (nitroglycerine). Two, the possibility of Ng trace persistence and transfer on hands. Three, the possibility of heart tablets providing a source of contamination.

The May enquiry in 1990 found that RARDE scientists knew throughout the trial that PETN was confusable with Ng. They misled the court by failing to mention it. Further second tests using a different TLC system were said at trial not to be necessary. The enquiry discovered there had been second tests with negative results. Knowledge of the tests was denied by Mr Higgs and Dr Hayes, RARDE scientists, and even though they had examined the notebooks before they first gave evidence to the enquiry they did not mention them on that occasion.

The enquiry also discovered that various experiments were conducted during the trial and not revealed. Mr Higgs had said he did not see how Ng could be transferred under the fingernails after merely clenching the hand and Mr Elliott maintained presence under the nails indicated manipulating and kneading. Hand trials at RARDE demonstrated that transfer could occur. As far as Sustac tablets are concerned, Mr Elliott had told his jury that you might get a positive result from crushed tablets but not if the hand was left for some time. Again experiments during the trial refuted this by showing a three-and-a-half hour gap still permitted positive results.

The Guildford Four fared little better at the hands of our blind justice. After fourteen years in prison and a vociferous public campaign, the Home Secretary announced that he was referring the case back to the Court of Appeal. One of the matters to emerge related to the alibi of the supposed ringleader of the four, Gerry Conlon.

Gerry Conlon claimed to have spent the day of the Guildford bombings, 5 October 1974, in and around the Kilburn hostel where he was living at that time. He claimed that not only had he nothing to do with the explosions at Guildford but that he had never even been there until he was taken by police following his arrest.

He maintained there was one person who could prove he was innocent and that was a man who also lived in the hostel and had been with him on the day in question. Gerry Conlon's defence lawyers were aware of the importance of this witness but discovered that he no longer lived at the hostel and had left no forwarding address. Despite enormous efforts to track him down he seemed to have disappeared without trace.

At the trial, Sir Michael Havers (subsequently ennobled but now deceased), was leading the prosecution and in his closing speech referred to the fact that Gerry Conlon had no alibi. In the polite and diplomatic niceties which frame conversations in court, he was reminded by the judge, Lord Donaldson, that it wasn't so much that Mr Conlon didn't have an alibi, he did, it was simply that he had no witnesses to support it. Either way, the jury could be in no doubt that Gerry Conlon had a wafer-thin defence as far as alibis were concerned.

Many years later, when the case was first referred to the Court of Appeal, Conlon's defence lawyers made more strenuous efforts to find the elusive witness but again without result.

The truth of the disappearing witness is that he was far from being a mystery man and the Surrey police had interviewed him prior to the trial. They had taken a witness statement from him and he fully supported Gerry Conlon's alibi. He could even be certain of the date because it was the day before he checked out of the hostel. There was also a statement from a hostel worker to confirm his departure on that day.

It would be shocking enough if that piece of vital evidence was withheld on the authority of some junior. In fact, while prosecution lawyers were standing in court claiming that Conlon had no alibi, the prosecuting authorities knew this to be untrue and had made a decision to withhold the information. These statements were in a bundle which had been stamped 'NOT to be disclosed to the defence'.

It is probably fair to say that had there been safeguards in our system which ensured that any material available to the prosecution was also available to the defence, these unforgivable miscarriages would not have happened. As with so many aspects of the present system, I believe the need to win prosecutions is so inculcated in both the police and some of the Crown Prosecution Service that tinkering with the system will have no effect. What is needed is the kind of independent control offered by the *juge d'instruction*.

The dossier which she begins to compile at the very beginning of a case and in which every single incident is recorded, negative as well as positive, is what we should have in Britain. When the *juge* has finished her investigation, a copy of the dossier is handed to the defence and both sides begin with exactly the same information.

Such independent control, working to an established code of conduct, would also ensure that tighter control was exercised over the quality of evidence. For example, there could be no examination of a suspect without first establishing probable cause. This would outlaw 'fishing expeditions' in which people are pulled in on chance. It would be necessary for the police to establish reasonable suspicion that the suspect had committed the crime before they could take any action. This criterion would have outlawed the detention and swab testing of the Birmingham Six.

We should move to a system where no scientific examination can be carried out and testimony provided by anyone but an 'accredited' scientist. In some cases this would require a commitment to providing independent training for forensic scientists and the establishment of a recognised qualification. In other disciplines, the existing qualifications might suffice though accreditation would not be automatic but awarded on the basis of the type of work carried out and length of experience.

All scientific testing must be double-checked, first by the Home Office scientist and then by the defence. It would not simply be a case of confirming what each had found but independent analysis based on the overall context. As in the café case, Waite's blood inside the café would have to be identified as being his grouping but where it was found and the nature of the blood would also have to be established – whether smeared or pooled and its distribution.

Any tests carried out must be 'inter verifiable'. That means that a one-off, individual test which cannot be reproduced afterwards by another scientist would not be admissible. They must also be tests which are recognised and commonly accepted by the scientific community. This was not the case with the Griess test used on the Birmingham Six and neither was it with the thin layer chromatography test used in the Maguire case. In both instances the tests were non-specific and virtually useless for their intended purposes.

All samples must be contamination free with no possibility of adulteration from other sources – and that includes the police. The term 'Scenes of Crime Officer' or SOCO, sounds quite impressive but SOCOs are ordinary policemen who double in the role. Some of them are experienced but others are anything but. That is another reason why it is vital for any investigation to be overseen by a trained, independent, accountable person in the form of a *juge*. All samples must be handled correctly to avoid cross-contamination. There was contamination in both the Birmingham Six and the Maguire cases.

The importance of established and verifiable procedures is vital. There was an incident in Manchester in which hundreds of breathalyser cases for drunken driving had to be dropped because ethyl alcohol was used in breathalyser equipment and could influence the result of any test.

Science can so easily be seen as the provider of unarguable truths but today's truths often become tomorrow's miscarriages. And we don't seem to learn. The current scientific holy grail is DNA and as much caution needs to be exercised over this as over other fallible tests. For this reason amongst others, there should be no prosecution on forensic evidence without corroboration from another source. Just as with confessions, there must be a second source of evidence.

Again I can hear the cry that no one will ever be convicted. In reply I point to the Birmingham Six and all the other miscarriages. Even without these safeguards they didn't get the right people and perhaps the need to conduct proper investigations might be more fruitful than the hunch, the prejudice and the presumption of guilt on which the present system so widely operates.

Having ensured that the evidence gets into court, and that means all the evidence, having ascertained that it is sound and trustworthy and both sides start with a level playing field, then we have to reform the court.

Talat Sarwar sat in a dock, separated from his defence team, alone and solitary. He couldn't talk to anyone, discuss the prosecution evidence as it was presented, give opinions or counter accusations. He also carried the stigma of guilt or why else would he be segregated in a prominent box. In 'terrorist' cases, the addition of bullet-proof glass and armed snipers surrounding the court leave little doubt in a juror's mind as to the status of the accused. They are obviously dangerous men and women and almost certainly guilty, otherwise there wouldn't be any need for all the precautions.

As always, Talat Sarwar's prosecution and defence counsels wore their wigs and gowns and the judge sported a wonderfully colourful outfit. The pomp and ceremony of these occasions is the remaining visual reminder of privilege and preference. All professionals wore similar garb at some time in history but have had the sense to discard it. Such ostentation in court is a meaningless pantomime designed to scare the life out of the 'lower classes' and remind them of their position in the pecking order. It all has to go.

The archaic and extraordinary process a barrister has to endure in order to be called to the Bar must exercise the incredulity of lawyers from other countries. It is laughable and has its roots deep in the selective soil of public school and Oxbridge. The upshot is that you become extremely well fed in the process of qualifying.

You are obliged to eat a minimum number of dinners at one of the four Inns of Court to which all barristers must belong – Lincoln's Inn, Gray's Inn, Middle Temple and Inner Temple. These dinners take place every evening during what is known as the dining term. There are four terms a year each lasting about eight weeks.

Everyone dresses up in their gowns and sits at long refectory tables. Benchers, the qualified barristers, sit at the head table and all the aspiring barristers at the lower tables. They are formed into groups of four known as messes, with each mess having its senior and junior member. There are rules, of course, rules which are strictly adhered to. The food is ritually passed in one direction while the wine goes the other way. Should you be so socially inept as to make a mistake then a fine will follow.

At the end of dinner, the most junior person in hall, the one at the bottom of the table furthest from the high table, stands on the table and asks permission to smoke. The most senior person in hall might ask if any rules have been broken or any misdemeanour committed and may well impose a forfeit – a song to sing or something obnoxious to eat.

The benchers then retire upstairs for port and the dining hall takes on the appearance of a public school, often complete with thrown bread rolls and mayhem. The whole purpose of this system is to socially vet juniors to ensure they are the 'right type'.

Aspiring barristers will probably have a law degree and until comparatively recently had to pay for their pupillage. Now some chambers do provide a subsistence salary of about £3000 for the first six months and £6000 for the second six months. Out of this they have to pay for their books, their wig, gowns and neck bands, their suits and all travelling and living expenses. There are only a few scholarships and exhibitions granted.

My path was slightly different in that I did a philosophy degree at Keele University and then promptly failed the Land Law element of the Bar exams three times. I took it a fourth time and was convinced I had failed so took up cutlery design, one piece of mine ending up in Harrods! More in hope than expectation I took an Exhibition at Gray's Inn and passed it.

Against the pomposity of the British system, the US system has a lot to offer. There is no stigma attached to being a defendant and they sit in the most obvious place – alongside their legal representative. That must also be introduced here.

It is quite extraordinary that there is no transcript of the trial available to anyone unless they are prepared to pay a huge amount of money for it. If defence lawyers want a record of what is said in court then they have to arrange for someone to take notes – usually a junior who doesn't know shorthand. The official shorthand notes are taken by a private company and like all other products of private companies, they are sold. The figure quoted to Talat Sarwar's defence, £3000, for a comparatively short trial, is the going rate. Transcripts of longer trials cost *pro rata*.

In the Guildford Four case, investigations into the possible corruption of police witnesses was thrown into disarray because there was no copy of the official trial transcript available. As one person put it: 'How can you charge a person with perjury when you can't prove what they said in court?' Trial transcripts must be a matter of public record and available on request.

After a jury has been selected for a trial it is given virtually no instruction but told to choose a foreman and get on with it. There must be proper instruction to jurors on their role in the proceedings and they must be encouraged to participate. If they have questions they should feel free and confident in asking them. In the first Orgreave 'riot' trial, one juror did the unthinkable and passed a written message to the judge during an instance when the court was trying to recognise a police inspector from some rather blurred, coloured photographs. There had been other pictures implicating the inspector in serious acts of violence but in this particular and important shot his face was obscured. There appeared to be no other way of recognising him. The juror's note simply said, 'Do all inspectors wear brown gloves?' The answer was yes and sure enough the brown gloves could just be detected. It was a valuable contribution to the case.

At the moment, jurors are not encouraged to ask questions and they are positively discouraged from taking notes. Judges frequently tell jurors that note taking will interfere with their ability to assess the demeanour of a witness. This must also change and they must be encouraged to become an active part of the proceedings.

There should be two spare jurors, again as in the US, in case of illness or accident. These 'ghost' jurors should participate in the same way as the other twelve but would be excluded from the jury's deliberations. If they were required as replacements they would then join in with the jurors' debates.

Some trials prove painfully harrowing for many witnesses, particularly murder, abuse and rape cases. They often describe the ordeal of giving evidence as being worse than their original experience. It is not uncommon to see young or vulnerable people emotionally taken apart on the witness stand when their only intention was to provide a testimony as to what they had seen or experienced. There is nothing to prepare such witnesses for the ordeal they have to undertake and absolutely no support or counselling once they leave the witness stand. They can be distraught, tearful and hurt but they have nowhere to go but out of the door and into the street. That is something else which ought to change. Admirable but poorly resourced facilities, witness support schemes, have been established at some London Crown Courts.

The present system has endured for centuries while everything else around us has changed. Even a few decades ago, working-class children would be dressed up in their Sunday best for a visit to the doctor because of the elevated status held by doctors. Fortunately that attitude has changed but still the judiciary and many lawyers try to cling on to practices and customs which are part of a privileged past.

The real issue facing us is the best way to improve justice. I suggest that all the changes I have outlined are vitally needed in pursuit of that goal.

TWENTY

The Seat of Judgement

There are many great questions in life which confound intellectual analysis and are almost impossible to answer. 'How long is a piece of string?' is one of them. 'How are judges chosen?' is another. How they operate is a fairly baffling mystery as the handling of Talat Sarwar's case shows, but how they are chosen is a conundrum worthy of Ruth Rendell.

It would be fair to say that the present system for appointing judges has emerged from the complete dark ages when, like mushrooms in the night, judges simply appeared. We now have that great British substitute for democracy and accountability, the nudge and the wink.

That isn't to say that the whole field has become open and people can choose to be judges as they would choose to become an engineer or a teacher or a social worker. No, that would be far too visible and what's more, it might lead to a diminution of power for existing judges, a reduction in privileges and even the loss of a few jobs.

As the Lord Chancellor, Lord Mackay, so succinctly puts it: 'Those who are appointed (as judges) are the best qualified to deal with these matters.' In other words, the self-perpetuation of like choosing like will continue regardless of the seniority of the post and the power it wields over society.

A perfect example is the appointment of Lord Justice Bingham as Master of the Rolls in August 1992. So out of touch with the judiciary is the majority of the population that it's doubtful if more than a tiny percentage could actually say what the Master of the Rolls does. In truth he holds a powerful and influential post, one of the most powerful judicial posts in the country, and heads the civil division of the Court of Appeal. The position was once held by Lord Denning, whose name most people do know.

Officially, Lord Justice Bingham was appointed by the Prime Minister, John Major, 'after wide consultations, the details of which are secret'. As the act of a government which claims it is committed to an open society, it is laughable. Whom did the Prime Minister consult, who else was in the running, what qualities were sought, who made the final recommendation? Why should the details of the consultation remain secret?

The reality is that all judges are chosen in a similar cloak-and-dagger manner, regardless of the importance of the office. What actually happens is that senior judges recognise someone they believe will possibly make a judge. How they arrive at this decision is unknown and in what forum they discuss the proposal is equally obscure but, nevertheless, they make a choice – 'and he made them in his own image' would be a good biblical summary of the event.

The name is then passed to the Lord Chancellor who approaches the nominated person and in an informal way asks him (and it usually is a him) if he fancies having a go at being a judge. If he accepts and is approved then he undergoes a one week course, sits alongside another judge for a couple of weeks before sitting in his own right – in the first instance for twenty days a year.

There are a number of constants which apply to nearly all judges. For a start they are almost exclusively chosen from the ranks of the Bar, they are almost always men, they are almost always middle-aged, they are almost always white and because of where they are recruited they are almost always middle class.

There is a hierarchy for judges, beginning at the top with the High Court and descending down to the District judges. There are 84 High Court judges of which 80 per cent are Oxbridge. Three of them are women. Of the 471 Circuit judges, 21 are women. There are 781

Recorders of which 43 are women and 440 Assistant Recorders, 38 of which are women. Of the 243 District judges, twelve are women. Of all judges, less than 1 per cent are black or from ethnic backgrounds.

The imbalance is obvious but the answer is not simply to appoint more women and more black people if those appointees bring a similar set of experiences and prejudices to the job. For instance, in a recent television interview, one of the few high-ranking female judges, Dame Elizabeth Butler-Sloss, was able to show amazingly blinkered vision without really trying. When asked if the judiciary had been hurt by the recent spate of miscarriages, she replied: 'I haven't heard such criticism of the existing system as to think it needs to be changed. There's a great danger, particularly these days, of change for change's sake. I think there are areas where we need to change and improve but I don't know that the judiciary is one of them.'

In the same interview she had already replied: 'Oh really, is that right? I'm never quite sure,' when told by the interviewer how much she earned. While the rest of the population shakes its head in disbelief at the state of criminal justice; while economic mismanagement and Conservative dogma cut a swathe of poverty and unemployment through society, this particular judge believes that she leads an 'ordinary life' and is not out of touch with the wider world.

In the top echelons of the judiciary, the High Court, there are three female judges and the latest to be appointed, by the Lord Chancellor, Lord Mackay, created history: Judge Ann Ebsworth is the first woman High Court judge not to be assigned to family law cases. In fact she sits in the Queen's Bench Division.

One change which has come about in the selection of judges is that it is now permissible to apply to the Lord Chancellor and actually ask if you can become a judge. The one pace forward of these changes is more than counterbalanced by the two paces back which allow the Lord Chancellor to turn the application down flat without an interview or any need to provide a reason for the refusal. And so the control over who shall or shall not become a judge remains unaltered.

That our judicial system should be so archaic is disturbing; that anachronistic, privileged and sheltered judges should have the power

they do is alarming. There is a misconception that a trial is played out
in a courtroom, a kind of adversarial saga performed in front of a jury
and at the end of the day it is the jury which makes its mind up on the
basis of the facts alone. The role of the judge is simply to advise the
jury on matters of law. If only!

I'm going to return to the case of the Birmingham Six, not because the
conduct of that case was exceptional but rather because it was common-
place. Despite the time which has elapsed, the judge responsible, Judge
Bridge, has only just retired and has been ennobled to become Lord
Bridge of Harwich. And in the bizarre world of the judiciary he hasn't
really retired at all but at the (current) age of seventy-three will still
make an occasional appearance in the seat of judgement.

Mr Justice Bridge, as he then was, made a meal of the summing-
up in this case, such a meal that it lasted for nearly three days and in
transcript took up some 300 pages. In time and detail this summing up
was not unusual. Its content, approach and thrust was no different from
summings-up in many cases I hear today. Many of the judiciary still see
it as part of their role to steer and cajole the jury into the verdict which
they believe to be correct or the one they believe is necessary.

One accusation which could never be levelled at Lord Bridge was
that he was not frank. In his opening remarks to the jury, he set his stall
out very clearly: 'Members of the jury, some judges tell juries that . . .
they will express no views of their own on the weight of the evidence or
on the conclusions which may or may not be drawn from the facts, they
will be utterly detached and utterly objective in their consideration of
the facts.

'I never say that to any jury because I think that it is attributing to
oneself a superhuman capacity. I do not think that any of us can be
detached. We all see things differently but I have naturally formed an
impression of the conclusions to which the evidence leads, as I dare
say some of you already have and I think, however hard a judge tries
to be impartial inevitably his presentation of the case, his summary of
the evidence, is bound to be coloured by his own views.

'So I am of the opinion, not shared by all my brothers on the
bench, that if a judge has formed a clear view it is much better to let

the jury see that and say so and not pretend to be a kind of Olympian detached observer and try to hide the views that one has formed . . .'

And, of course, he didn't! In a careful, almost total, demolition of every defence witness and the lauding, sometimes verging on deification, of prosecution witnesses, the jury was corralled into the guilty pen as though driven by a diligent sheepdog.

At the start of his summing-up he ensured that the jury's emotions were honed and polished:

'As you have heard in the course of the evidence, feelings ran very high, not surprisingly when you reflect that twenty-one persons lost their lives and one hundred and sixty-one were injured.

'To us, that grim roll call of one hundred and eighty-two victims are no more than names on schedules but it does not require very much imagination, does it, to translate the names on those schedules into terms of all the human grief and suffering which they represent and all so senseless. Tragic, yes, but what in God's name did the explosions achieve?'

None of this has anything to do with matters of law nor even matters of fact and should form no part of a judge's summing-up. Of course, the more a judge can include a jury in his thinking, the more he can show them what a jolly reasonable and nice chap he is, the more he can ingratiate himself with them perhaps the more chance there is that they will listen to him: 'Now I turn to the facts, members of the jury. I do not know about you but when I open a book, having read the preface, the next thing I see is the contents. In any serious book I like to see the scheme of the work before I get into detail, so may I outline in detail the scheme of my summing-up so you can see how I'm trying to present the picture and I will call them chapter headings!'

Perhaps the most bizarre twist of all was the judge's assessment of how the jury should determine which scientist was accurate and which wasn't. Firstly he tried his own hand at interpreting scientific evidence, but not too successfully: 'I am sorry, I have lost the thread of what I was saying. May I start the sentence again? Mr Field-Evans argues that if you find ammonium and nitrate on one hand, as Dr Black did in the case of Power, and you find nitrate in isolation, without identifying any ammonium ions, on the other hand, the presence of nitrate alone in some way detracts from the significance of the presence of ammonium and nitrate on the other hand as a pointer to the subject having handled commercial explosives containing the compound of ammonium nitrate . . .'

But not to be defeated, he knew precisely how to make the best sense of these complicated arguments: 'Members of the jury, the resolution of scientific argument of this sort is difficult, particularly difficult for a jury of lay people, and I say once again that I am not going to try and go into the technicalities in detail because I would be in great danger of misleading you. The only way you can resolve these differences is by your impression of the witnesses. Use any technical knowledge you may have but I suspect that in the end you will judge primarily by your impression of the witness.'

It beggars belief that a jury was, effectively, told not to bother about the factual evidence of witnesses' testimonies but to judge them on how they looked and how they sounded. In this instance the scientific witnesses were middle-class professionals so the impression they made on each individual member of the jury would be somewhat subjective. But it doesn't take a huge leap of imagination to realise what effect this attitude could have if one of the witnesses were working-class, black, campily homosexual or bizarrely dressed.

Just in case impressionism wasn't sufficient to point the jury in the right direction when it came to assessing the evidence of scientific witnesses, Judge Bridge gave them more than a little nudge of his own. It's important to remember that the prosecution's case against the Birmingham Six was largely based on only two contentions – the scientific evidence and their own confessions. On that basis the scientific evidence assumes enormous importance.

'. . . the forensic scientists were able to infer so much that one is lost in admiration for the precision of their science . . .'

The scientist to whom Mr Justice Bridge was largely aiming these remarks was Dr Frank Skuse, later to be totally discredited for his role in this and other cases, and to be retired early from the forensic service. Perhaps science does require more than impressionism. But he continued: 'Dr Skuse is a Bachelor of Science, a Doctor of Philosophy and a forensic scientist employed as such at the Home Office forensic science laboratory for this area. He is a man whose working life is spent detecting the evidential value of such samples as can be found, for example, by swabbing a man's hands to see if they have been in contact with explosives. The evaluation of the evidential significance of samples of the kind he took in this case is part of his everyday work, and you heard from him of the many experiments he has carried out on his own hands in particular to try and exclude the possibility that the kind of positive results he relies on may be produced by what is referred to in the evidence as spurious substances. He has given evidence in many similar cases.'

Just in case the jury should be of the inclination that, after all, Dr Skuse was a witness for the police and they should therefore treat him as a prosecution witness, Judge Bridge had an addendum: 'Of course, just as Dr Skuse in this case has said, "some of my results were negative and some were positive" – and I therefore say that it is not fair to call him a prosecution witness. . . .'

The defence scientist, Dr Black, in his evidence cast doubt upon the reliability of the tests used by Dr Skuse and therefore stood to puncture the rather inflated position of infallibility bestowed on Dr Skuse by the trial judge. The situation was remedied in the summing up: 'What is his experience, however, in the very different field of forensic science, a rather specialised field of detecting the evidential significance of infinitesimal traces of various substances? I hope I am not being unfair to Dr Black but we do not need to look beyond his own admissions to see how very limited his experience in that field is.'

One of the most common approaches of judges during their summing-up is to say something which indicates precisely what they think of a particular piece of evidence or a witness and then benignly to back-track from it, as though they have been ever so slightly naughty. In demolishing John Walker as a witness, Judge Bridge did precisely that. A man called Murray also stood trial with the Birmingham Six but was found guilty on other charges. He had exercised his right to question Walker. Judge Bridge summed up this action with the following words.

'The inhibition against cross-examining co-defendants was only lifted in the case of Walker, and that presumably because the evidence of Walker was too much even for Murray to stomach but, member, of the jury, if that is an unfair comment, disregard it.'

He also attempted to demolish Paddy Hill in a similar manner: 'You will remember Hill very vividly as a witness. He was very forth-right in the manner in which he gave evidence. Some might have said that he was perhaps a little arrogant in the manner in which he gave his evidence. But that is a matter entirely for you.' This is one of the most frequently used anodyne phrases but it is often reversed: 'It is a matter for you, members of the jury, but you may think . . .'

From the very beginning of the trial, all six defendants had main-tained that their confessions had either been beaten or frightened out of them. Alongside the sketchy scientific evidence against them, it was the only ammunition held by the prosecution. Whether the jury believed the Six or not was vital to this second plank of the prosecution's case.

'Mr Skinner, in his final address to you, likened the police behaviour alleged by the defendants to that of Hitler's Gestapo. In my recollection, Hitler's Gestapo did not bother with confessions. They were going to execute you whatever you said. But my mind went even further back in history. It seems to me that the kind of treatment to which, as they say, these defendants were subjected was reminiscent of the days of the Star Chamber, the rack and the thumbscrew under the Tudor monarchs of this country about four hundred years ago.'

The Six had also consistently maintained that they were first beaten into signing confessions in the police station and were then beaten again when they were admitted to prison on remand. Judge Bridge had views on this: 'But the other plain implication from the circumstances that these men were, as they clearly were, attacked in prison, is that if the defendants' complaints of serious assaults upon them by police officers are true then the attack in Winson Green prison came as a Godsend to the police, because, but for the attack in Winson Green prison, which the police could not have anticipated, then inevitably what the police had done would have been exposed . . . There would have been an enquiry, no doubt, disciplinary proceedings and very probably criminal proceedings and many police officers' careers in London – very senior police officers' careers – would have been blighted if indeed a number of them would not have finished up in prison.'

One by one Judge Bridge went through each retraction of the confessions and, on the basis not of fact or law but of conjecture, tried successfully to demolish the rebuttals.

'The other question is this: if the police in this case are the double-time villains which they are painted as being by these defendants, why should two police officers waste practically a whole morning interviewing a suspect and recording in a long-hand note a perfectly innocuous account of what Hunter now says is a perfectly truthful version of his movements on that Thursday?'

The naive assumption that if police are going to lie then every single thing they say will be a lie is difficult to comprehend. Similarly incomprehensible is the belief that the police, when they are lying, which they were in this case, are not capable of subtlety: 'You may think it odd – it is a matter entirely for you – that if the police are inventing all the incriminating parts of the evidence which they put forward, they should have had the subtle artistry to, in Hunter's case, single out these two different reactions: at one moment arrogant defiance, at another moment remorse at the realisation of the horror of what he had done, to which he had been a party.

'Once again, as with the other two cases I have dealt with, I remind you of the extent of the conflict between Hunter on the one hand and the police officers on the other. If Hunter is telling the truth then the following officers are certainly telling lies: superintendent Reade, inspector Moore, sergeant Buckley of the Lancashire police, sergeant Millichamp, detective constable Bell, sergeant Morris, sergeant Ball and chief superintendent Robinson.'

It was a similar assessment in the case of Billy Power: 'If Power is telling the truth, then the officers who are directly telling lies are, of course, Watson and French, Kelly and Brand . . . Ingram and Pinder . . . the assistant chief constable and, indirectly, superintendent Reade.'

Of Hughie Callaghan, Judge Bridge was almost dismissive: 'What happened in Callaghan's case was that a fist shaken under his chin and the threat that he would be beaten up were sufficient to induce him to agree to everything that the police suggested.'

Such a dismissal of an environment of fear, oppression and intimidation reveals either disingenuity or a total lack of understanding of what it means to be arrested under this type of circumstance. It is the kind of attitude which leads to rape cases being dismissed because the victim exhibits no evidence of assault.

But perhaps the finest extract from the whole summing-up is one desperate attempt to support the validity of the confessions and to make the evidence fit the prosecution's scenario. It is the perfect illustration of a presumption of guilt. The confessions made by the men differed in considerable detail from the reality, almost certainly because at the time police concocted the confessions they were not in possession of the full facts from the scene of the explosions. In one instance, Hughie Callaghan 'confessed' to leaving bombs outside one of the pubs. In fact they had exploded inside but this didn't deter Judge Bridge.

'... it is a common experience, at least for those of us who are in court day in day out, that men often seek release from their inner tensions by making confessions. It also teaches us that when they make confessions they are not always necessarily either accurate or complete in what they say.

'Men are often ... anxious to minimise their own fault, their own blameworthiness. They are often anxious to show that someone else has really induced them against their better judgement to do what they have done, to shift the main responsibility on to someone else's shoulders. Read through if you will ... the statements of Power and Walker in particular to see whether you can detect that psychological process at work.

'Again, could that not account for Callaghan saying that the bombs planted at the Mulberry Bush had been planted not inside but outside the pub. When he realised, if you remember, what a state he was in, the enormity of what had happened and how many people had been killed and injured because the explosive device had been planted in the pub, would it not be a way of seeking to minimise the extent of his own responsibility?'

These few quotes from the many pages of comment are not selected carefully but almost at random. It is possible to open the transcript of the summing-up at any page and find comments like these. As Arielle Jarret, the US defence attorney put it: 'If this were the US, I would be looking at this document for reversible error. I have done just that and there's at least one on almost every one of the three hundred pages.'

Reversible error would indicate misdirection by the judge and would be grounds for the defence attorney to have the verdict set aside and a new trial ordered.

Now, seventeen years later, the convictions of the Birmingham Six have been found to be unsafe. The system failed to protect them from conviction. Who is responsible? Is it Lord Bridge? 'I feel unhappy but I don't feel guilty, no!' Striking a dispassionate, third-party pose he maintains: 'Yes, I suppose the judiciary have to bear a share of the responsibility. I think it's very difficult. It's easy to be wise after the event as to who was responsible for what went wrong. I don't think it is the most important question. The important question is how do we prevent it happening in the future. It's water under the bridge!'

Water under the bridge? Of the string of policemen named by Lord Bridge as being in collusion, not a word; of the very senior officers who would be in prison should the defendants have been telling the truth, not a word; of the unreliable and inaccurate forensic evidence, not a word; of the lack of disclosure of evidence, not a word; of his own directions to the jury to return a guilty verdict, not a word. In one sense he is right, that now the most important question is, how do we prevent it from happening in the future? And on this subject, not a word!

The truth is that within our secretive and closed judiciary there are no means whereby any judge can be called to account for the decisions he or she takes, there are no known methods of discipline or of being called to account for error, neglect or negligence. A sexual indiscretion can lead to their being asked to fall on their sword, do the honourable thing and retire but to contribute to the wrongful conviction of a person will pass without comment.

Juries are daily faced with a bewigged man dressed in red, who has all the authority of the judiciary behind him, who belittles the defence to such an extent that there is really little or no option for that jury. And that is really what happened in the Birmingham Six case and again in the case of the Guildford Four and many, many other cases. But it does not have to be like that. It does not require a revolution, it can be stopped tomorrow.

Firstly, judges should be given no discretion whatsoever in the case of confessions. If there is no corroboration there should be no prosecution. If the preconditions for admissibility are not met the confession is automatically excluded. Perhaps even more importantly, judges should have absolutely no right to make any comment at all, at any stage of the proceedings, about the witnesses, their defence or anything else. This is a situation which already exists in the United States where judges do not sum up on the facts and do not make comments, in fact they are allowed only to sum up on the law and nothing else – a situation which should pertain here.

To gain an insight into how the case of the Birmingham Six would have been handled in the US, I showed a copy of Lord Bridge's summing up to Judge Joan Carey, who practises in Manhattan. She was first appointed a judge at the age of thirty-seven and so has seventeen years' experience in the job at an age where she might just have a toe on the first rung of the judicial ladder had she worked in Britain. Like many American judges, she had followed the case of the Birmingham Six so the details were not completely new to her.

'I believe that the Birmingham Six case would never have been brought to trial in the US. For a start they would never have been held in custody on the evidence which existed because they simply had nothing to articulate and there was no just cause.

'Police can't go from one stage of questioning to the next stage without reasonable evidence. They have to state certain facts to justify that and the evidence required from them grows as they move from one stage to another. You really can't go very far without an identification and you just can't scoop people off the streets and hold them for long periods. From what I have read of the case, the discrepancies are so clear that they couldn't possibly have been the men. For instance, Hill had many previous convictions for petty larceny and he is precisely the kind of man the IRA have never used and never would use.

'The defence solicitors appeared to do no kind of investigation whatsoever and sounded to me as though they were afraid of the judge. The confessions were not in synchronisation with what happened. All the way along the line everyone kept adding to this atmosphere, this circus.

'The silence of the police was unbelievable with so many different crime squads involved, so many different ranks of policemen. It's extraordinary that no one broke the vow of silence. It simply could not happen here!'

One of the things which struck Judge Carey most forcibly was that throughout the whole of Judge Bridge's summing-up there was not one mention of the presumption of innocence only a mention of the need for proof beyond a reasonable doubt. This was particularly surprising to her considering the time he took to deliver his summing-up – three days. The summing-up of the case she prepared for me would have taken somewhere between one and a half and two hours to deliver.

'It is extremely important that a person be presumed innocent. It is the person who points the finger, the person who brings the charge, the person who brings the accusation, that's where the burden stays, not with anyone else. Nobody should ever be required to prove his or her innocence.

'Certainly in my role as a judge I would never attempt to steer a jury towards a particular verdict and if I attempted it I know that the defence lawyers would be rubbing their hands together, thinking, "reversible error, reversible error!"

'Judges in this country say very little about the facts, if anything at all. I make it very clear to a jury immediately that in order for me to give any credibility to the oath which I have been sworn to uphold, the facts are not my job. I have no opinion in respect to the facts, the jury members are the sole and exclusive judges of the facts and no one can take that role away from them, certainly not the court.

'I think our system works. I think that giving the facts to the jury, the peers of the accused and the peers of the witnesses, and allowing them to make all the decisions with respect to the facts is the right way. If a judge takes a truly impartial position during the course of a trial, just gives the jury the law and lets them apply the law to the facts, you very often come up with the right result. Sometimes for the wrong reasons but under the proper guidelines and the proper guidance from an impartial court, you come up with the right result.

'In the Birmingham case, H.H. Judge Bridge spoke of the two items which he said were the most important and most damaging pieces of evidence – which was the forensic evidence and the confession statements. And from that point on he started talking about the credibility of witnesses. You can go through page after page of the record and it's clear that he found – and gave the impression to the jury – that the defendants were obviously incredible and the police were extremely credible witnesses.

'In my opinion, that summing-up amounted to Judge Bridge telling the jurors to find the defendants guilty.'

Judge Carey was appointed to her role openly and publicly, selected by the State on the basis of her knowledge of the law, her litigation experience, on her merit: 'Black members and many more women are now sitting on the judiciary and many of them are younger people. For quite a few years the attitude in this country has been that being a judge should not be a retiring position. People should bring to it a certain youthful quality and an interest in things other than going to clubs and having sabbaticals. We are interested in an energetic workday and the merit selection process has brought that about.'

The judiciary I would like to see in Britain is much closer to the US model than the anachronistic system we currently have, one which enshrines power and privilege and does not serve the people well.

I would like to see a system in which judges are not culled almost exclusively from the ranks of the Bar but come from all walks of life. Being a judge should be a normal career structure like any other which you decide on when you leave school. It should be no different to deciding to become an engineer, a doctor or a social worker and judges should be open to public scrutiny and accountable, subjected to the control of a Ministry of Justice.

Of course, this is precisely what many of the Law Lords want to avoid because there will be no guarantee that they are the ones who finish up with the power and the jobs. However, we shouldn't have to wait for even more miscarriages before these people begin to feel the wind of change on the back of their necks. The present Lord Chancellor envisages only creeping change to the judiciary by adding the occasional woman or sometimes a black person to the ranks and perhaps sometimes even a radical. It is essentially done to allay people's fears and seemingly to put the judicial house in order prior to the findings of the Royal Commission. It does not reflect a desire to provide the public with a judiciary which represents a cross-section of society. Lord Mackay has dissociated himself from any such concept that the judiciary should perform this role.

Such a proposition as mine is neither outrageous nor unique. In France a similar system already operates and it operates well. The *juge d'instruction* is a part of that system.

The French magistrature is divided into two branches: there are the 'sitting judges', those who physically sit in the courtroom and decide and pass sentence and these judges are, in theory at any rate, independent of the executive and legislative powers and their independence is guaranteed by the President of the Republic.

The second group are the Prosecutors of the Republic and come under the auspices of the Ministry of Justice. They are commonly referred to as 'standing judges' as that is precisely what they do in court when they make their contribution. While they are part of the court's hierarchical structure and are obliged to respect that, they are, again in theory at any rate, free to speak out and have their own opinions. They can, if they wish, specialise in areas such as juvenile, matrimonial or probation. The *juge d'instruction* comes in this category as does the public prosecutor.

Initially they are appointed for a period of three years to one particular court but can remain for much longer than this. To uphold the principle of independence a *juge d'instruction* can't be moved except at their own request. The prosecutor doesn't have this protection.

There is a career structure and it starts at the National School for Magistrates either in Bordeaux or Paris. Anyone with a suitable degree from university and under twenty-seven years of age can apply to become one of the 250 students who are accepted each year. Once accepted they become an *auditeur de justice*.

The course lasts for two-and-a-half years, with one year spent in class and another in court. During this time a student learns the functions of both judge and prosecutor. In the remaining six months, the *auditeur de justice* works with organisations such as the police, *gendarmerie*, the Bar, prisons and even private companies.

I am not advocating the wholesale adoption of the French system nor even the system of *juge d'instruction* without some amendments. But I believe there is a deep malaise at the heart of our criminal justice system which cannot be cured by tinkering at the edges. The judiciary must be more in touch with ordinary people and represent their interests rather than the perceived interests of the state. This can only happen when they no longer constitute a part of the state and its controlling powers.

While we are heading towards a criminal justice system based on cost effectiveness, where the only debate is about costs and not the delivery of justice, there are systems which are moving in the other direction. In a recent French parliamentary debate, the budget of the Ministry of Justice was raised. The debate finished with almost unanimous approval of the statement, 'Justice is much more a virtue than a bureaucracy!' It couldn't happen here.

TWENTY-ONE

The Court of Appeal

Perhaps the one thing for which Talat Sarwar should be most grateful is that he wasn't found guilty and did not have to rely on the Court of Appeal to correct the verdict.

'There are many innocent people in prison who have more chance of being released by Hezbollah than by the Appeal Court!' These were the words of Mark Braithwaite after being released from prison and cleared of the murder of P.C. Keith Blakelock. On that day of his release, which followed a long and vociferous public campaign, he added: 'Today is not jubilation. I haven't won a raffle. This is my life. This is not happy. This is bitter.'

The reality is that he may well have stood a better chance had the appeal system been a raffle rather than what it appears to have become – a means of reinforcing bad decisions reached in lower courts. And just as Hezbollah, in the end, did deliver the people it had falsely imprisoned so the Court of Appeal does sometimes disgorge innocent people who should not be in prison. More often than not, it does not.

This book has been about many different aspects of the criminal justice system where change is vitally needed but nowhere is change more necessary than in the present system of appeal.

After a trial has been held there is a period of twenty-eight days in which the verdict can be appealed. There are essentially two grounds; on a point of law, the basis for which is that it is felt the judge got something wrong. It could be that he excluded evidence which should have been allowed or allowed evidence which should have been excluded. The second ground is that of fresh evidence. Nowhere in this book will I address the first area which should be left to judges to determine. In the case of fresh evidence, however, there must be a fundamental reappraisal of how the system operates.

If material was available to the defence at the time of the trial but wasn't called then it is up to the defence to explain why. Their reasons may not be accepted. There are other fundamental problems surrounding fresh evidence, one of the biggest being how it is defined. There is currently a big debate about what should and shouldn't be allowed.

For me, the situation is relatively clear. If fresh evidence is relevant and not incredible it means that the original jury must have therefore reached a decision on only some of the evidence. But the situation with fresh evidence is that it does not go back in front of a jury but is considered by judges who, because the Act is so loosely worded, have only to decide whether the original verdict was safe and satisfactory. In performing this task they substitute themselves for a jury 'here and now' rather than assessing what effect the fresh evidence might have had on the original jury. This is a factual decision which I believe only jurors are equipped to take and therefore this decision must be removed from the Court of Appeal.

After a conviction a defendant has twenty-eight days to submit an application for leave to appeal. Once out of time or after an unsuccessful application or appeal the only course left is to go to the Home Office. The Home Secretary has the power to refer a case to the Court of Appeal for their consideration. This is a laborious, time-consuming route, and the Home Office has not established a large, efficient, well-resourced miscarriages department capable of taking its own initiative. The final decision to refer will depend greatly upon the incumbent Home Secretary – Kenneth Clarke demonstrating a real reluctance to have matters reopened – (Bentley and Carl Bridgewater). It is no wonder that one of his predecessors, Douglas Hurd, felt the time had come to remove this function from the Home Office.

I believe there should be a standing commission for fresh evidence cases with its own secretariat, its own investigations department and its own legal department and to which aggrieved parties can take a fresh evidence case. They will get the trial papers together and will have the authority to initiate their own cases. The only criteria will be that the fresh evidence must be relevant to an issue in the case and might have affected the outcome; it must not be incredible or fabricated.

If it is unopposed then the jury will rubber-stamp the appeal purely on the basis of a paper hearing but if opposed there will be a hearing. At this hearing, both sides will be represented to argue the relevance and credibility of the fresh evidence and a jury of lay people will make the decision, which is no more than they do every day of the week in any criminal trial.

I firmly believe that appeal cases should not be heard by judges or even a judge, not even at arms' length. Judges should have nothing to do with them for the reason that the presumption of guilt again comes into play and they cannot be trusted to deal with the facts in a fair manner. In fact I think the powers of the Court of Appeal to hear fresh evidence cases should be ended completely.

Although gradually being diminished, still our system pays lip service, in most serious cases, to the need for an accused person to be tried in front of a jury of his or her peers. When it comes to appeal, despite the fact that it requires new evidence to be considered and despite the fact that witnesses may be called to present that evidence, none of it takes place in front of a jury. That has to be altered. It is again the Birmingham Six case which illustrates the need for such change and again it is important to stress that this case is not the exception.

Breda Power, Billy Power's daughter and one of the guiding lights in the sixteen-year-long campaign to free the men, sat through the first appeal, held in 1987. It made an indelible impression on her: 'The atmosphere was not nice at all, you could cut it with a knife. It seemed to me that the judges treated the men's defence team very badly – at the time I thought they were cruelly treated. The judges kept interrupting them every couple of minutes and they pretended not to understand even the most simple detail, making them repeat it over again. With the prosecution, on the other hand, they treated them as though their case was flawless. It was heartbreaking to watch.

'There were completely new witnesses. There was Tom Clarke, the ex-policeman man who said that the six had been subjected to intimidation and violence at the police station. His evidence was dismissed as the product of bitterness. There was Joyce Lynas, a policewoman who said she had seen the six beaten by police. Her evidence was also dismissed as was her report of having been telephoned at night and threatened during the course of the appeal. Even when Dr Frank Skuse contradicted himself in court and it was conceded that tests he carried out were not specific to nitroglycerine but could give similar results if someone had been touching playing cards or cigarette packets, even this was dismissed as not being of any consequence.

'At the original trial it was stressed that the two main planks of the prosecution's case was the confession evidence and the forensic evidence. And here were witnesses throwing serious doubt on both these aspects.

'But the cruellest part of the appeal was the last day when the judges said they would come back with a verdict after Christmas. Although since the opening hours in court we had thought there was no hope, suddenly this delay to consider the evidence gave us fresh hope – not much faith but an awful lot of hope. If there wasn't a chance, why delay?

'When we came back on 28 January, six weeks later, Lord Lane turned down the appeal with those, by now, famous words: "The longer this hearing has gone on the more convinced this court has become that the verdict of the jury (in the original trial) was correct." Why did they make us go through the whole of Christmas and January thinking there was a chance when obviously the whole thing was cut and dried?

'Although I'm only in my twenties, I have now watched many important cases very closely and I think the rot runs from the very bottom to the top of the system but I think it is the judges who are most to blame. If you get a trial judge who is biased and strongly influences a jury then the result is obvious. The only remedy is appeal where you go before not one judge but three with no jury and that makes the situation even worse. It seems that the main aim of the judges is to cover up for what went wrong rather than trying to put it right.'

That is one person's view which will no doubt be dismissed as impressionistic and biased by some. But compare Breda Power's views with those of one of the judges who has been involved in and has commented on the case – not just any old judge but the then Master of the Rolls, Lord Denning, one of the most powerful judges in the country. Halting the Birmingham Six's civil action against the police for assault in 1980, he said: 'If the six men win, it will mean that the police were guilty of perjury, that they were guilty of violence and threats and that the convictions were erroneous . . . This is such an appalling vista that every person in the land would say: "It cannot be right that these actions should go any further." '

That on its own is probably one of the most undemocratic, impressionistic and biased views ever uttered by a judge but to prove that it was no momentary aberration nor simply the unguarded comment of a normally fair and concerned judge, he managed to improve on it in 1988 when he said, again in reference to the Birmingham Six and the growing clamour for their release: 'It is better that some innocent men remain in jail than the integrity of the English judicial system be impugned.'

The greatest condemnation of any judicial system is that it should imprison innocent people, allow them little chance of redressing the balance and then place the interests of that system above the interests of those it was designed to protect. That is perhaps one of the most compelling reasons why the whole system of appeal must be changed.

There are those, of course, who present the recent discovery of so many miscarriages as a triumph for the English system of criminal justice and as proof that the Court of Appeal does work. The truth is, had we waited for the judicial system to correct the injustices in many of these cases, the innocent people involved would still be behind bars.

It wasn't the Appeal Court who got them out in the end, it wasn't the judicial system, it wasn't lawyers and it wasn't the Home Office. It was, in the case of the Birmingham Six, because a television company as far back as 1985 commissioned research which cast doubt on the forensic evidence; it was because they persisted in the investigation without any contribution from legal aid; it was because Gareth Peirce the defence solicitor gave up a lot of time without payment to pad around the streets hour after hour, to dig up the evidence to present to the Home Secretary – again because legal aid was lacking; it was because for sixteen years, families and friends journeyed from one end of the country to the other, over and over again, campaigning and working ceaselessly to draw attention to what had happened.

That is why these men were released, it is why the Guildford Four were released, it is why the Maguire Seven were released, it is why the Tottenham Three were released. These cases were not proof that the appeal system works but that public pressure works.

While the eventual release of these innocent victims says a huge amount about the faith and energy and determination of ordinary people, it says nothing about the ability of the judicial system to correct its mistakes. It is a huge sadness that it requires people to join together to correct miscarriages. We should have a system after all these years that doesn't require the public to stand up and risk themselves on the streets of London and Paris and wherever else they had to go to campaign. The system should have in-built safeguards.

I believe that in the forefront of these safeguards should be a system which depends upon lay people, precisely the same type of people who constitute the original jury. Instead of twelve as in the original jury, there should be a review panel comprised of six but they should be selected in exactly the same way that a jury is selected. They will form part of a standing commission empowered to deal with fresh evidence appeal cases.

Their first task will be to consider any new material put forward as evidence for appeal. They will have the ability to sift and reject to ensure that an appeal is not frivolous or irrelevant. Just as importantly, they will have the power to initiate their own investigation into a miscarriage in the event of public concern over a case. The case would not necessarily have to be raised by lawyers but could be brought to their attention by third parties such as relatives, journalists or TV programme makers.

This commission will have its own secretariat, its own legal bureau and its own investigative branch which will not be staffed by police. A commission along the lines I have in mind has been successfully established in Hong Kong to investigate corruption within the police and legal institutions.

The present position with the granting of legal aid for appeal cases leaves a lot to be desired. In most of the big miscarriage cases I have written about, there was no legal aid until the cases were actually referred back to the Court of Appeal. The years of slog and investigation were completely unfunded. It is possible occasionally to receive small amounts of aid for specific advice or very particular, small enquiries but it's impossible to have a case referred back without first having done a great deal of the investigative work. That has to change and that work has to be paid for. Few solicitors have the time or resources to take the risk of no remuneration for months of intensive work preparing a fresh evidence case for submission to the Home Secretary.

As part of the panel's deliberations, all the interested parties will be present and represented by advocates if that's what they want. The commission will have the power not only to hear submissions, witnesses and representations but will be able to initiate its own investigations.

When it reaches the end of its investigation it will not normally have the power to declare the innocence of an appellant but simply to decide whether to recommend to the Court of Appeal whether they should order a retrial, a power rarely exercised by the present Court of Appeal.

Speed is of the essence both in reaching a decision about the retrial and in carrying it out. The greater the passage of time after the original trial, the more difficult it is to hold a retrial. Witnesses may well have died, papers may have been lost or destroyed or people's memories may be called into question.

Where too much time has elapsed, as could have been the case with the Guildford Four or the Birmingham Six, the commission will have the power, if they have serious doubt about the original conviction, to recommend to the Court of Appeal that the conviction should be quashed as unsafe and unsatisfactory. There will be no need for a retrial.

Under this system, the Court of Appeal would retain its overall position but would only have the power to uphold convictions when the review panel did not recommend a retrial.

Until ordinary people can have their confidence in the system restored there will be no real justice. By confidence in the system I mean confidence in the people who administer it, the judges and lawyers, and in their commitment to the sanctity of individual rights and freedoms.

Paramount in all this is the presumption of innocence. If people are presumed to be innocent from start to finish, if we keep our eye on that ball and that ball alone, then we have a chance of much-needed and meaningful change. If that right is conjoined with a genuinely democratic form of judicial disposition – by that I mean jury systems with accountability to all of us – then there is real hope for the future.

Through serving on juries or through witnessing the response of the police and others to their decisions, we can monitor the administration of justice. Only this way can we have some confidence that the risks which have been exposed over the past five years or so will never happen again.

We have a Royal Commission currently investigating the state of our criminal justice system and so we are faced with a golden opportunity for change. If it misses this opportunity then in fifteen years' time we may well be witnessing another session of public hand-wringing and embarrassment by the establishment as someone else is released from prison after having been wrongfully convicted.

Of course there is a slight penalty in many of the changes I have advocated that some guilty people may go free. That may be the case but it is infinitely better than innocents being locked behind bars, in brutal and brutalising regimes of custody, for so many years.

TWENTY-TWO

Conclusions

In the short time since this book was begun even more examples of miscarriages of justice and police corruption have emerged, each of them equally disturbing and each of them with common threads running through them. There is the case of Wayne and Paul Darvell, two unemployed and homeless brothers tried and convicted for the murder of a Cardiff sex shop manageress in 1986. The new public protection, the Police and Criminal Evidence Act (PACE), was in operation at the time.

The basis of the appeal was that the judge, jury and the court at the original trial were seriously misled and, in the words of the Lord Chief Justice, '... the integrity of the whole conduct of the original police investigation is thrown into grave doubt.'

What caused this grave doubt was the fact that supposedly contemporaneous notes taken by detective sergeant Jones and detective constable Collins were entered in notebooks, one of which was not issued until two months after the interviews.

Again the technique of electrostatic deposition analysis (ESDA) came to the rescue and showed that D.S. Jones's long witness statement bore impressions showing versions which differed in content from the final version. The conclusion was that far from the interviews with the two accused men being made up from notes taken at the time, they were cribbed from their witness statements.

It was also never revealed in court that Wayne Darvell was highly suggestible and was prone to confessing to crimes he had not and could not have committed. So fantastic were his confessions that he had even admitted to handbag thefts which had taken place while he was in the police station.

But perhaps the most disturbing discrepancy of all was the result of fingerprint analysis of a bloody palm print found close to the dead woman's body. The print was found on a board to which was attached a pay 'phone. It engaged the efforts of eight fingerprint experts for several days and at the end of that time they concluded that it didn't belong to the dead woman nor did it belong to either of the accused. This vital piece of evidence was never produced in court. To add insult to injury the results of these tests were disposed of even before the trial took place despite the obligation to retain indefinitely all photographs, negatives and lists of fingerprints.

Following hard on its heels came another Welsh case, the Cardiff Three, referred to in a previous chapter, and early in 1993 four more were released in the Court of Appeal when the Crown were unable to support the evidence of officers from Stoke Newington in four unrelated drugs cases.

The eighteenth victim of a miscarriage of justice involving terrorist crimes was freed on 11 May 1992 after serving eighteen years, three months and five days in prison for a crime she did not commit. I am pleased to have represented Judith Ward but saddened by the familiar litany of prejudice, incompetence, blinkered vision and arrogance which led to imprisonment. I am angered by the complacency which kept her there. Above all this case reflects the collapse of a criminal justice system in which a young vulnerable woman slips through all the various stages of the preparation of a prosecution and at each stage those responsible make selective decisions about what needs to be disclosed. Without firm clear rules and without an independent check on those rules from the outset it will all happen again.

One of the most disturbing elements of Judith Ward's case is that forensic information held by the prosecution was never revealed at her trial. Her trial preceded the Birmingham Six, the Guildford Four and the Maguire Seven trials and the knowledge which was in the hands of the Crown, had it been revealed, would almost certainly have had a considerable effect on the outcomes of those cases.

The Royal Armament Research and Development Establishment (RARDE) carried out tests, the results of which contradicted the prosecution's claim that Judith Ward must have been handling explosives. They knew that contamination from boot polish and floor polish would produce similar results to traces of explosives. They also determined that it was possible to be innocently contaminated with residues produced from firing an explosive device – Judith Ward was arrested at Euston station hours after an IRA blast there.

Once again Douglas Higgs, principal scientific officer and head of Forensic Section, was to deny knowledge of these results even though some tests were being done just before and as the trial began.

In an historic judgement by the Court of Appeal Glidewell LJ observed that in relation to the boot polish tests Mr Elliott must have known about these results and that it was inconceivable Mr Higgs was unaware of them. 'We reject Mr Higgs' evidence and find that he was fully aware. But Mr Higgs did not want the prosecution and the defence to know about these experiments.' With regard to the firing cell tests Mr Higgs claimed he had forgotten about them and the court considered this to be a 'deliberate falsehood'. 'The consequence is that in a criminal trial involving grave charges three senior government forensic scientists deliberately withheld material experimental data on the grounds it might damage the prosecution case. Moreover Mr Higgs and Mr Berryman misled the court as to the state of their knowledge about the possibility of contamination coming from debris of an explosion . . .

'Three senior RARDE scientists took the law into their own hands, and concealed from the prosecution, the defence and court matters which might have changed the course of the trial. The catalogue of lamentable omissions included failures to reveal actual test results, the failure to reveal discrepant Rf values, the suppression of boot polish experimental data, the misrepresentation of the first firing cell test results, economical witness statements calculated to obstruct enquiry by the defence and most important of all oral evidence at the trial in the course of which senior RARDE scientists knowingly placed a false and distorted scientific picture before the jury. It is in our judgement also a necessary inference that three senior RARDE scientists acted in concert in withholding material evidence.'

The 'lamentable catalogue' of non-disclosure, however, was not confined to forensic scientists. For one reason or another the police, the staff of the Director of Public Prosecutions and counsel who advised them, and the psychiatrists who prepared medical reports on Judith Ward all failed to disclose relevant and material information.

West Yorkshire Police took over 1700 statements but only 225 were forwarded to the DPP. The significance of some of the non-forwarded statements lay in their relevance to a proper assessment of the unreliability of Judith Ward's 'confessions'. Some related to conversations with detective chief superintendent Oldfield, who handled the Yorkshire Ripper case. These conversations were held without the knowledge of Ward's solicitor and were not disclosed.

The staff of the Director of Public Prosecutions decided that other statements, three of which clearly suggested serious shortcomings in the mental welfare of Judith Ward, need not be revealed. Further interviews with her after her arrest were also withheld. They were conducted by detective superintendent Wilson on 15 February 1974, the day after she had been found in a doorway in Liverpool and detained. The defence were told about the existence of the interviews but that they concerned 'antecedent and certain peripheral matters'. Mr Bibby of the DPP phrased the letter on the advice of counsel for the Crown Brian Walsh QC. When cross-examined by me Mr Bibby accepted that the interviews were central to the issues in the case and he could not explain the use of the word 'peripheral'. The court concluded: 'It was wholly wrong for Mr Walsh to draft and for Mr Bibby to adopt the language adviser.' The letter seriously misrepresented the position.

Finally the defence solicitor never saw the psychiatric reports Dr Lawson and Dr Mather prepared for the Crown. The reports indicated a psychiatric problem and the defence solicitor told the Court of Appeal that had he seen them he would have taken that into consideration. These reports described a diagnosis of acute psychiatric depression and attempted suicide. From office diaries produced at the hearing there were entries showing the reports had been sent to the three prosecuting counsels, to the DPP, to New Scotland Yard, to Thames Valley and West Yorkshire Police. In fact everyone save the defence! Furthermore there was a note in the diary about the reports having 'nothing in them'!

Dr Lawson's second report was an attempt to tone down the serious nature of Judith Ward's plight. The court was unable to accept Dr Lawson's new statement that he had signalled his views of the defendant's mental state loud and clear in the first sentence of his opinion. Besides failing to record in the statement a second suicide attempt in August shortly before the trial, of which Dr Lawson had no recollection, 'that sentence records in muted terms Dr Lawson's assessment of the appellant's powers of deception and self-deception but it fails to meet Mr Mansfield's submission that Dr Lawson has put the interests of secrecy and of scrutiny before the interests of the appellant who was his patient.' Dr Lawson admitted that he had not told the appellant's family, let alone her solicitor about the acute psychosis which he had diagnosed. Dr Mather likewise made no mention of the second suicide attempt and gave the impression of a prompt and complete recovery. When asked by the court whether he attached any significance to the second attempt, he said, 'Not particularly because one quite often gets behaviour of attempted suicides and this sort of thing in a large remand prison.'

Glidewell LJ observed: 'these answers are astonishing both in their own right and in the light of the anxiety caused by the earlier court cutting incident.'

This lamentable catalogue resulted in a conviction but those who committed the offences went free. Encompassed in this one case is much of what this book is about. There is here still grave cause for concern.

And what is the response of the new Director of Public Prosecutions, Barbara Mills QC? It is this: 'Disclosure is in the forefront of prosecutors' minds. The public is rightly concerned but the circumstances and atmosphere of seventeen years ago were quite different.'

In Northern Ireland, an independent enquiry by the Haldane Society of Socialist Lawyers into the killing of two army corporals, and the subsequent sentencing of three men to life imprisonment, also raises great cause for concern. The report maintains that such convictions would have been impossible in an English court.

The case arose out of the arrival at a Republican funeral in Casement Park of two plain-clothes army corporals who were subsequently killed in horrendous circumstances.

The society's disagreement with the verdicts focuses on five main issues. The only photographic evidence was shot from a helicopter and the quality was so poor that precise facial details could not be made out (this was not denied by the Court of Appeal); there was an assumption by the trial judge of a concerted network of actions which in reality were chaos and panic; guilt was inferred because one defendant decided to remain silent; all three men had clean records and were not members of nor involved with Republican organisations; the judge failed to establish the context within which the funeral took place – a Republican funeral had been attacked and people killed only three days previously.

None of the convicted men actually carried out the shootings and so their convictions – two life sentences for murder, two ten-year sentences for grievous bodily harm, two fifteen-year sentences for false imprisonment – were based on the assumption of 'joint common enterprise'. Like so much of the administration of law in Northern Ireland, the outcome of this case is very troubling. What is just as troubling is that we are gradually importing elements of that system into England and Wales.

Another recent Northern Irish case, this time an inquest into the deaths of three unarmed IRA men killed ten years ago, was halted by the coroner. There was suspicion that the jury had been packed by the police.

In yet another case, the chief constable of the Royal Ulster Constabulary has refused to hand over police interview notes which were instrumental in convicting a man accused of being a Republican paramilitary. Seamus Mullen's solicitors wanted to subject the notes to ESDA testing but they have been refused access because to have acceded to their request 'would lead to many other similar requests'. This is not the administration of law but of anarchy.

I wonder if it could have anything to do with the fact that three UDR men were recently released after more than eight years in prison. ESDA tests were used on notes made by police during the original interviews of the three accused men and these were shown to have been rewritten and false authentications had been appended to some of them by senior police officers.

Meanwhile, back on the mainland, one of the biggest enquiries ever conducted by the Metropolitan police is underway in Hackney. They are investigating the behaviour of Hackney police after numerous allegations of brutality, interfering with witnesses and selling drugs. Twelve firms of solicitors and nineteen barristers have contacted the Home Secretary about the enquiry and this level of intervention is seen as unique.

A drugs case has collapsed because of the unreliability of police evidence, some officers have been moved to other stations and a local community group, the Hackney Community Defence Association, is coordinating a large number of complaints of police brutality. Some have already been fought and won.

The West Yorkshire police, who conducted an enquiry into the West Midlands Regional Crime Squad, recommended that sixteen detectives should face charges. The Director of Public Prosecutions, Barbara Mills QC decided not to proceed with any prosecutions against the officers as there was 'insufficient evidence'. The reaction of many people including myself was that of complete amazement. However, seven former members of the West Midlands squad are now to face disciplinary charges concerning falsehood and prevarication.

And, of course, once that announcement was made, the arrogance of those involved was allowed to blossom and take voice through the words of chief inspector Robert Goodchild. He addressed chief constable Geoffrey Dear, who had disbanded the West Midlands squad in 1989, through the columns of the *Police Review*. He said:

'The time has now come to show that you have the courage of your stature and publicly apologise to those officers, their wives and families at whom you pointed the finger of corruption. If it is not forthcoming perhaps it is time for you to go – in silence.'

Of the many men who spent years in prison, wrongfully convicted, not a word; of the families broken and thrust into poverty, not a word; of a police squad which was out of control and wrote its own rule book, not a word; of the cynical and callous disregard for human rights and individual liberty, not a word. It is a chilling comment from a man who is supposed to uphold the law.

The government's answer is to urge the police to win the hearts of middle England. Speaking to the 270 most senior policemen in the country, Kenneth Clarke, the Home Secretary, recently told them how to improve their image: 'Offences such as speeding, neglecting to wear a seatbelt and failure to carry an up-to-date road fund licence should be dealt with but with a style that fits the style of misdemeanour. The indignant middle-class motorist will be much more likely to support the police if he has not recently been outraged by the way he was treated when he committed a traffic offence.'

In response, the chief constable of Essex said that police were aware that there had been cover-ups in the past and he accepted that there was public disquiet that no members of the West Midlands Serious Crime Squad had been prosecuted but the Director of Public Prosecutions had been quite right not to do so. And so everything is all right and cosy and there is no need for alarm.

While this mutual admiration is going on police are still calling for the restoration of the death penalty, totally unabashed by what would have been a string of totally innocent corpses. They are demanding greater powers of stop and search which broaden the scope of PACE.

Meanwhile, the Police Complaints Authority also promotes the pretence that nothing really is wrong within the police force by calling for the rooting out of 'rotten apples' – the assumption being that it is only the odd one or two who are spoiling an otherwise admirable service. 'Police officers who report their colleagues' misbehaviour must be given full support,' it maintains.

Meanwhile the ultra-secretive, uncontrolled and completely unaccountable MI5 is to take over some police work. Desperate to find a role since the disintegration of the USSR, it has won the battle to take on security and 'terrorist' work from the Special Branch. This is likely to be only a first step and the portents for the future of accountable, democratic, consensus policing takes another enormous step backwards.

What else has come to light? Well, despite fine words on altering the regimes inside our prisons, and despite the warnings offered by the riots at Strangeways and elsewhere, spending on prison education is being cut by 50 per cent. This flies in the face of Lord Justice Woolf's recommendations on prison conditions and shows last September's White Paper on prison reform to be a hollow shell. It's an irony that Strangeways, the prison which led to the Woolf report, may well be the first to go private.

Obviously the future of convicted and remand prisoners in Britain now lies in the hands of the private sector as a programme of prison privatisation gets underway and the principle of profiting from punishment is established. It is quite breathtaking how the current administration can introduce legislation in almost every walk of life – education, health, energy, transport, environment – which has absolutely nothing to do with the real issues and needs. We have sacrificed rule by parliamentary democracy for rule by the public relations man, the advertising executive and the gloss and glitz of corporate image.

They have learned their lesson well from the private sector but the painted smile, colourful uniform and bow-tie of the McDonalds' worker can't alter the fact that pay and conditions are abysmal and hundreds of thousands of creatures are needlessly slaughtered annually, in barbaric conditions. The answer here as in government appears to be if the blood and guts gets on your shoes and defiles your image then let's paint the image even thicker and pretend the gore doesn't exist.

The lack of action in tackling the problems in our prisons continues and is personified by the conditions in which young people are locked up. These have worsened and regimes of bullying and the most obscene brutality have been allowed to grow and prosper with nothing but fine words to ameliorate the misery. In the last year alone, nearly 3000 teenage prisoners injured themselves in acts of desperation. Their ages ranged from as young as fourteen and the injuries included self-mutilation, wrist-slashing and attempted suicide.

Perhaps it's also not surprising that three organisations concerned with justice – Liberty, the National Association of Probation Officers and Conviction – have compiled a dossier of 110 other possible cases of miscarriage, chosen from a list of 'hundreds'. The probation officers go even further and maintain that on the basis of studies carried out by them, the number of people wrongly convicted could total 500 or more.

No one will ever know the true picture and in reality the total is almost certainly higher. Once sentenced, there is no incentive for a prisoner to contest his or her conviction because parole is rarely given to those who insist on protesting their innocence. Keep quiet and you get out earlier – considerably earlier because the granting of parole effectively halves the length of a sentence. Normal remission for 'good behaviour' knocks about one third off.

It is in this climate that the Royal Commission on Criminal Justice sits. The terms of reference given to them by government are as follows:

> To examine the effectiveness of the criminal justice system in England and Wales in securing the conviction of those guilty of criminal offences and the acquittal of those who are innocent, having regard to the efficient use of resources and in particular to consider whether changes are needed in
>
> (i)   the conduct of police investigations and their supervision by senior police officers, and in particular the degree of control that is exercised by those officers over the conduct of the investigation and the gathering and preparation of evidence;
>
> (ii) the role of the prosecutor in supervising the gathering of evidence and deciding whether to proceed with a case, and the arrangements for disclosure of material, including unused material to the defence;
>
> (iii) the role of experts in criminal proceedings, their responsibilities to the court, prosecution and defence and the relationship between the forensic science service and the police;
>
> (iv) the arrangement for the defence of accused persons, access to legal advice and access to expert guidance;
>
> (v)   the opportunities available for an accused person to state his position on the matters charged and the extent to which the court might draw proper inferences from primary facts, the

conduct of the accused, and any failure on his part to take
advantage of an opportunity to state his position;

(vi) the powers of the courts in directing proceedings, the possibility of their having an investigative role both before and
during the trial and the role of pre-trial reviews; the courts'
duty in considering evidence, including uncorroborated confession evidence;

(vii) the role of the Court of Appeal in considering new evidence
on appeal, including directing the investigation of allegations;

(viii) the arrangements for considering and investigating allegations of miscarriages of justice when appeal rights have
been exhausted.

During the course of this book I have addressed each one of
these terms of reference and laid out how I believe the system
should be changed and why. I have called on my twenty-five years
of experience as a defence lawyer and that same experience causes
me some concern when I look closely at these guidelines.

Top of the list is the lack of reference to justice in Northern
Ireland, where a particularly oppressive and undemocratic criminal
justice system has been developed. It is a system which should not
and would not be tolerated in any developed country. It is only
possible to guess at the number of miscarriages for which it has
been responsible – but of this, not a word.

In paragraph ii, the decision to consider the disclosure of all
material to the defence is vital, as the string of miscarriages I have
written about testify. But that isn't quite the end of the story. This
paragraph allows the Commission to consider instructing the defence
to provide all its material to the prosecution. On the face of it that
might sound only fair but in reality it would demolish defence cases
alleging collusion, corruption and lies by giving advance warning and
allowing those involved to get their stories right. Also it is another
incursion on the presumption of innocence and the right to silence
particularly where there is no parity of resources between prosecution
and defence.

The most disturbing clause of all is number v. This charges

the Commission to consider abolishing the right to silence. It is a complete and utter diversion. The right to silence or lack of it was not a factor in any one of the recent spate of miscarriages and the inclusion of this clause is simply to further the government's own political agenda. If the Commission does abolish the right to silence the effect will be felt in how police handle interrogations and the liberty they will feel in pressuring detainees to answer or be seen as guilty. The number of miscarriages which flow from this decision will be legion. The thought of abolition of this right is anathema to the US Judge Joan Carey:

'It's absolutely fundamental to retain the right to silence because under an accusatorial system of justice it is those who make the accusations who must furnish the proof. A person should not be convicted by virtue of the words he or she does or doesn't utter and the abolition of the right will do nothing to stem miscarriages.

'In this country, from the time you begin kindergarten you are taught to respect rights, property rights yes, but more importantly individual rights. Many of the abuses that have occurred would not have done so if you had a Bill of Rights or a written constitution. I think the problem in Britain from the very beginning is that you have laid much more emphasis on property rights rather than the rights of the individual. What I have found is that the rights of the individual should be paramount and of far greater importance than any other rights.'

It is fascinating to listen to the hypocrisy of many British politicians, particularly over the past decade or so, as they pay lip service to a belief in human rights and yet with every new piece of legislation ride rough-shod over those rights. Every new Act, which is usually cloaked with the words 'freedom' or 'choice' or 'democratic', invariably erodes those concepts for the majority of citizens. Without a written, inviolate and wide-ranging Bill of Rights, the steady erosion of our liberties will continue and the concentration of power and money in the hands of a very few will continue.

While we are force-fed and accept illusions of participation and democratic accountability, the hands behind the scenes will continue to pull the strings of control with ever greater confidence and contempt. The bow-ties will grow brighter, the painted smiles grow broader and the corporate greed will grow ever more demanding. And behind the facade, the dispossessed, the abused and the ignored will grow in number.

It was in the United States that British expatriate Thomas Paine, some two hundred years ago, wrote his book *Common Sense* which led to the inspiration behind the Declaration of Independence. He was, in the writing of his book *The Rights of Man*, trying to uphold the principles of the French revolution. It's easy to forget history and occasionally it is worth rereading.

In the chapter headed 'Declaration of the Rights of Man and of the Citizen', Thomas Paine spells out what are the real dangers to those rights, how they are so easily undermined: 'Ignorance, neglect ... or contempt of human rights are the sole causes of public misfortune and corruption of government.'

It is for these reasons that the Royal Commission should not be tinkering around the edges of our criminal justice system, changing a bit here, altering a bit there. They should, for all our sakes, be going back to basic principles.

Thomas Paine sets out nineteen principles within his book and principle nine begins with these words, 'Every man being presumed innocent until he has been convicted.' That is the basic principle to which we must return.

INDEX

Pakistani names are entered under the first part of the name. Witnesses are concerned with the Lloyd Waite murder case.

FENTON BRESLER

INTERPOL

A history and examination of 70 years of
crime solving

This unprecedented study of the secretive international police organisation focuses the forensic gaze on the crime-fighters themselves.

Interpol's biggest enemy – and the world's No.1 crime – is drug trafficking, an industry worth, at $500 billion a year, more than the oil industry and less only than the international arms trade.

30 per cent of the organisation's effort is geared to fighting white-collar crime, with computer fraud netting an estimated £2,500 million in Britain alone.

Interpol's Twelve Most Wanted list currently includes notorious terrorist Carlos the Jackal, fugitive American fraudster Tom Billman and Alois Brunner, the most notorious Nazi war criminal still at large.

Founded in 1914 by Prince Rainier's great grandfather, Interpol now has 169 member states, ten more than the UN, coordinating its work in four official languages (English, French, Spanish and Arabic) from a bullet-proof, state-of-the-art HQ in Lyons.

In researching this highly illuminating account of a unique and little-known organisation, Fenton Bresler, a distinguished criminologist and barrister, has worked with the full support of Interpol's current Secretary General, Raymond Kendall.

'A fascinating and uncomfortable story'
John Stalker, *Sunday Express*

TOM BOWER

THE RED WEB

MI6 and the KGB Master Coup

This is the extraordinary and untold story of how the KGB first compromised, then controlled, the whole of MI6's intelligence network in the Baltic States of the USSR, completely deceiving the western world.

Between 1944 and 1955 MI6 thought it had established a major spy network inside the Soviet Union – while in reality the KGB had organised a massive sting operation. For more than a decade, British agents were dropped by boat on the Soviet coast, many to lose their lives. Once the betrayal was revealed, MI6 officers abandoned their agents in Russia, hoping that the bungle could be explained away by Kim Philby's treachery.

The Red Web is based on newly declassified information from Washington, Bonn and Stockholm, and from over two hundred interviews – including access to KGB files and officers. Here, for the first time, Tom Bower exposes the truth behind the entire botched operation and reveals the shameful cover-up that followed.

A Selected List of Non-Fiction Titles Available from Mandarin

While every effort is made to keep prices low, it is sometimes necessary to increase prices at short notice. Mandarin Paperbacks reserves the right to show new retail prices on covers which may differ from those previously advertised in the text or elsewhere.

The prices shown below were correct at the time of going to press.

All these books are available at your bookshop or newsagent, or can be ordered direct from the address below. Just tick the titles you want and fill in the form below.

Cash Sales Department, PO Box 5, Rushden, Northants NN10 6YX.
Fax: 0933 410321 : Phone 0933 410511.

Please send cheque, payable to 'Reed Book Services Ltd.', or postal order for purchase price quoted and allow the following for postage and packing:

£1.00 for the first book, 50p for the second; **FREE POSTAGE AND PACKING FOR THREE BOOKS OR MORE PER ORDER.**

NAME (Block letters) ....

ADDRESS ....

....

☐ I enclose my remittance for ....

☐ I wish to pay by Access/Visa Card Number

Expiry Date

Signature ....

Please quote our reference: MAND